WITHDRAWN FROM CLARK UNIVERSITY LIBRARY

# Hungary
**A Century of Economic Development**

## NATIONAL ECONOMIC HISTORIES
General Editor W. E. Minchinton

*The Argentine Republic 1516–1971* by H. S. Ferns

IN PREPARATION

*Poland* by M. Malowist

*Norway* by F. Hodne

*France* by G. Holmes and P. Guillaume

NATIONAL ECONOMIC HISTORIES

# HUNGARY
# A Century of Economic Development

❋

I. T. Berend
and
G. Ranki

DAVID & CHARLES : NEWTON ABBOT
BARNES & NOBLE BOOKS : NEW YORK
(a division of Harper & Row Publishers, Inc.)

This edition first published in 1974
in Great Britain by
David & Charles (Holdings) Limited
Newton Abbot   Devon
in the U.S.A. by
Harper & Row Publishers, Inc.
Barnes & Noble Import Division
0 7153 6269 0 *(Great Britain)*
06–490371–0 *(United States)*

© I. T. Berend & G. Ranki 1974
All rights reserved. No part of this publication may be reproduced, stored in a retrieval system, or transmitted, in any form or by any means, electronic, mechanical, photocopying, recording or otherwise, without the prior permission of the publishers

Printed in Great Britain by
Latimer Trend & Company Ltd Plymouth

# Contents

List of maps and tables ... 7
Foreword ... 11
Introduction ... 13

Part One: EVOLUTION OF A MODERN CAPITALIST ECONOMY, 1848–1914: THE AGE OF INDUSTRIAL REVOLUTION

  1  Foundations of modernisation: changes in population, development of a credit system and infrastructure ... 24

  2  Transformation of the economy: agriculture, industry, commerce ... 40

  3  Development of the economy: results, peculiarities, contradictions ... 69

  4  The prime social consequence of economic transformation: emergence of the proletariat and its organisation as a class ... 77

Part Two: A STAGNANT ECONOMY IN A NEW POLITY, 1914–44

  1  Wartime destruction and new economic circumstances ... 92

  2  Markets and financing: the role of the state and of foreign capital ... 99

  3  Effects of the depression: government intervention ... 111

|   |   |   |
|---|---|---|
| 4 | Development of the economy between the wars | 123 |
| 5 | Changes in the composition and situation of the working class | 153 |
| 6 | The years of war economy | 167 |

Part Three: SOCIALIST TRANSFORMATION AND INDUSTRIALISATION OF THE ECONOMY SINCE 1944

|   |   |   |
|---|---|---|
| 1 | Expropriation and recovery | 184 |
| 2 | Development of a socialist economic strategy | 197 |
| 3 | Changes in economic structure | 210 |
| 4 | Social consequences of economic development | 247 |

|   |   |
|---|---|
| Bibliography | 257 |
| Index | 261 |

# List of maps and tables

**MAPS**

Hungary before World War I     20
Hungary today     21

**TABLES**

| | | |
|---|---|---|
| 1 | The growth of population | 25 |
| 2 | Development of banking system | 33 |
| 3 | Growth of railway network | 38 |
| 4 | Land distribution in 1895 | 42 |
| 5 | Production of main crops | 46 |
| 6 | Animal stocks | 47 |
| 7 | Gross agricultural production | 48 |
| 8 | Coal production | 56 |
| 9 | Iron and steel production | 57 |
| 10 | Horsepower capacity of machines in industry | 60 |
| 11 | Value of industrial production | 61 |
| 12 | The structure of manufacturing industry | 63 |
| 13 | Growth of national income | 74 |
| 14 | Distribution of gainfully occupied population | 74 |
| 15 | Structure of gainfully occupied population in 1910 | 95 |
| 16 | Production of principal industries in postwar territory | 95 |
| 17 | Depreciation of the gold crown | 104 |

## List of maps and tables

| | | |
|---|---|---|
| 18 | Agricultural production and prices during the great depression | 112 |
| 19 | Volume of foreign trade | 120 |
| 20 | Distribution of population according to settlement growth | 124 |
| 21 | Distribution of agricultural holdings, 1895 and 1935 | 127 |
| 22 | Production of principal crops | 130 |
| 23 | Value of the principal crops | 130 |
| 24 | Livestock | 131 |
| 25 | Output of coal | 132 |
| 26 | Output of iron and steel | 133 |
| 27 | Horsepower and workers in manufacturing industry | 139 |
| 28 | Index of industrial production | 139 |
| 29 | Structure of Hungarian industry | 143 |
| 30 | Value of foreign trade | 146 |
| 31 | Structure of foreign trade | 146 |
| 32 | Banks and credit institutions | 148 |
| 33 | Occupational structure | 151 |
| 34 | Average yearly labour force | 156 |
| 35 | Budgetary expenditure during World War II | 172 |
| 36 | Value of industrial output in 1938 territory | 176 |
| 37 | War losses in manufacturing industry | 182 |
| 38 | Distribution of land in private ownership after land reform in 1945 | 186 |
| 39 | Public and private sectors in Hungarian manufacturing industry at 24 April 1948 | 189 |
| 40 | Changes in the industrial structure in the postwar period | 195 |
| 41 | Industrial production per capita | 195 |
| 42 | Investment in the economy | 205 |
| 43 | Size and density of population, distribution of population in different branches of economy | 211 |

| | | |
|---|---|---|
| 44 | Index of industrial output | 215 |
| 45 | Coal output | 219 |
| 46 | Output of iron and steel | 223 |
| 47 | Structure of industry based on total output at 1965 prices | 228 |
| 48 | Gross output of agriculture (1959 prices) | 231 |
| 49 | Foreign trade | 239 |
| 50 | Annual changes in national income | 243 |
| 51 | National income (1959 prices) | 244 |

# Foreword

Until some twenty years ago, the economic history of Hungary in the nineteenth and twentieth centuries was little studied or was treated only very sketchily, by Hungarian and Western historians alike. This situation has changed, either because Hungarian history has become better understood or because interest in economic theory has aroused the desire to apply it to the economic history of Hungary. Books published in the 1950s dealt principally with the period before World War I and with the industrialisation of Hungary. Subsequently, studies of the inter-war period and of Hungarian economic history since 1945 have appeared, not only dealing with the country's economic growth but treating it as part of European economic history in general and as a type of east-central European development in particular.

The existence of these studies, largely the work of the present writers, and of much statistical and archive material, very little of which is available in languages other than Hungarian, encouraged us to accept the invitation of David & Charles to write a short economic history of Hungary in the nineteenth and twentieth centuries. We deal with the economic modernisation of Hungary in its historical context: to 1918 as an independent but integral part of the Austro-Hungarian Empire; and after 1918 as it emerged from the break-up of that empire and from the Trianon treaties. Despite great territorial changes in Hungary, the element of continuity was a decisive factor in this period. After 1945 Hungary's territory remained unchanged, but considerable political changes occurred when Hungary became a people's democracy and its economic development began to follow a socialist pattern. Throughout, we have tried to show the development of Hungary and its economic growth in the context of European and world economic history.

We would like to express our thanks to Professor Walter Minchinton for his guidance as general editor of the series. We also owe a great debt to Mr Brian Clapp for the care with which he edited our manuscript, as regards both style and subject-matter, though of course the responsibility for any errors is entirely ours.

We are also especially grateful to Mr Richard Allan, our American colleague who was kind enough to undertake the heavy burden of translation of our Hungarian manuscript.

IVÁN T. BEREND
GYÖRGY RANKI

# Introduction

In the ninth century, on the last wave of the great migrations, the pastoral Magyars arrived in the Carpathian basin; in the tenth they settled down permanently, organised their state, and gradually accommodated themselves to the European feudal system. The adoption of Christianity, the transition to agriculture, and the appearance of serfdom set in motion, from the eleventh to the thirteenth centuries, the same tendencies of social and economic development which characterised other parts of Europe at the time. This movement reached its peak in the middle of the fifteenth century. The evolution of an agriculture based on peasant production, and the spread of money rents, pointed toward Western European levels of development; but the lag in urban growth, the predominance, among the cities of Hungary, of large peasant towns (*mezővárosok*), and the weakness of the craft and commercial bourgeoisie, reflected a lower level of maturity.

Those phenomena, however, which spread across Western Europe in the sixteenth and seventeenth centuries—upswing in the production of agricultural commodities, weakening or disappearance of serfdom, marked extension of handicraft industry, and, as a concomitant of all these, flourishing trade and urbanisation—these were not to be found in Hungary.

The displacement of European trade routes to the Atlantic, and the change in the composition of the products exchanged, basically altered the situation of Hungary and the other Eastern European countries. Together with this went the advance of the Turks into Europe, an extended period of warfare, and the

Turkish occupation of central Hungary for 150 years during the sixteenth and seventeenth centuries. The end of Turkish occupation brought with it, again, the ever closer incorporation of all of Hungary into the domains of the Habsburgs, who had been called to the Hungarian throne in the sixteenth century.

All these influences prevented or retarded the dissolution of the old feudal relationships, the transformation of agriculture, and industrial and urban development along Western lines; they contributed to the preservation of backward, traditional relations, and to a stagnation lasting several centuries. Modernisation could proceed only weakly, at an extraordinarily slow tempo.

In the sixteenth to eighteenth centuries—to use Frederick Engels' widely known phrase—a 'second edition of serfdom' appeared in Hungary, as in most of the other east-central European countries. The manorial bonds of the serf, already beginning to loosen in the fifteenth century, tightened again; money rents, which had slowly begun to replace feudal labour service and dues in kind, faded into the background again, while forms reminiscent of an earlier era of serfdom became prominent once more.

One legislative act after another cancelled the peasant's right of free movement, won at the end of the thirteenth century, binding him firmly to the soil again. This was far from being a mere legal change; it was closely connected with the new method of cultivation. In contrast with the Western tendency toward production on a capitalist basis by peasants or tenant farmers employing wage labour, production developed on large estates using labour service exacted by the lord.

All these circumstances powerfully affected the position of the cities as well. Politically and economically the landed aristocracy gained the upper hand over the weak urban bourgeoisie, inhibiting the growth of the cities. Urban industry was weak; commercial capital, restricted to a narrow sphere, was incapable of filling the role of industrial entrepreneur. Industry stagnated within its guild limitations, the cities retained their medieval appearance. Inadequate urban-industrial development in turn had its effect on agriculture, whose advance was further limited by a narrow internal market.

The progress of the Western European economies, the growth of large-scale industry, and the industrial revolution of the late eighteenth and early nineteenth centuries did not leave Hungary unaffected. At the end of the eighteenth century and in the first half of the nineteenth, late serfdom began, slowly and in its own way, to yield to modern capitalist development.

It was the Habsburg Monarchy which provided an ambiguous setting for this slow transition. In the eighteenth century Hungary had become an organic part of the Monarchy economically. On the one hand this promoted a division of labour based on comparative natural endowments and levels of development, lending impetus to the capitalist development of agriculture by providing a large internal market for foodstuffs. On the other hand, however, it allowed the absolutist Habsburgs to put into effect a deliberate economic policy more favourable for the western part of the empire.

The historical turning-point in the modern capitalist transformation of the Hungarian economy is bound up with the revolution of 1848–9. With the abolition of serfdom and of noble privileges, and the introduction of legal equality and free access to land and office, new socio-economic conditions came into existence. In the middle of the nineteenth century, on the heels of the revolution's accomplishments, new possibilities appeared for industrial entrepreneurship and the acceptance of free wage-labour on a wide scale, and for a modern credit system.

None of this, of course, brought an immediate revolution in economic development. Despite basic changes in the conditions of economic life, too many old institutions, customs, and legal forms survived. As a result of the earlier weakness of urban-bourgeois development, the country's political and social leadership—indeed, even its economic leadership—remained in the hands of the former nobility, which only slowly took bourgeois features. The retention virtually unchanged of the system of latifundia formed the basis of this leadership; but many medieval institutions and enactments—eg, the guild system, or the law on ownership of mines—still stood in the way of further development.

Inseparable from all these factors, the grave consequences of the defeat of the revolutionary struggle against Austria weighed heavily on the country. Years of military administration, in an atmosphere of armed force, at first made any advance impossible, failing to assure even the minimum conditions for economic development. That basic, irrevocable achievement of the revolution, the liberation of the serfs, was confirmed by imperial patent in 1853—with, it is true, revisions to the benefit of those great landowners who had remained true to the court. Many other reforms were effected only at the end of the decade. The unsettled political condition of the country, the centralising efforts of the Habsburgs, the absence of constitutional public life, the persistence of sharp political conflicts, and the stubborn passive resistance of the Hungarian political élites all left their mark on the Hungarian economy for decades afterward. Austria, too, sought during these years to exploit her military victory economically. An early measure suspended, from 1 October 1850, the customs duties between Hungary and the Austrian provinces; on 1 July 1851 the duties were permanently abolished.

In 1867 the Austro-Hungarian Compromise put an end to the stage of uncertainty which had prevailed since 1849. The aristocratic and bourgeois élites of Austria and the house of Habsburg, defeated politically and militarily, excluded from a united Germany, and struggling with financial difficulties, were obliged to reach agreement with Hungary. On its side the Hungarian landed aristocracy, weary of resistance, fearing for its hegemony over the non-Magyar half of the population, and desirous of a strong central authority *vis-à-vis* its own peasant masses, was equally anxious to seek agreement. By the terms of the Compromise Austria abandoned her efforts to centralise the empire, which was converted into a dualist state with two centres. Within this framework Hungary received its own government and its own civil administration. The new system secured for a long time to come the hegemony of the Hungarian landowners over the country, and over the Slovak, Rumanian and Croat minorities as well. As regards the tariff community, the Compromise established a customs and trade agreement lasting ten years, with provision for extensions every ten years. At the same time a uniform currency was created for Austria and Hungary. In 1878 the Austrian National Bank was converted into an Austro-Hungarian Bank.

Here we may observe a circumstance characteristic of the economic development of modern Hungary, and more or less typical of Eastern Europe in general. Not only did the revolutions fail to clear the way completely for the development of capitalism; in addition, subsequent capitalist development took place not within the framework of an independent national state, as in most of the Western European countries, but in the context of a great empire, the Habsburg Monarchy.

The Empire-wide framework created peculiar conditions of development for all the nations of the Monarchy. In Hungary, these peculiar circumstances affected the economy in an extremely contradictory way, and strongly influenced the course of developments in the following decades. Hungary was at one and the same time a ruling nation within the Monarchy and an oppressor of other nationalities, and yet was also exploited by the more economically developed territories of the Monarchy. Even disregarding, for purposes of economic history, involved political aspects of the matter, the economic situation itself was contradictory. For the lands of the Monarchy, this contradictory situation brought both mutual advantages and disadvantages. The imperial setting led to the emergence of a special Empire-wide integration, opening to each region the possibility of co-operation in a broader market and of realising the benefits of comparative advantage. Amidst the varied influences making themselves felt on this common market the individual lands could not, of course, develop every branch of their industry and economy; rather they concentrated their relatively limited resources on those areas which were, in the circumstances, the most promising.

This concentration favoured, above all, the industrialisation of the Austrian and Czech lands and the capitalist development —rapid for Eastern Europe—of Hungarian agriculture, to a comparatively high level. At the same time, it created opportunities within industry for a specialised division of labour.

Along with the Austrian and Czech textiles and other consumer-goods industries (wood, leather, glass), Hungarian milling and, in part, sugar industries found great opportunities. But mutual advantage extended beyond these individual branches, before which spread the wide markets of the Monarchy. The advantages of a so-called 'closed economy'—a common monetary system, the possibility of trade among various regions, and the absence of foreign exchange problems—facilitated the financing of the economy, enabling backward areas to develop to a degree exceeding their own internal resources and potential for accumulation. In Hungary these advantages were reflected, in particular, in the existence of a Monarchy-wide infrastructure, a transport network of European calibre, and a developed banking system. Again, capital from the advanced parts of the Monarchy not only took a share in financing investments in the backward regions; it also grew apace by exploiting the cheap foodstuffs and raw materials, and the secure protected markets for goods and credit, of the backward areas. Given the internal laws of free competition, the formally equal conditions assured by a common market naturally favoured the stronger. For Austria this was all the more advantageous, since its degree of development assured it of superiority only within the Monarchy and in relation to other Eastern European or Balkan countries; it would have held its own less well on equal terms in the European market.

In this connection one must point to the reciprocal disadvantages which formed the other side of the comparative advantages assured by the framework of the Monarchy. Austrian and Czech agriculture suffered from the competition of the Hungarian latifundia, Hungarian industry from the murderous competition of Austrian and Czech industry. Nor were the disadvantages simply reciprocal: they naturally weighed more heavily on the more backward areas. Economic co-operation in a common market offering formally equal advantages, while on the one hand it lent impetus to modern economic development, on the other it set limits to that development, preserving elements of backwardness. The fact that Hungary and the Monarchy's other underdeveloped regions could not employ the weapon of protective tariffs against the more industrialised partners contributed in no small measure to this state of affairs—whereas from the 1870s and 1880s onward virtually all Europe was making repeated and forceful use of protection. The situation was not changed by the fact that the tariff walls surrounding the Monarchy powerfully served the interests of large-scale Hungarian agriculture; high agricultural duties protected the Monarchy's markets, and at times economic policy even accepted the risk of a tariff war with the Balkan countries in defence of agrarian interests. In spite of all this, the absence of an *internal* protective tariff in the Monarchy generated the demand for an independent Hungarian customs area, a demand which grew stronger particularly in the early twentieth century.

*Note:* In the text a billion is used in the US sense, a thousand millions. Similarly a trillion is taken as a million millions.

Hungary before World War I

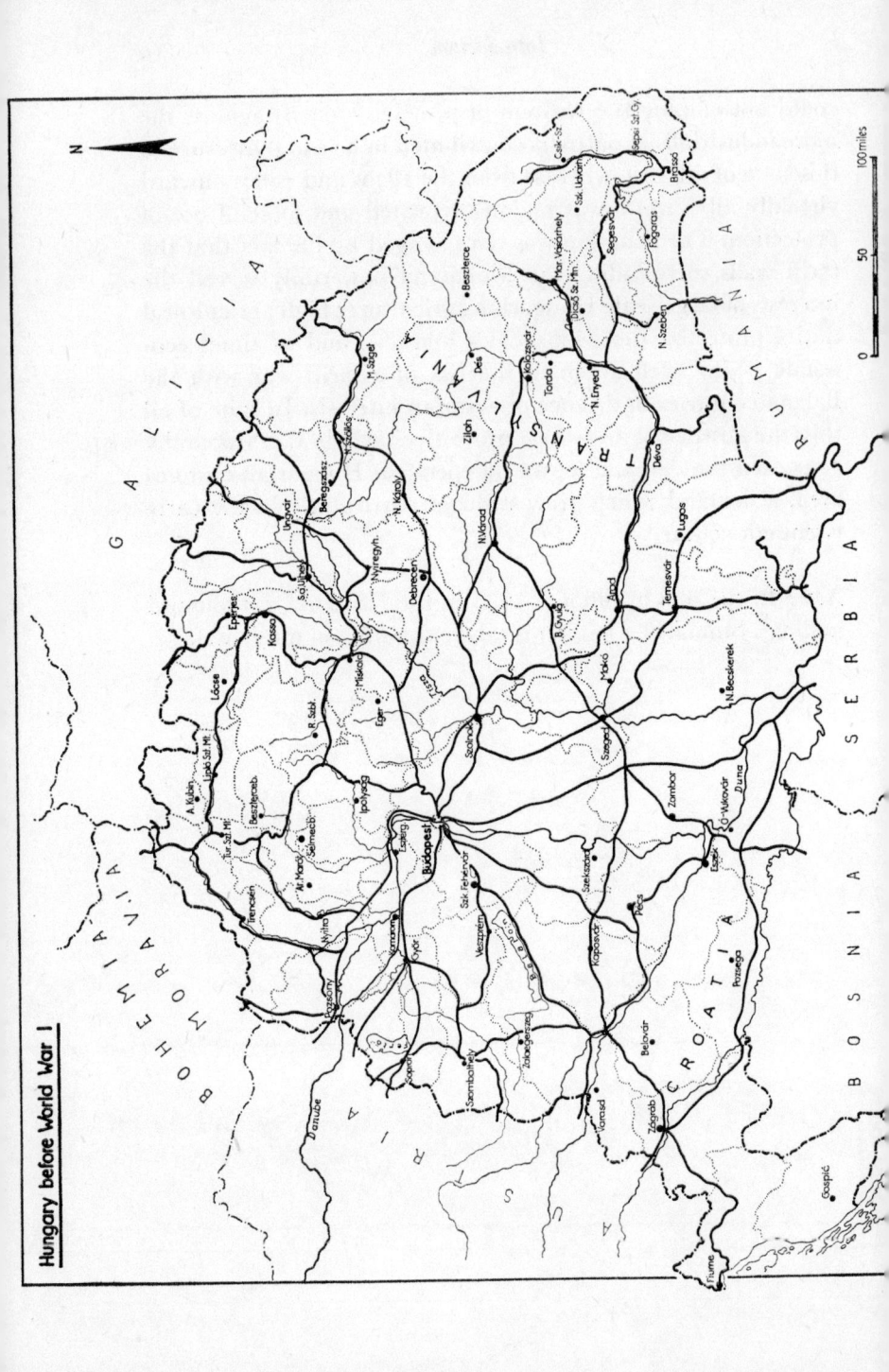

## Hungary today

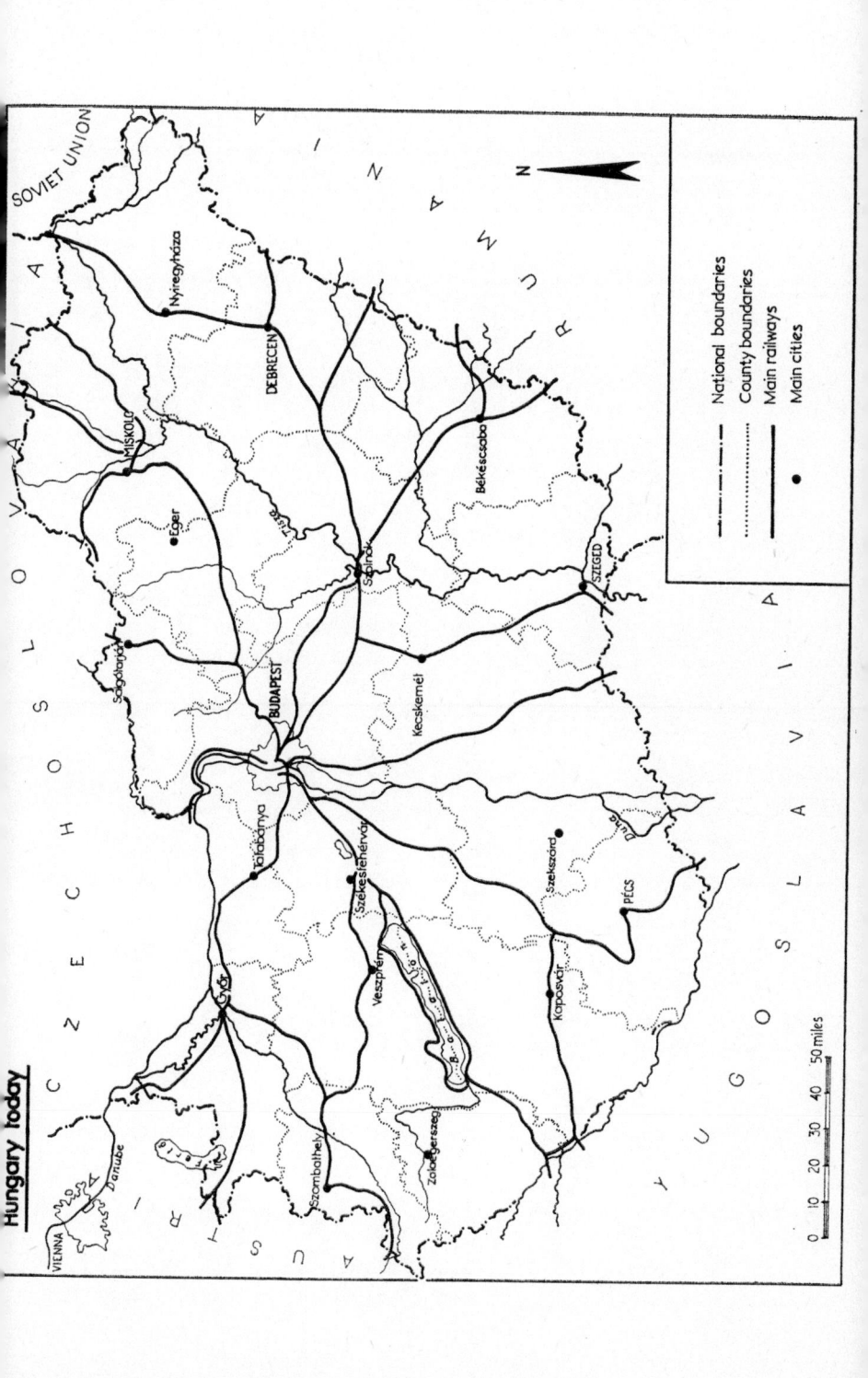

# 1
Evolution of a Modern Capitalist Economy 1848–1914: The Age of Industrial Revolution

# 1 Foundations of modernisation: population changes, development of a credit system and infrastructure

As it emerged from the revolution of 1848 and the Compromise of 1867, Hungary was a multi-national state inhabited by Magyars, Rumanians, Croats, Slovaks, Serbs, and Germans. It covered 325,000 square kilometres in the Danube–Carpathian basin. The country's frontiers largely coincided with the line of the Carpathians in the north and east, and with the river Sava and the Adriatic in the south.

The central part of the country was occupied by the Great Plain of Hungary, a wide, flat, sandy expanse with excellent humus soils in its southern part. The western part of the country —Trans-Danubia—was a hilly region, better endowed with water and more suited for industry, all the more so after the discovery in the nineteenth century of two important coal-fields. Later, in the first half of the twentieth century, discoveries of bauxite and petroleum figured in the further development of the region. In the north and west, the ridges of the Carpathians were covered with rich forests, and contained important reserves of coal, iron ore, non-ferrous metals, and salt. Even richer sources of raw materials were to be found among the Carpathians of Transylvania.

The country had a continental climate, with relatively light rainfall and dry summers.

These geographical and climatic characteristics provided suitable conditions for the development of a modern economy.

## DEMOGRAPHIC CHANGES AND THE ROLE OF EDUCATION

Hungary's population grew rapidly in this epoch. According

to the census of 1787 the country had 9,300,000 inhabitants. In 1850 there were already 13,800,000; in 1869, 15,400,000; and in 1910, 20,900,000. The average annual rate of growth of population between 1869 and 1910 was 0·75 per cent; the birth rate fell from 42·5 per thousand to 33·5 per thousand, but the death rate from 34·5 to 22·7. It may seem surprising that actual population growth was at its most moderate—only 35 per cent—between 1869 and 1910, precisely the time when economic growth was most dynamic. But even in this period

TABLE 1*

*The growth of population*

| Year | Number (000s) | Decade | Yearly average growth (per cent) |
|------|---------------|--------|----------------------------------|
| 1857 | 13,768 | — | — |
| 1870 | 15,512 | 1857–70 | 0·93 |
| 1880 | 15,739 | 1870–80 | 0·15 |
| 1890 | 17,464 | 1880–90 | 1·03 |
| 1900 | 19,255 | 1890–1900 | 0·98 |
| 1910 | 20,886 | 1900–10 | 0·82 |

\* The sources for this table and those that follow, unless otherwise stated, are statistical yearbooks, censuses, and industrial and agricultural statistics.

the growth of population was affected, at the beginning of the 1870s, by the last great cholera epidemic, estimated to have claimed at least a quarter of a million victims. Population thus stagnated between 1869 and 1880. Thereafter, large-scale emigration drained off much of the increase. In the last decades of the nineteenth century roughly half a million people left the country; another 1,400,000 followed them in the first fifteen years of the twentieth century. Even allowing for return migration, the net loss still totalled 1,300,000 to 1,400,000. Thus between the 1880s and World War I emigration consumed about one-fifth of Hungary's natural population increase.

In the last analysis, the growth of population in Hungary was not negligible. The country, however, still lagged noticeably behind the contemporary West: the birth rate of 34 per 1,000 and the death rate of 23 per 1,000 were both significantly higher than in most European countries. Here the explanation is obviously to be sought in the relatively backward state of public hygiene, a very high rate of infant mortality, and the extremely widespread incidence of tuberculosis (in 1905 Budapest was first among European cities in incidence of tuberculosis).

The relatively rapid growth of population went side by side with an increase in mobility which transformed both the country's social structure and its geographic pattern of settlement. Internal migration gradually rose until, in 1910, almost one-third of the population—6 million people—lived and worked in some other place than the locality of their birth. The capital and a few provincial centres were naturally the principal foci for internal migration. Among its consequences were a marked shift in the proportion between rural and urban population, and the loss of population by the outlying (especially northern) areas to the central part of the country, above all to the county of Pest and the region between the rivers Danube and Tisza.

In the last three decades of our period (1880–1910) nearly 400,000 people migrated to Budapest; between 1869 and 1910 the population of the capital rose from 270,000 to 880,000. The modern process of urbanisation centred disproportionately on the capital, of course—even its adjacent communes showed a gain of 200,000 people; still urbanisation extended to every commercial or administrative centre which was drawn into the current of industrialisation. Overall the urban population nearly doubled during this period; in 1913 about a quarter of the population lived in cities. In the larger cities the population living from trade and industry already exceeded 50 per cent of the total.

As a concomitant of these demographic changes, important alterations took place in the schooling and cultural level of the populace; these worked to raise considerably the level of manpower skills.

From the end of the eighteenth century, educational reforms in most European countries laid the basis for mass schooling. In the nineteenth century free, compulsory popular education was introduced generally—in Hungary by Law 38 of 1868, passed while József Eötvös was Minister of Education. The Act established compulsory education for children from 6 to 12 in the elementary schools, and up to 15 years of age in the so-called Repeaters' Schools. The building of schools was made obligatory upon the communes. In 1869 there were 2,300,000 children of school age in the country, but only about 1,100,000 of them (48 per cent) attended the 13,600 schools then in operation. Nothing shows the low cultural level of the populace, at the time compulsory education was introduced, so well as the fact that according to the census of 1870 only 31 per cent could read and write.

During the school year 1910–11 some 44,000 teachers taught 2,700,000 children—89 per cent of the school-age population—in 17,000 elementary schools. By this time 68 per cent of those of an age to have attended school could read and write. The rate was better among wage-earners (illiteracy was always higher among women and the elderly); in 1910 only 25–28 per cent of wage-earners were illiterate. Among them, however, there were differences of significance for modern economic development: the illiteracy rate reached 36 per cent among those engaged in agriculture and about 25 per cent in mining and metallurgy, while it was under 12 per cent in industry, and under 10 per cent in transport, commerce, and finance.

Thus the conquest of illiteracy went forward with giant steps in Hungary, until it was restricted more and more to the older generation. In most of the newer branches of production only a tiny fraction of those employed were illiterate.

The relative developed level of mass education in Hungary could, of course, guarantee little more than the abolition of general illiteracy. Primary education in general did not aim at more than preparing the masses of the population to acquire the rudiments demanded by a modern economy, or the knowledge required for a skilled trade. For most, elementary school offered not just the basis of an education; it was their whole education, and its completion meant the close of their studies. Only a tiny fraction went on to further studies.

The Education Act of 1868 required every locality of more than 5,000 inhabitants to open an upper school; but in spite of this secondary education remained extremely restricted throughout the period under consideration. By the turn of the century only 4 per cent of children of secondary-school age were in school, and just before the World War the figure had risen to barely 5 per cent.

In these exclusive, well-equipped secondary schools a real élite education was provided, with high-level curricula and a well-trained teaching staff, and with exacting demands made on the students. The Hungarian secondary-school system reached the best European standards. This kind of education, however, with its classical bias, was not oriented toward economic usefulness. In 1910 only 15 per cent of secondary-school graduates were to be found working in industry and agriculture.

This characteristic feature, uneconomic orientation, is even more noticeable in higher education. By the end of the century the number of university students had risen to more than 10,000, by the academic year 1910–11 to 14,000. Although excellent instruction was available in some subjects, the whole structure of university education was thoroughly antiquated. Before World War I 43 per cent of Hungarian students studied law, while another 15 per cent studied theology. Engineering students made up less than 12 per cent of the total.

Because of the extremely small number of university graduates, and the antiquated structure of university education, the economic importance of higher education was virtually negligible. In the main sectors of the economy, so few graduates were employed that their number can scarcely be expressed as a percentage.

## DEVELOPMENT OF A MODERN BANKING SYSTEM

In Hungary, as in other countries of Central and Eastern Europe, conditions during the second half of the nineteenth century and at the beginning of the twentieth lent themselves to the capitalist transformation of the economy.

The establishment of a modern banking system in Hungary began before the revolution of 1848, with the founding of the First Domestic Savings Bank of Pest (Pesti Hazai Első Takarékpénztár, 1836) and the Hungarian Commercial Bank of Pest

(Pesti Magyar Kereskedelmi Bank, 1841). Between then and 1848, however, only small savings banks came into existence; at the latter date there were, all told, thirty-six financial institutions in the country. Following the defeat of the revolution and the War of Independence the development of the banking system came to a standstill; only after the stagnation of the 1850s did a certain upswing make itself felt. In 1866 there were already eighty financial institutions functioning (most of them still savings banks), but in their operations they encountered numerous obstacles. The government in Vienna, for example, extended to Hungary an old Austrian decree applying to benefit societies, which obliged the savings banks to restrict their charters within narrow limits, even though at this time most of them were already functioning as joint-stock companies. Government measures also limited the rate of interest which savings banks could collect on mortgages: 5 per cent was the maximum. The only large institution founded during this time was the Hungarian Land Credit Institute (Magyar Földhitel-Tintézet, 1863), partly on the initiative of the Hungarian National Economic Union (Országos Magyar Gazdasági Egyesület, OMGE), the interest group of the great landowners.

Following the Compromise, the Hungarian banking system began to grow by leaps and bounds. Above all, a large-scale influx of foreign, mainly Austrian, financial capital began, attracted by the political consolidation and economic boom which succeeded the political crisis and moderate prosperity of the pre-Compromise years. In 1867 the Austrian Rothschilds founded the Hungarian General Credit Bank (Magyar Általános Hitelbank), with the participation of the Vienna Creditanstalt and of representatives of Hungarian capital and agriculture; in 1868 Austrian and English financiers set up the Anglo-Hungarian Bank, with the participation of the Anglo-Austrian Bank of Vienna and of Hungarian capital; three other big institutes were founded, also with the contribution of foreign capital.

Alongside the five great banks representing foreign interests a great variety of other credit institutions sprang up in the years following the Compromise, among them smaller banks with foreign and domestic capital, and savings banks based principally on internal capital accumulation. The wave of joint-stock company formations which accompanied the boom all over Europe, reaching its peak in 1872, centred first and foremost on financial institutions.

The great banks founded after the Compromise were modelled on the French Crédit Mobilier, as it had developed and spread in the 1850s. This type of bank dominated Austrian credit; the leading Austrian bank, the Creditanstalt, was of the same type, and it was this model which was carried over into Hungarian practice too.

Large and small banks, large and small entrepreneurs, vied with one another in setting up companies and in stock-exchange speculations, hoping to drive up the price of their shares.

In the years between the Compromise and 1873 the number of banks and savings banks mushroomed, from 78 to 429; their capital assets more than trebled, from 169 million crowns to 531 million (£1 was equal to 24·9 Austro-Hungarian crowns). In the latter year depression shook Hungary for the first time, forcibly bringing the era of company formation to a close. In accordance with the general level of development of the economy, the effects of the crisis were felt most powerfully in the financial sphere.

On 9 May 1873 came the great crash on the Vienna exchange, inaugurating the most severe crisis yet seen in the history of capitalism. The Pest exchange soon followed the Viennese example: a host of fraudulent enterprises, mostly credit banks, collapsed like a house of cards, carrying down with them numbers of otherwise sound firms. As a result of the crisis, 74 credit institutions closed. Of the five great banks formed after the Compromise, only the Credit Bank survived the crisis; only the strongest foreign interest group, that of the Rothschilds, was able to maintain the position it had won in Hungary.

From the beginning of the 1880s, as a new boom slowly built up, the development of the Hungarian banking system also gained new momentum. This time, too, it was chiefly foreign banks and financial groups which took the initiative in the Hungarian market. In 1879 the Austrian Union Bank and its French associates (Société Générale and Banque de Paris) substantially increased—to 20 million crowns each—the original capital of the Hungarian Discount and Exchange Bank (Magyar Leszámitoló és Pénzváltó Bank) and the Hungarian Mortgage Credit Bank (Magyar Jelzáloghitelbank). With this action both these once-small banks become significant factors in the Hungarian credit system.

An Austro-French group doubled the original capital funds of the historic Hungarian Commercial Bank of Pest (Pesti Magyar Kereskedelmi Bank) so that by the beginning of the 1890s there were—counting the Rothschilds' Credit Bank—five great banks representing foreign interests in operation in the country. In 1890 an Austro-German group founded the Hungarian Bank of Industry and Commerce (Magyar Ipar és Kereskedelmi Bank).

Thus, alongside a few new establishments, several historic but hitherto small-scale financial institutions rose into the ranks of the great banks. At the same time, another significant portion of the capital being accumulated was invested in the foundation of more financial institutions: a large number of savings banks, savings and loan associations, and provincial banking houses appeared. By 1900 the number of banks and savings banks came to 1,011. The number of financial institutions had more than doubled since 1873; but more significant for growth during this period was the almost fivefold increase in their capital assets (original and reserve capital, plus savings deposits), from 531 million crowns to nearly 2,400 million. Within this generally rapid development the large banks with foreign ties —especially the increasingly prominent Commercial Bank, Credit Bank, and Discount Bank, as well as the First Domestic Savings Bank of Pest, which worked to a considerable extent with domestic capital but also belonged among the leading banks—achieved a much more rapid concentration of resources than the average. Between 1880 and 1900 the Commercial Bank's capital grew from 38 million to 503 million crowns, that of the Discount Bank from 19 to 110 million. The four great banks, together with a few other institutions under their influence, controlled 47 per cent of the total capital resources of the Hungarian credit system.

The leading banks towered above the others around the turn of the century not only through their enormous resources, but also because they had come to monopolise the financing of important areas of the economy, and through this business activity their influence in the economy grew. After the panic of 1873, for example, the Credit Bank acquired a monopoly over the floating of state loans, becoming 'banker to the Hungarian state'. It also played a decisive role, from the early 1880s, in financing the renewed construction of railways. Between 1873 and 1894 the bank undertook about sixty large domestic financing projects, more than half of them connected with state loans or railway construction. Good connections, especially with the aristocracy, smoothed the way for these transactions. From 1881 the Hungarian Mortgage Credit Bank monopolised the offering of municipal loans. The rich profits earned in these operations had no small part in the seventy-fold growth of the bank's assets during the last two decades of the century, after a modest start.

Finally, there was the Hungarian Commercial Bank of Pest, which acquired this kind of monopolistic business only in the course of the 1890s, though afterwards it proved all the more profitable; it specialised in the financing of local railway lines.

Naturally the extension of agricultural credit played a decisive role in the activity of the banks throughout our period. In the second half of the nineteenth century mortgages generally accounted for 50–60 per cent of the assets of these financial institutions. From 1867 to 1914 the banks' securities portfolios—ie their supply of credit to trade and industry—were never as large as their mortgage credit outstanding.

These features of the Hungarian banking system typify the Central and Eastern European situation. The peculiar role of the banks does not end with the primarily agricultural orientation of banking activity, however. In Central and Eastern Europe—and thus in Hungary—the banks played a far greater entrepreneurial role than in the West.

Early in the twentieth century the Hungarian banking

## TABLE 2
## Development of banking system

| Year | Number of credit institutions (1848 = 1) | | Share capital and reserve fund (crowns, 000s; 1848 = 1) | | Deposits (crowns, 000s; 1848 = 1) | | Bills of exchange (crowns, 000s; 1848 = 1) | | Mortgage stock (crowns, 000s; 1848 = 1) | |
|---|---|---|---|---|---|---|---|---|---|---|
| 1848 | 36 | 1·0 | 3,724 | 1·0 | 19,138 | 1·0 | 2,696 | 1·0 | 17,250 | 1·0 |
| 1860 | 38 | 1·1 | 5,026 | 1·3 | 76,244 | 3·9 | 44,966 | 16·7 | 108,384 | 6·3 |
| 1867 | 107 | 2·9 | 28,874 | 7·8 | 143,126 | 7·5 | 81,208 | 30·1 | 170,050 | 9·9 |
| 1873 | 637 | 17·7 | 199,588 | 53·5 | 348,416 | 18·2 | 267,648 | 102·6 | 333,676 | 19·3 |
| 1890 | 1,225 | 34·1 | 348,532 | 93·5 | 1,104,595 | 57·7 | 662,890 | 245·9 | 938,658 | 54·4 |
| 1900 | 2,696 | 74·9 | 833,379 | 223·8 | 1,773,631 | 92·7 | 1,313,391 | 487·2 | 1,924,679 | 111·6 |
| 1913 | 5,993 | 166·5 | 2,568,397 | 689·6 | 4,123,596 | 215·5 | 3,266,227 | 1,211·5 | 3,941,786 | 228·5 |

system went through another important period of expansion. The number of financial institutions grew rapidly once again, reaching a figure of 1,842 and covering even the most backward districts with a network of banks. Even more rapid was the growth of their assets. Within a decade and a half capital stock and savings deposits more than doubled, approaching 5·7 billion crowns.

This extensive development of the banking system, however, was far from limited to purely quantitative changes. Most striking was the completion of a process already visible at the end of the century: alongside the rapid growth in the number of banks and their assets, the leading banks of Budapest advanced even more rapidly. The four banks which had been prominent at the end of the century, joined by a fifth, the Hungarian Bank and Trading Company (Magyar Bank és Kereskedelmi Rt), extended their influence over the smaller city and country banks, still centres of local importance. At the end of the century the five great banks still had only 16 branches, and an interest in 19 other financial institutions. By 1913 the number of branches had grown to 76, that of affiliated institutions to 153. By 1913 the emerging bank groups had brought under their control the greater part (58 per cent) of the capital assets of the entire Hungarian credit system.

Associated with this process, was a change in the whole character of the banks. Assured of a powerful position, the great banks ever more rapidly extended their advances to industry. The predominantly Crédit Mobilier-type banks of the 1860s and 1870s, engaged in lending and speculative investment, were transformed into investment banks of the German type, involved in entrepreneurial and financing activities and retaining permanent control over a wide range of industries.

### RAILWAY BUILDING: CREATION OF A MODERN COMMUNICATIONS SYSTEM

Demands for the construction of a modern communications system in Hungary, as a first step toward modernising the Hungarian economy, were practically contemporaneous with the first appearance of railways in Europe. In view of the primitive condition of the roads and the limitations of water transport, railways seemed the only possible way of shipping agricultural surpluses abroad, and exports the only way of overcoming the shortage of capital which hampered development of the great estates. Thus it is understandable that, from the 1830s, the great Hungarian reformer of the first half of the nineteenth century, István Széchenyi, worked out comprehensive plans for the creation of a modern system of communications. Lajos Kossuth, who in the 1840s emerged as the leading political exponent of bourgeois revolution and national independence for Hungary, himself placed great stress on the initiation and development of railway building and steamboat transport. The public debates about railway routes soon gave way to action; in 1846—relatively early by East Central European standards—the first line was opened, connecting Pest and Vác. It was 46 kilometres long, and was planned as part of a Pest–Vienna line. By 1848 a total of about 200 kilometres of railway had been built.

As part of the imperial system which had evolved since the 1830s the Hungarian railways were greatly extended, after the creation of a joint customs area in 1850, in response to the Austrian demand for imports of foodstuffs and to Imperial political considerations. First Vienna and Pest were joined by rail; but more important was the linking of the capital with the great agricultural centres, mostly from the latter half of the decade, with rail lines totalling 2,160 kilometres in length by 1866. The Vienna–Pest–Szeged–Temesvár line connected the metropolises with the most important grain-producing region to the south, the Vienna–Szolnok–Debrecen line made a similar link with the centres of stock-raising east of the Tisza.

Ninety-seven per cent of the lines constructed were in the hands of three great railway companies; two of these were owned by the Rothschilds and the third was under their influence.

The years after the Compromise of 1867 saw an extraordinary surge of railway building in Hungary. During the great railway boom which stretched from the mid-1850s to the 1870s, the Hungarian railways were privately built, especially after the policy of state support for private construction was accepted in 1854; of the Hungarian lines which were opened before 1873, only 16 per cent were publicly owned. State support for private railways took the form of a guaranteed 5 per cent interest on capital invested, if reported earnings did not reach that figure; this commitment was given—usually for ninety years—at the time the government issued a concession for each new project. The system of guaranteed interest opened the way for unexampled speculation and profiteering. The great age of railway building became an age of great financial scandals as well.

A private-railway deal began with the acquisition of a concession. This was a fair field for aristocrats and other political 'personalities', who could use their good connections to obtain a railway-building franchise, either in their own name or for a group of financiers associated with them.

Frequently the bestowal of such a franchise was followed, not by the start of construction, but by speculation in the licensing papers. These documents were regularly bought and sold; it often happened that before a railway finally began to be built, a whole series of concession-owners, international swindlers, and politically well-connected domestic 'licensees' made their appearance in turn.

In 1870 the government paid only 2 million crowns in interest guarantees; but between 1871 and 1873 it paid, on a yearly average, 16 million, and, in 1874, almost 32 million crowns.

The main railways of Hungary were built in the years after the Compromise, at an enormous profit to the 21 banks which collaborated in their financing; of these 15 were Austrian, led by the Austrian Rothschilds, who also acted as intermediary for French, Belgian, German, and English capital. The lines of mainly industrial importance made up only 10 per cent of the whole system at the time of the laying out of the main routes.

As a result of the unscrupulous, tumultuous railway fever, the pace of rail construction quickened markedly in the years after the Compromise. In the 1850s an average of 250 kilometres was put into service annually; in the years after the Compromise the average was 600 kilometres a year. Between 1867 and 1873 over 4,000 kilometres of new railway were opened; by the latter date the extent of the whole system exceeded 6,000 kilometres, almost three times its length in 1866.

The panic of 1873 put a stop temporarily to the railway-building boom. But early in the 1880s, after several years of stagnation, another big upswing began. In these years the main lines built earlier were connected by a dense network of local lines. In 1900 17,000 kilometres of railway were being operated in the country; in 1913 over 22,000 kilometres.

During these years a marked change took place in the system of railway construction. Where previously the government had supported the building of a private system of railways, now, following the panic, the role of the state grew significantly. In December 1877 Austria returned to a system of state railways. In Hungary the greater part of the railways came into the hands of the state. By the end of the century only about 3,000 kilometres of privately owned railway were in operation in the country, out of a total railway system of almost 14,000 kilometres. Nationalisation not only meant taking over and redeeming the securities of railway companies ruined in the crash; it also served purposes of political and economic policy as well. The state sought to develop the transport system more rapidly, and to compensate, through its power to set railway rates, for the limitations imposed by Habsburg customs policy. The state thus played an important part in Hungary in the creation of a railway system well-developed even by European standards.

By Central and Eastern European standards, the density of the Hungarian railway system was especially advanced. At the end of the century there were 5 kilometres of railway line for every 100 square kilometres, and about 87 kilometres of railway for every 100,000 inhabitants. These figures were essentially identical with those for the Austrian and Czech lands, far surpassed the level of development of the other countries of Eastern and South-eastern Europe, and approached the Western European standard.

This developed railway system naturally transformed the country's communications radically. The importance of the railways, however, was far from being limited merely to the expansion of transport facilities. The railways acted as a multiplier; their extension exercised an extraordinary influence on other branches of the economy, creating markets on every hand. Above all, they expanded the labour market, stirring enormous masses of people from their traditional immobility and enabling

TABLE 3
Growth of railway network

| Year | Length of railways (kilometres) | Length of railways (km) per 100 sq km |
|---|---|---|
| 1846 | 35 | 0·0 |
| 1850 | 222 | 0·08 |
| 1867 | 2,285 | 0·8 |
| 1873 | 6,253 | 1·9 |
| 1890 | 11,246 | 3·4 |
| 1900 | 17,108 | 5·2 |
| 1913 | 22,084 | 6·8 |

hundreds of thousands to become wage workers. But wide-scale railway building also significantly affected the markets for land and capital; and, during the age of railway fever, railway construction itself became, through the orders it provided, the prime market for industry.

Side by side with the spread of railways went the beginnings of modern water transport. In the 1830s steamboats made their appearance on the Danube. At first progress was at a modest pace: in pre-Compromise Hungary 135 steamboats and 532 barges provided water transport.

Thereafter, however, the development of shipping was extremely rapid. As a result of the extension of waterways and the continual improvement in rivers—including the works begun on the lower Danube after the Treaty of Berlin (1878) and completed, in five stages, in 1896—the country possessed 3,500 kilometres of waterways navigable by steam vessels by the time of World War I. River transport was given a strong impetus by the constant expansion of the Danube Steamship Navigation Company's (Donaudampfschiffsfahrtgesellschaft) fleet, and by the creation in the 1880s of a division of the Hungarian State Railways for water transport, made into an independent company in 1894 as the Hungarian River and Ocean Transport Company (Magyar Folyam és Tengerhajózási Rt, MEFTER). By 1914 338 steam vessels and 1,500 barges were serving the needs of water traffic in Hungary.

During these decades of the Austro-Hungarian Empire, then, enormous investments went to build a modern infrastructure, which in turn became a decisive factor itself in the growth of production.

## 2  Transformation of the economy: agriculture, industry, commerce

### DEVELOPMENT OF AGRICULTURE

In the middle of the nineteenth century Hungary was a predominantly agrarian country, where 80–88 per cent of the population earned their living on the land. Moreover, serfdom and other feudal institutions inhibited the growth of the main branches of production.

The revolution of 1848 abolished serfdom in Hungary. Laws promulgated in March 1848, and approved by the king in April, put an end to manorial jurisdiction, to the payment of feudal dues to the lord, and to tithes. While abolition extended to all the serfs, only some of the former serfs received the land which they had previously cultivated. This affected—counting family members—about 3 million leasehold serfs, while another 4 million received a plot too small, for the most part, to provide a living by itself. In addition, serfs who had worked on the lord's estate remained without land. All in all, and taking into account special cases, regional variations and meadow and pasture lands retained as communal property, about half the land came into the peasants' possession, the other half remaining with the landlords. Moreover, emancipation did not do away with a good many minor feudal obligations, making it possible for disputes to be settled to the disadvantage of the emancipated serfs in many cases. On the other hand, the legislation relating to the emancipation of the serfs was not reversed after the defeat of the War of Independence; essentially, the Urbarial Patent of 1853 did not alter the basic principles of the emancipation; but it did confirm practices in its execution which favoured the landlord, and it created a situation where disputes about the final division of lands between lord and peasant dragged on for decades.

This settlement, and the lawsuits connected with it, troubled great landowners, the courts, and sometimes the gendarmerie, for many years; but the course of future Hungarian agricultural development had been set. The former manorial estate worked by serf labour was gradually transformed into a capitalist enterprise employing wage labour, while large numbers of peasants remained landless, earning their living on the great estates as seasonal wage labourers or permanent farm servants (*cselédek*).

In itself, of course, the emancipation of the serfs did not create conditions for the emergence of modern agriculture. Markets were lacking, or else the transport facilities needed to exploit them; capital and a modern organisation of labour were lacking. All these developed only gradually.

Above all else, it was railway construction that helped to overcome these obstacles. Soon after the building of the first main lines it became possible to compete in the Austrian market, now open following the abolition of the old customs barriers.

The credit situation improved somewhat too, though here one can hardly speak of a fundamental change. With the expansion of the banking system, mortgage loans outstanding grew eightfold. With this development, too, went the increased use of machinery on the great estates: several thousand seed-drills and reaping machines made their appearance, and in 1871 2,420 steam threshers were recorded. Signs of change appeared in the pattern of agricultural production too: the area sown to potatoes, sugar beet, and hemp increased, and the area of fallow land diminished. All in all, however, the rapid commercialisation of agriculture did not begin until the end of the 1860s.

In the half-century after the Compromise no essential change took place in the structure of Hungarian landownership. To the end the system of great estates dominated, reflecting the way the emancipation had been carried out. According to the census of 1895, estates over 1,000 *hold* (about 1,400 acres), representing 0·2 per cent of the number of holdings, occupied more than 32 per cent of the country's land surface; while at the same time peasant holdings under 100 *hold*, 99 per cent of the total number, occupied only 52 per cent of the land.

TABLE 4

Land distribution in 1895

| Size of holdings (in hold*) | Percentage of all farms | Percentage of total land area |
|---|---|---|
| 0– 5 | 53·6 | 5·8 |
| 5– 20 | 35·3 | 23·6 |
| 20– 100 | 10·1 | 22·9 |
| 100–1,000 | 0·8 | 15·4 |
| 1,000– | 0·2 | 32·3 |

\* 1 *hold* = 1·4 acres.

Measures were even taken to preserve the latifundia. A law of 1867 strengthened the system of entails (*fidei commissi*) which had existed earlier; under it sixty-four new entailed estates were created, raising to 2,300,000 *hold* the area of indivisible and inalienable estate land.

At the same time, however, several measures worked to strengthen the existing peasant properties. Among these were laws which settled questions left over from the emancipation in favour of the peasant (eg, abolition of the surviving tithe on vineyards), the consolidation of scattered plots to form more viable peasant holdings, and settlement schemes at the end of the century which, with the co-operation of the state, made available to the peasantry small amounts of land not needed by the great landowners.

As already mentioned, the supply of credit—during the entire nineteenth century a central question for agricultural development—improved only very slowly up to 1867. But after the Compromise, along with the development of the Hungarian credit system, Austrian capital increasingly took a direct interest in the Hungarian mortgage market. The mortgage department of the Austrian National Bank (after 1878 the Austro-Hungarian Bank), together with other Viennese credit institutions, made larger and larger loans to great Hungarian landowners. The total amount of mortgage credit extended to landowners by domestic banks increased rapidly as well. The Hungarian mortgage loans of the Austro-Hungarian Bank and the Hungarian credit institutions—170 million crowns in 1867—increased roughly eleven-fold by 1900; and in the next decade they doubled again, reaching 3,800 million crowns in 1913. From two-thirds to three-quarters of these loans were made on landed property. They naturally played a great part in the technical development of agriculture. However, a rather large part of them went to perpetuate the landowners' free-spending way of life or, in the case of peasants, to buy new pieces of land.

After the Compromise the practice of leasing land spread too. Renting out part of his estates—more precisely, the income thus obtained—enabled the landowner to modernise the property which he still cultivated directly. At the end of the century nearly a fifth of the total area of all holdings over 100 *hold* was in the hands of capitalist tenant farmers. Improved credit facilities and good sales outlets led to a rise in the profitability of Hungarian agriculture. The industrialisation of Western Europe—of Austria and Germany especially—expanded external markets significantly, and the rapid progress of railway construction eased the problem of reaching the markets by linking up the best farmlands with the transport system. Hungarian agricultural exports grew by leaps and bounds; at the end of the 1870s they averaged between half and three-quarters of a million tons per year, but by the eve of World War I the export of grain alone had jumped to over one and a half million tons. The internal market expanded too, though at a slower rate.

This advance was temporarily interrupted by the agrarian crisis which broke out in the mid-70s, largely as a result of the appearance of cheap overseas grain on the European market. Once the transport problem was overcome, American produce reached the Western European market in great quantities, where, because of its lower production costs, it sold more cheaply, driving out Hungarian foodstuffs. The crisis struck Hungarian agriculture particularly hard, burdened as it was with feudal survivals and (partly because of them) with excessive specialisation on cereal growing. High costs of production were the consequence of backwardness. Mechanisation was still on a fairly primitive level, and productivity was low.

Spurred by the agrarian crisis, the countries of Europe (England excepted) introduced, from the end of the 1870s, a policy of protective tariffs. After the changeover to the protective system it became more difficult to sell Hungarian exports in markets outside the Monarchy, where high duties and cheaply produced American wheat made it almost impossible for them to compete. As a part of the Austro-Hungarian Monarchy, however, Hungary could enjoy the benefits of its new protective system, which assured the products of Hungarian agriculture a secure position in the Monarchy's internal markets. It was not possible to stop the fall in prices which occurred as a result of the crisis—17 per cent from the 1870s to the 1880s—but a greater decline was avoided. The Monarchy's market thus compensated for the loss of markets elsewhere. At the same time the grain crisis encouraged mechanisation in Hungary, and promoted the development of other, more intensively cultivated crops at the expense of grain. The modern technical transformation of Hungarian agriculture began in the 1860s; in the 1870s and 1880s it began to catch up with the Western European countries.

The level of mechanisation, an important factor in the technical development of agriculture, was still extremely low at the beginning of the 1870s. Progress at first took the form of improvements in the traditional implements (ploughs and scythes), and of producing more and better tools. New animal-drawn equipment was introduced too; but the greatest change was the application of the steam engine to agriculture. Between 1871 and 1895 the number of steam-driven threshing machines nearly quadrupled, and the number of those driven by animal power increased fifteen-fold; horsedrawn seed-drills multiplied nearly seven-fold, horsedrawn reapers and harvesters tripled. In the years up to World War I the number of steam threshers tripled again, to about 30,000, compared with 2,500 in 1871. This made possible the complete mechanisation of the threshing process, the only agricultural operation completely mechanised in Hungary at this time.

By the end of the nineteenth century most large and middle-sized estates collected and used substantial amounts of animal manure. Before the end of the century the available supply of manure allowed, nationwide, for fertilising on average once every nine years.

Artificial fertilisers, which were becoming increasingly important alongside farmyard manure all over Europe in the later nineteenth century, appeared in Hungary about the end of the century. While in 1898 only about 5½lb of artificial fertiliser were used per *hold* (1·4 acres) of arable soil, in 1913 the figure had risen to about 26½lb.

The productivity of the land was also increased by various other forms of soil improvement, which were used with growing frequency in this period. The most important of them were the reclamation works, dating from 1879. About 2½ million *hold* (4 million acres) were drained between 1879 and 1918.

Under the influence of technical progress in agriculture, the area under cultivation grew, and important changes took place in the relationship of the various branches of agriculture. Between 1873 and 1913 the area under crops grew by nearly one-third, to 5½ million *hold* (about 8 million acres). The increase in cropland sprang primarily from the reduction (by about one-third) of the amount of unproductive soil, and from the conversion of pasture and meadow land. As a result of the changed relations among the various branches of cultivation, the proportion of arable land rose from 35 per cent in 1873 to 45·5 per cent in 1913.

The extension of arable land is inseparable, of course, from the expansion of the area sown to crops and the shrinkage of the fallow. The backwardness of Hungarian agriculture at the time of the Compromise could be seen in the unusually high proportion of fallow land: in the first half of the 1870s about 22 per cent of the arable land was lying fallow. By the second decade of the twentieth century this figure had fallen to 8 per cent.

If one examines agricultural production, one is struck by the great increase in the quantities produced of certain commodities. Between the decades 1871–80 and 1900–10 the production of wheat increased two and a half times (from about 1·7 million tons to over 4·1 million); the production of maize more than doubled, while that of rye, barley, and oats grew by 55 per cent to 80 per cent. Particularly large was the increase in the output of certain industrial and fodder crops: potato production grew 3·7 times, that of sugar beet six-fold, of root fodder 7·6 times, of hay and grain fodder five-fold. This great increase in crop production sprang partly from the expansion of the area sown, partly from increased productivity, ie, higher yields per acre.

TABLE 5

*Production of main crops (tons, 00,000s)*

|  | 1864–6 | 1911–13 | 1911–13 as percentage of 1864–6 |
|---|---|---|---|
| Wheat | 17·2 | 49·1 | 285·5 |
| Rye | 11·2 | 13·2 | 117·9 |
| Barley | 6·7 | 16·8 | 250·7 |
| Oats | 6·2 | 13·6 | 219·4 |
| Maize | 13·4 | 48·5 | 361·9 |
| Potatoes | 7·3 | 54·9 | 752·0 |
| Sugar beet | 2·0 | 43·3 | 2,165·0 |

An increase in the area planted is observable only in the case of certain crops: of the increase in arable between the decades 1871–80 and 1901–10, 44 per cent fell to wheat, 23 per cent to corn, and 25 per cent to hay and grain fodder. During this period the acreage under these three crops grew by 50 per cent, 34 per cent, and nearly 200 per cent respectively. A substantial increase can also be seen in the amount of land planted to root fodder, sugar beet, and potatoes, while the area under rye, oats, legumes, and several industrial crops (tobacco, hemp, and rape) declined.

The other important factor in the growth of agricultural output was the significant rise in average yields per acre of wheat. The increase was 66 per cent between the decades 1871–80 and 1901–10; for maize it was 60 per cent, for rye 71 per cent, for oats 79 per cent. The growth of the average yield was especially rapid in the case of potatoes (160 per cent) and root fodder (119 per cent).

Stockbreeding was characterised by notable progress too,

especially from the 1880s. Between 1870 and 1911 the number of pigs grew by 74 per cent, the number of horned cattle by 34 per cent. In 1895 the aggregate value of all livestock was more than 1,540 million crowns, of which cattle accounted for 53 per cent, horses for 28 per cent and pigs for 13 per cent. Stock-raising was an important component of the national income.

TABLE 6

*Animal stocks (millions)*

|  | 1870–5 | 1910–14 | 1910–14 as percentage of 1870–5 |
|---|---|---|---|
| Pigs | 4·44 | 7·58 | 170·7 |
| Cattle | 5·28 | 7·32 | 138·6 |
| Horses | 1·67 | 2·20 | 131·7 |
| Sheep | 15·08 | 8·55 | 56·7 |

At the end of the century more than 40 per cent of the income from farming—915,600,000 crowns out of 2,210,000,000 using the annual average for the years 1899–1901—came from stockbreeding.

The development of stockbreeding cannot be sketched in purely numerical terms, however; attention must be paid to the qualitative changes too. During the period under consideration significant progress took place in this area. Some advance was observable in the decade before 1895, but it was principally after that date that the really important qualitative improvements took place.

There was particularly great progress in cattle-raising. In 1884 more than 80 per cent of the cattle in the country were of the native Hungarian variety, giving low yields of meat and milk, and useful primarily as draught animals; but by 1895 only two-thirds were of this variety, and in 1911 fewer than one-third.

The growth of the number of cows is a significant index of the changeover to a more intensive form of cattle-raising. By 1911 more than 46 per cent of the cattle in the country were cows (compared with 37 per cent in 1884), which in itself led to increased production of milk and other dairy products.

As in the case of cattle-breeding, great qualitative improvements were made with other farm animals. Between 1884 and 1911 the proportion of pigs raised for meat rose from 11 per cent to 20 per cent.

Despite the general predominance of large estates, Hungarian stock-raising was based primarily on peasant property. The great bulk of domestic stock was in the hands of the peasantry. In 1911 more than four-fifths of the cattle were on farms under 100 *hold*, along with nearly 85 per cent of the pigs and more than 87 per cent of the horses. Estates over 100 *hold* led only in sheep-raising, with about 62 per cent of the national stock.

Despite a visible slackening in the pace of development of field crops, Hungarian agriculture continued to display notable progress after 1900, thanks chiefly to qualitative advances in stockbreeding. The rate of development of agriculture was lower than that of industry, but all in all can still be deemed extremely rapid. The annual increase in production of non-animal crops, from the time of the Compromise to World War I, reached 2 per cent; for animal products the rate of growth was 1·7 per cent per annum.

Based on these figures, the gross annual rate of growth of Hungarian agricultural production was 1·8 per cent (according to other calculations, 2·2 per cent).

TABLE 7

*Gross agricultural production, 1867–1913* (%)

| Year | Crowns, millions* | Yearly average growth | Crowns, millions† | Yearly average growth |
|---|---|---|---|---|
| 1867–70 | 1,814 | 2·2 | 3,060 | 1·8 |
| 1911–13 | 5,265 | | 6,935 | |

\* According to the calculation of I. T. Berend—Gy Ránki, 'Nationaleinkommen und Kapitalakkumulation in Ungarn 1867–1914', *Studia Historica*, No 62 (1970), Calculated on prices of 1900.

† According to the calculation of L. Katus, 'Economic Growth in Hungary During the Age of Dualism, 1867–1918', *Studia Historica*, No 62 (1970). Calculated on prices of 1913.

Before World War I agriculture played a decisive role both from the standpoint of employment, and for its contribution to the gross national product.

## DEVELOPMENT OF FACTORY INDUSTRY

In Hungary in the first half of the nineteenth century the social division of labour had not gone very far. According to available statistics, only one out of every twenty inhabitants lived in a town in the 1840s. Independent artisans made up the bulk of the modest industrial population. They numbered about 230,000, plus 78,000 journeymen and apprentices; in addition there were 23,000 'factory operatives', workers employed in large establishments using mechanical or manual power. Thus the industrial population, with their families, made up about 5 per cent of the population of the country.

As these data indicate, not only was the role of industry negligible, but such industry as existed was predominantly small handicraft industry. The greater part of industrial activity still went on within the limits of the guild system which had survived from the Middle Ages and which, indeed, enjoyed a renaissance in Hungary in the eighteenth century, following the expulsion of the Turks.

There were very few large enterprises which broke up the labour process into simple operations. According to some figures, the majority of the 450 or so 'large works' employed only 20–40 workers. Some of these were operated as a sideline on landed estates, to process crops grown on them (mills, distilleries) or other raw materials found there (iron foundries, glass works). Their workers frequently came from the serfs on the estate. Steam engines scarcely existed in Hungary. The census of 1841 found nine steam engines in the country, generating 100 horsepower; but only four of these were being used in industry.

From the late 1830s a few larger and more typical factories came into existence, as a result of a new policy of deliberate support for industry and promotion of new establishments. In 1838 the Pest Rolling Mill Company (Pesti Hengermalom Társaság) was founded, the first Hungarian steam mill, through the reforming efforts of István Széchenyi; it was followed by a number of factory-type sugar refineries processing sugar beet, and by breweries and distilleries.

Coal mining for all practical purposes began in these years, and, in spite of antiquated technique, the manufacture of iron grew significantly in quantity. Little rural machine shops working on agricultural equipment developed into the first small machine-tool factories; their number was increased by the establishments of foreign manufacturers settling in the country, such as Ábrahám Ganz, and by the first Austrian establishments, such as the Danube Steam Ship Navigation Company in Óbuda which with a thousand workers was one of the largest enterprises in the country. Lajos Kossuth's great agitation on behalf of industrialisation encouraged the growth of the textile industry, marked by the founding or expansion of the first important factories.

In the environment of absolutist repression which weighed upon Hungary after the defeat of the revolutions of 1848–9, the decade of the 1850s was not a favourable one for industrial advance, even after the introduction of a common customs area in 1850. Even so, it was at this time that mechanised large-scale industry began to spread, following the beginnings of railway construction by (largely) Austrian capital. Substantial enterprises appeared, especially in the extractive branches of industry. The Austrian State Railway Company and the Danube Steam Ship Navigation Company almost monopolised transport in Hungary, and played a leading role in the development of Hungarian coal mining. The hard-coal mines were around Stájerlak-Anina, Resica-Domán, and Pécs. The two companies greatly increased the output of the mines; almost the entire hard-coal production of the country was in their hands. The role of Austrian capital in the extraction of brown coal also grew significantly from 1849 to 1867. Seventy-five to eighty per cent of Hungary's growing coal production—ten times that of pre-1848 days—was in the hands of Austrian capital at this time.

Iron production, increasing principally to meet the demands of railway-building, also came to a great extent from mines and foundries established by Austrian capital. On the site of its iron ore mines the Austrian State Railway Company built what was even by European standards a formidable industrial complex, producing crude iron from its own ore with the aid of its own coal and charcoal from its own forests, then refining it and rolling it into rails and other equipment in its plant at Resica for use on its own railways.

Since the Austrian railway system's foundries produced essentially to meet its own needs and Austrian iron manufacture in general stagnated until the mid-1850s, the growth of demand for iron created opportunities for Hungarian entrepreneurs. Thus in 1852 the Rimamurány Iron Works Company (Rimamurányi Vasmű Egyesület) was formed by the merger of three smaller foundries. In 1865 the output of crude iron in Hungary approached 100,000 tons. Despite the relative backwardness of its productive and technical level, it filled an important role in Hungarian industry.

Agricultural prosperity also contributed to the development of industry. Along with the Austrian transport companies' installations, producing essentially to cover their own needs, several other shops founded before 1848 began to expand. One of the most prominent of them was the Ganz works, producing mainly railway wheels and milling equipment, and the Röck, Vidats, Schlick, and Ötl factories, which made various kinds of agricultural implements, from iron ploughs to threshing machines. In 1863 the power sources of Hungarian foundries and shops amounted altogether to 218 horsepower, one-ninth of the Austrian figure.

In these decades the greater and more easily mobilisable part of the capital accumulated domestically was in the hands of merchants. Within the joint customs area it was trade in agricultural produce, relying on the demands of the industrialising Austrian and Czech lands and the opportunities offered by a rapidly developing Hungarian agriculture, which provided the main source of capital accumulation. The best opportunities for the profitable investment of the sums accumulated by the great merchants were offered, from the 1860s, by the export of certain Hungarian agricultural products, mainly grain processed into flour. Even before the Compromise there was an extraordinary growth of interest in the establishment of flour mills.

During the 1860s a number of large milling companies made

their appearance in Pest and Buda. By 1867 fourteen 'major' mills had been founded in the capital, but in the country, too, mills were set up one after another with more than local importance, for they worked for export as well. Between 1852 and 1863 the quantity of horsepower used in the milling industry multiplied almost thirteen-fold. Significant progress was recorded in distilling as well.

Important foreign investments were made outside the extractive and heavy industries, especially in the sugar industry.

In spite of the progress made in the years before the Compromise we can speak at most of the sporadic appearance of machinery. In all Hungarian industry 480 steam engines were in operation, with a total capacity of only a little over 8,100 horsepower.

After the Compromise of 1867 more rapid industrial growth was assured, in part, by the entrepreneurial activity of the new banks, which extended to industry as well, but more especially by the unprecedentedly powerful stimulus of the railway mania and by the growing opportunities for accumulation offered by a booming society in general. It was the post-1867 boom which first linked the development of Hungarian industry—hitherto based primarily on individual accumulation of capital—with the joint-stock form of organisation.

Only a minority of the industrial corporations founded at this time were entirely new enterprises, most of them having existed before as individual proprietorships; still, the establishment of joint-stock companies marked an important stage, for by permitting increased investment it made possible the introduction of newer, more advanced technology. Those industries flourished most whose development could already be observed in the decades before 1867. Thus food-processing continued to lead the advance. One-third of the new firms founded as joint-stock companies (and a good many of those established by individuals as well) were in the milling industry.

In 1866 the mills of Budapest ground about 50,000 tons of wheat; by 1875 the figure was close to 300,000 tons, in 1879 430,000, or more than an eight-fold increase, and their capacity grew even more rapidly. A notable factor in the development of this industry was the introduction of modern equipment. Particularly important as a technical innovation was the use of the new roller-milling methods in place of the traditional millstone. Its technical advancement contributed to a considerable extent to the rise of Hungarian milling, after the Compromise, to a position of dominance in the Monarchy-wide common market, and beyond that to an important place in the world market.

Second only to milling among food-processing industries, the sugar industry continued the growth already begun in the 1850s. In the decade following the Compromise the quantity of sugar beet processed rose by more than 80 per cent, and sugar production itself by 124 per cent.

The development of heavy industry after the Compromise was evident first and foremost in coal mining. Between 1866 and 1873 coal production more than doubled, from 700,000 tons to 1,630,000, but it still failed to keep pace with the growth of coal consumption. Technical progress was signalled by the replacement of wooden rails by iron equipment in the mines, and of animal or water power by steam in moving the coal to the pithead.

Iron mining, too, quickened after the Compromise: between 1869 and 1873 output almost doubled, from 290,000 tons of ore to nearly 550,000. Austrian capital owned about one-third of the iron mines, and at least one-fifth of the ore—an average of 100,000 tons a year in the 1870s—was sent to Austria for smelting. For this reason the production of pig iron grew more slowly than that of iron ore, by scarcely 50 per cent (from 110,000 tons to 160,000, 1869–73).

One-fifth of Hungarian pig iron production was turned out by the Austrian State Railway Company's operation in southern Transylvania; the Rimamurány Iron Works occupied second place with one-tenth of total output. These plants also stood in the forefront of technical development in the field. The Austrian company during these years was the first in Hungary to employ the Bessemer process and the Martin method of steelmaking in its mills. The iron and steel works at Diósgyőr, founded by the Treasury in 1868, also put Martin smelters into operation at the end of the 1870s.

In 1868 the Ganz works adopted the corporate form of organisation; in the 1870s, alongside its first main product, cast railway-carriage wheels, Ganz began to exploit its other, even more important patent, for the roller-milling which was to revolutionise the milling industry. With its introduction Ganz acquired a place of importance on the Central European market, and even on the world market. At the same time it earned rich profits from deliveries of munitions (eg, cannon) to the Austro-Hungarian and German armies. The year 1873 saw the opening of the Hungarian State Railway Machine Works (Magyar Államvasuti Gépgyár, MÁVAG), which introduced the manufacture of steam locomotives into the country, and was also equipped to make locomotive equipment and threshing machines. In a short time it became the second largest engineering works in the capital.

Hungarian machine production, concentrated almost exclusively in Budapest, was closely bound up with the needs of the transport system and, secondarily, with those of agriculture and the food industry. The number of modern plants making other kinds of machinery was insignificant. Austrian and Czech factories supplied the greater part of Hungarian domestic demand. Even the relatively advanced Hungarian farm machinery industry was no exception to this rule.

All over the country, the boom which followed the Compromise was accompanied by an upsurge of construction, leading to the founding of a number of new construction companies, principally in Budapest.

Thus, beginning in the years before the Compromise, but more especially in succeeding years, the foundations of Hungarian industry were laid. The spread of the steam engine was already notable at this time. During the years between the censuses of 1863 and 1884 the steam-power used in Hungarian industry jumped almost eight-fold, from 8,100 to 63,900 horsepower. The distribution of steam engines, however, remained fairly uneven; 36,700 horsepower, almost 60 per cent of total capacity, was concentrated in the food industry. But in these years in the iron industry steam engines increased six-fold and other achievements of modern technology were introduced.

Charcoal was replaced by coke in the smelting process, the water wheels which had formerly driven the bellows were withdrawn from service, and, after the introduction of the Bessemer and Martin processes (1868 and 1873) a good many of the furnaces employing an older technology were closed down.

Following the depression of the years 1873-9, which affected many areas of production, Hungarian industry in the last decades of the century acquired new momentum. This process was closely connected with the beginnings of state support for industry.

In Hungary, the idea of state support first arose in connection with the renewal of the Austro-Hungarian economic compromise in 1878, as a kind of compensation for the impossibility of introducing protective tariffs because of the common customs area. The first law to stimulate industry, passed in 1881, offered tax exemptions and the like to new factories, but it was not very effective. Somewhat more effective was a law of 1890 which made possible the extension of subsidies and interest-free loans to industry. They were supplemented, after the nationalisation of the railways, by rate schedules designed to favour industry. After the law of 1899 this series of laws to promote industry was crowned by a statute of 1907 which, for the first time, indicated the direction of future development on the basis of systematic prior studies: it concentrated the greater part (57 per cent) of the projected subsidies of about 50 million crowns on the textile industry. In all, however, the subsidies of 76 million crowns paid to private industry amounted to a mere 2 per cent of their total investment. Much more important was the fact that the state purchased 13 per cent of industrial production—indeed, in some branches, like machine-building, it bought almost one-third of output.

From the end of the century, however, the state's most important function was not so much to mobilise its own resources, as to attract foreign capital into various industrial fields. The new boom was clearly marked by the establishment of large foreign-owned enterprises.

It was from the 1890s that the influx of foreign capital led to the development of the country's greatest mining companies. In the early 1890s the Hungarian General Coal Mining Company (Magyar Általános Kőszénbánya Rt) was formed with French and Austrian capital to exploit one of the country's most important brown-coal fields, around Tatabánya. The second largest coal operator, the Salgótarján Coal Mining Co, was jointly run by Austrian, German, and Hungarian capital, and it was largely thanks to this circumstance that the firm was able to expand its production so rapidly. In 1899 the Salgótarján Coal Mining Co produced 28·8 per cent of the coal mined in Hungary.

Coal production rose rapidly, by more than three and a half times from 1880 (1,800,000 tons) to 1900 (almost 6,500,000 tons); by 1913 it had climbed nearly another 60 per cent, to 10,200,000 tons. Though substantial, this increase did not nearly cover the growth of internal demand, as is clearly indicated by the much more rapid rate of increase in coal imports (up seven-fold by the end of the century).

TABLE 8

*Coal production (tons, millions)*

| Year | Lignite | Coal | Total | 1860=1 |
|---|---|---|---|---|
| 1860 | 2·4 | 2·4 | 4·8 | 1·0 |
| 1880 | 10·1 | 8·0 | 18·1 | 3·8 |
| 1900 | 52·1 | 13·7 | 65·8 | 13·9 |
| 1913 | 89·5 | 13·2 | 102·7 | 21·7 |

When two of the largest Hungarian iron-makers, the Rimamurány Works and the Salgótarján Foundry (Salgótarján Vasfimomitó), undertook large-scale conversions of their plant requiring substantial amounts of capital, the great Austrian banks took the opportunity to extend their influence by making their supply of funds conditional on the merger of the two firms. Since the Wiener Bankverein already had a large interest in the Salgótarján works, the same banking house thus acquired a decisive influence in the newly created enterprise. At the same time, this merger was a step forward of great significance for the Hungarian iron industry. It created one of the country's largest industrial enterprises, which in the decade after 1900 reorganised its production, streamlining and modernising its plant. Steel production was centralised at Ózd, which big new

Martin furnaces were built, while Salgótarján became the centre for the production of iron goods. Thanks to successive investments in new equipment, the firm developed a power capacity in the years before the war of over 45,000 horsepower; it employed 16,000 workers. The State Iron Works, the country's second largest producer of iron and steel, embraced numerous mines, foundries, and other processing plants. Its most important installation was the factory at Diósgyőr, where even in 1913 8,000 workers were employed. The Diósgyőr plant was designed to supply the state railways' need for rails, and also to produce munitions.

The Austro-Hungarian State Railway Co also owned an important ironworks. These large enterprises, owning 57 per cent of the large blast-furnaces amongst themselves, furnished over 90 per cent of all pig iron production and more than 96 per cent of steel production.

On this basis the output of iron ore, pig iron and steel progressed rapidly. By 1900 production of iron ore had reached 1,600,000 tons, and by 1913 2 million tons, 40 per cent of which was exported. Pig iron production rose from 140,000 to 460,000 tons, and then again to 620,000 tons. The newly developed steel industry, turning out 350,000 tons around the end of the century, had raised its output by 1913 to about 800,000 tons. Even on the eve of the war, however, per capita pig iron production remained far below the level of the more industrialised countries. In Hungary it was 64·6lb per head, in Austria 131·1, in Germany 550, and in the United States 717·2.

TABLE 9

*Iron and steel production*

| Year | Iron ore (tons, 000s) | index | Pig iron (tons, 000s) | index | Steel (tons, 000s) | index |
|---|---|---|---|---|---|---|
| 1867 | 294* | 50·2 | 105 | 75·0 | — | — |
| 1880 | 586 | 100·0 | 140 | 100·0 | 16 | 100·0 |
| 1900 | 1,666 | 284·3 | 456 | 325·7 | 427 | 267·0 |
| 1913 | 2,059 | 351·4 | 623 | 445·0 | 800 | 500·0 |

* Data from 1869.

After the Compromise a marked advance set in in the production of rolling stock. The manufacture of locomotives progressed side by side with the large-scale building of railways; in the last decades of the century production tripled in the shops of the state railways alone. Typical of the rapid pace of development is the fact that while 500 steam locomotives were turned out in the first twenty years of production in Hungary (1873–93), another 500 were produced in the next four years alone. In the 1880s only the Ganz works made railway trucks, but by 1898 five large plants were manufacturing them, and in the 1890s 28,000 trucks were produced, twice as many as in the previous decade.

Shipbuilding too flourished in the 1890s with the development of water transport. Besides the Danube Steam Ship Navigation Company's shipyard at Óbuda, the Danubius, Nicholson, and Röck yards also built ships.

Two-thirds of the Hungarian output of machinery consisted of transport equipment. Next, a large share was taken by the manufacture of farm machinery and equipment for the food industry, especially milling. Despite its distinguished past, however, the farm machinery industry no longer covered even half of the domestic demand.

Developments in the early twentieth century did not alter this situation. It was at this time (1900) that the country's largest farm equipment factory, the Hofherr, Schrantz, Clayton and Shuttleworth Co, was founded at Kispest on the site of the English merchants' one-time depot. In 1912 the first tractor was produced in Hungary at the Kühne Machine Works. In the years before World War I automobile manufacturing was introduced, at the Győr Waggon Factory, as well as the production of steam turbines, at the Láng Machine Works. By 1913 there were already ten engineering works in the country employing more than a thousand workers each.

An important event in the development of metal and machine production was the establishment of the Manfréd Weiss works on the island of Csepel, near Budapest. Organised as a private corporation in 1884, this modest tinned food factory soon made enormous strides, and by the beginning of the twentieth century was Hungary's biggest munitions maker.

As before, Hungarian manufacturing remained largely

limited to the primary processing of raw materials; here no essential change took place. Only 20–25 per cent of all machine tools and other industrial equipment was produced at home.

Among the more advanced lines the electrical industry acquired a growing importance. During the 1890s the manufacture of incandescent lamps and electric cables got under way on a larger scale, and the production of electrical energy in Hungary itself dates from this time. In 1890 two power stations were in existence, but by 1900 forty-three in all had been built, and thus even by European standards electrification began early in Hungary. The production of electrical energy rose from the pre-1900 figure of 36,400,000 kilowatt hours to a level of 220 million kilowatt hours in 1913 (despite which only 300 communes had electric light). This performance, however, still lagged far behind the pace of Western European development.

An important part in the development of the electrical industry was played by a number of outstanding Hungarian technical experts, whose inventions opened the way for a rapid expansion of production and, once patented, afforded a species of protection against foreign competition. Here the famous engineers of the Ganz works, Bláthy, Déry, and Zipernovszky, were especially prominent; it was they who developed the alternating-current transformer, opening the way to the development of high-powered electrical technology. The induction watt-meter designed by Bláthy was also of prime importance. In 1897 Kálmán Kandó began to experiment with the three-phase electric locomotive, and his name is linked with the construction of the first electrified railway, the Valtellina line in Italy. Thanks to the inventions of these unusually gifted engineers the Ganz Electrical Works soon became world famous.

During the course of its expansion at the end of the nineteenth century Hungarian industry retained its serious one-sidedness, in the substantial lack of a light industry in the strict sense. The backwardness of the textile industry is clearly illustrated by the fact that Hungary at the end of the century had altogether 110,000 cotton spindles, while Austria had $4\frac{1}{2}$ million and Germany nearly 10 million. The Hungarian textile industry met scarcely 14 per cent of domestic consumption, and the percentage was even lower for the most important articles: the production of woollens met not quite 10 per cent of the local demand, production of cotton cloth scarcely more than 3·5 per cent. The leather and paper industries, though they began to develop into large-scale mechanised industries in the 1880s and 1890s, were still characterised by serious backwardness.

After 1900 there was a new turn of events in the textile industry. The world boom in textiles, combined with substantial state support, offered such high and secure profits that many foreign and Hungarian entrepreneurs were induced to set up business. Between 1900 and 1913 three times as many textile factories were established as in the three previous decades together. Textile production grew three and a half times, and the number of spindles rose from 110,000 to nearly 500,000. Despite this rapid tempo of development, textile manufacturing in 1913 still satisfied only about 30 per cent of domestic demand.

Other branches of light industry developed faster. The paper industry's production more than trebled, but it mainly produced crude wares of inferior quality. Leather making began to turn into a large-scale mechanised industry at the end of the century, but still met only 40 per cent of domestic consumption.

A survey of the main branches of production demonstrates convincingly that the boom of the end of the nineteenth century and the beginning of the twentieth witnessed the triumph of the industrial revolution in Hungary. The statistics clearly demonstrate the spread of machinery and the triumph of large-scale industry. From 1884 to 1898 the capacity of the steam engines used in industry increased more than four-fold, from 63,500 to 262,100 horsepower. At the end of the century machine production based on steam power began to play a leading role in every industry.

TABLE 10

*Horsepower capacity of machines in industry*

| Year | Horsepower, 000s | 1863=1 |
|---|---|---|
| 1863 | 8 | 1·0 |
| 1884 | 81 | 10·1 |
| 1898 | 307 | 38·4 |
| 1913 | 886 | 110·8 |

The industrial base was still extremely narrow and one-sided, however, and it was only in the first decade and a half of the twentieth century that dynamic development set in in several branches which had hitherto retained the character of backward, small-scale manufacture, or had been lacking altogether. Once again the summary data place matters in an unmistakable light: between 1898 and 1913 the number of factories rose from 2,700 to 5,500, the number of workers employed from 302,000 to 563,000, and the capacity of the power equipment used in the factories from 307,000 to 930,000 horsepower, a more than three-fold increase.

The figures showing the growth of production bear witness to the rapid rate of development in the second half of the nineteenth century and at the beginning of the twentieth. Starting

TABLE 11

| Year | Value of industrial production In constant (1900) prices Crowns, millions | Index |
|---|---|---|
| 1860 | 175 | 100 |
| 1900 | 1,400 | 800 |
| 1913 | 2,539 | 1,450 |

from extremely weak foundations, Hungarian industry grew by leaps and bounds in the age of Dualism, and the pace was especially rapid around the end of the century. From the 1870s to 1900 the average annual rate of growth of industrial production was 6·2 per cent, between 1900 and 1913 5·1 per cent, giving an overall growth rate of 6·0 per cent for the entire period. As a result, industry became an important branch of the national economy, and one constantly growing in importance.

One of the most conspicuous traits of Hungary's industrial structure, early in the century, could be seen in the relation of small- to large-scale industry. The process of industrialisation described above naturally showed up not only in the rapid growth of industrial output, but also in the rapid triumph, within industry, of mechanised large-scale production. In 1880 the 110,000 factory workers made up 21 per cent of all industrial workers. At the end of the century, the 305,000 factory workers were more than 40 per cent of the industrial work force; after 1910 563,000 factory workers were over half of all workers. But factory industry at this time turned out nearly three-quarters of industrial production. At the beginning of the twentieth century, large industrial enterprises amounted to a mere 0·9 per cent of all industrial firms. But they employed more than half of all industrial workers (51 per cent in 1900). More than a third of all factory workers were found in plants with more than 500 workers, 3·8 per cent of all factories.

We may single out as another special feature of the industrial boom the peculiar distribution of the various branches of production. All over Europe, industry advanced most rapidly in those industries producing the most important articles of mass consumption. These branches could always rely on a broad consumer market; with their low level of demand for capital investment, the ease with which they overcame technical difficulties, and their ability to employ unskilled or semi-skilled workers (or train them cheaply), these industries offered a chance for high profits and a quick return on capital. All these things were true of the two great branches of light industry: textiles and foodstuffs.

In the leading countries of Western Europe the industrial revolution implied the primacy of textile manufacture. In England one may speak of the absolute predominance of the textile industry. Elsewhere, as in Belgium, Denmark, Sweden, and the Netherlands, food-processing played the largest part in factory production in the first period of the industrial revolution. The development of these countries' industries was pushed in this direction not only by the markedly agrarian nature of their economies, but also by the irresistible competition of their large neighbours, already partly industrialised (especially England), and at the same time by the powerful demand for foodstuffs generated in the neighbouring countries.

In the Eastern European countries the food industry not only played a leading role, surpassing that of textiles, but even came to acquire a one-sided dominance within industry. In Hungary this appeared in even more extreme forms, since the develop-

TABLE 12

*The structure of manufacturing industry in Hungary*

| Industry | 1898 Number of workers (000s) | Percentages of total | Value of production (crowns, millions) | Percentages of total | 1913 Number of workers (000s) | Percentages of total | Value of production (crowns, millions) | Percentages of total |
|---|---|---|---|---|---|---|---|---|
| Mining | 69·9 | 23·1 | 98·0 | 6·7 | 84·2 | 15·8 | 179·7 | 5·4 |
| Iron and steel | 44·5 | 14·7 | 184·1 | 12·6 | 62·1 | 11·5 | 503·1 | 15·2 |
| Engineering | 33·0 | 10·9 | 132·0 | 9·0 | 47·6 | 9·1 | 230·0 | 6·9 |
| Electricity | 3·0 | 1·0 | 35·1 | 2·4 | 12·8 | 2·4 | 75·0 | 2·3 |
| Building materials | 31·6 | 10·5 | 51·3 | 3·5 | 65·9 | 12·4 | 136·6 | 4·1 |
| Wood | 28·2 | 9·3 | 96·7 | 6·6 | 69·7 | 13·1 | 224·1 | 6·8 |
| Leather | 4·7 | 1·6 | 30·9 | 2·1 | 9·4 | 1·8 | 91·2 | 2·7 |
| Textiles | 13·7 | 4·6 | 53·5 | 3·6 | 46·4 | 8·7 | 208·6 | 6·3 |
| Clothing | 3·5 | 1·2 | 20·4 | 1·4 | 11·0 | 2·1 | 33·4 | 1·0 |
| Paper | 5·5 | 1·8 | 16·0 | 1·1 | 9·4 | 1·7 | 52·5 | 1·6 |
| Food processing | 46·1 | 15·3 | 646·0 | 44·1 | 77·2 | 14·5 | 1,287·7 | 38·9 |
| Chemicals | 12·1 | 4·0 | 83·8 | 5·7 | 25·5 | 4·8 | 242·0 | 7·3 |
| Printing | 6·1 | 2·0 | 17·1 | 1·2 | 11·1 | 2·1 | 50·5 | 1·5 |
| Total | 302·3 | 100·0 | 1,464·9 | 100·0 | 522·3 | 100·0 | 3,314·4 | 100·0 |

ment of the Hungarian textile industry was inhibited for a long time by the competition of Austrian and Czech textiles. At the beginning of the twentieth century the food industry turned out about 40 per cent of the output of Hungarian manufacturing; the textile industry produced only about 5 per cent. (In the Balkan countries the share of the food industry varied between 50 per cent and 60 per cent.)

## COMMERCE

Modern commerce appeared in Hungary in the second half of the nineteenth century. The internal trade of the mid-century still reflected to a considerable degree the traditional conditions of a subsistence economy and a low level of consumption. Its most characteristic figures were the wandering peddler, the tavern-keeper whose forebears had leased the feudal right of selling beverages, and who often dealt in money-lending too, and the general storekeeper, looking after the simpler needs of local trade. In the Hungary of the 1850s some 2,500 to 3,000 nation-wide fairs were held in 600 or 700 different places, and about 300 regular weekly markets were conducted, at which the bulk of internal trading was transacted.

Modern commerce developed in the environment of a rapidly growing Budapest. In the early decades of the nineteenth century the number of merchants there stood at about one thousand; the statistics of the 1850s give a figure (probably exaggerated) of substantially more than five thousand. In the years after the Compromise a little more than 7 per cent of the employed population of Budapest worked in trade and finance; by 1910 the figure had risen to over 13 per cent.

It was in Budapest that a network of permanent, specialised retail outlets first developed, with large, modern stores. The commerce of the capital grew rapidly; between the two periods 1876–85 and 1906–13 its physical volume nearly quadrupled, not least because of the precipitate growth of the population.

The spread of specialised stores continued. At the beginning of the twentieth century about 10 per cent of Budapest's shopkeepers dealt in the sale of fuel, another 7 per cent in wood, leather, and paper goods, and 2 per cent in books and pictures.

Thus a network of individual shops grew up above and beyond the traditional traffic in foodstuffs. Indeed, under the influence of a fashion emanating from Paris, the first modern department store in Budapest was opened in 1911.

Still, the conditions of underdevelopment preserved more traditional forms of trade, even in Budapest. In the first decade of the twentieth century market-women, door-to-door peddlers, and the like still made up more than a third of all independent merchants. More than one-third of all commerce still dealt with foodstuffs, and nearly one-fifth with textiles and other articles of clothing. In the provinces progress had scarcely begun: there markets still accounted for most transactions, and the general store and house-to-house selling still prevailed.

From the standpoint of commodity exchange, the development of foreign trade was more important for the growth of the Hungarian economy. All the features of the economy which we have hitherto examined point to the fact that one of the prime stimuli to the modern capitalist transformation of the Eastern European countries was the challenge presented by the industrialisation of the West: the appearance of extremely promising and almost unlimited opportunities for profit. Hence one of the first signs of capitalist development in Eastern Europe was the marked increase in agricultural exports from the middle of the nineteenth century, an extension of the east-west division of labour which had developed since the sixteenth century and which made Eastern Europe, traditionally, an exporter of foodstuffs.

In Hungary, export opportunities for agricultural products expanded after 1850 because of the demands of the industrialising Austrian and Czech provinces, and because of the existence of a common customs area and a unitary Empire-wide market. Detailed figures are not available for these years, but between 1848 and 1867 foreign trade increased about five-fold. After the Compromise, when the pace of economic growth quickened, exports and imports grew more rapidly, primarily as a result of the booming demand for Hungary's wheat and flour exports, but also because of the rapid increase in imports connected with the building of an infrastructure (which in 1874 even brought about an import surplus). Between the Compromise and the World War foreign trade expanded by a yearly average of nearly 2 per cent; during this period it trebled, following on the five-fold growth of the years 1850–67.

However, this extremely rapid progress of foreign trade displayed throughout the same structural traits virtually unchanged: the bulk of exports still consisted of raw agricultural produce and of food products like flour and sugar (though the latter increased in proportion), while imports were composed of finished goods, principally industrial articles.

At the end of the nineteenth century 70 per cent of Hungary's imports were finished products; the share of raw materials (21 per cent) and semi-processed goods (9 per cent) was small. By 1913 the proportion of finished-goods imports had fallen significantly, but it still exceeded 60 per cent of total imports. Meanwhile the share of raw materials and semi-processed manufactures rose from 30 per cent to over 38 per cent. In the course of industrialisation, however, not only did semi-finished and raw-material imports rise: the structure of finished-goods imports also underwent a change. Thus iron and non-ferrous metal products, and machinery, formed the fastest-growing item in the total import of finished goods.

The structure of exports showed fewer changes. During the entire period raw materials (principally agricultural) constituted somewhat more than half of all exports, while the proportion of finished manufactures remained at around 37–38 per cent. Two-thirds of the latter figure, however, was contributed by the products of the food industry.

Compared with the other indices, the distribution of foreign trade by country changed very little. The common market and common currency of the Austro-Hungarian Monarchy, and its unitary transport network—products of history and deliberate Austrian economic policy—made it almost inevitable that the great bulk of Hungarian 'foreign' trade should be conducted with the Austrian and Czech provinces of the Monarchy. In the second half of the nineteenth century 80–85 per cent of imports to Hungary came from these so-called hereditary provinces, right up to the end of the 1880s. In the course of the 1890s this figure fell a little, stabilising at around 80 per cent; after 1900 it dropped slowly and gradually to about 70 per cent. Hungarian exports to the other parts of the Monarchy did not display even this modest tendency to decline; during the entire period they remained virtually unchanged at 70–75 per cent of all Hungarian exports.

Germany played the largest part in Hungarian trade outside the Monarchy. Its share in Hungary's imports rose from an average of 4 per cent in the 1880s to 11 per cent after 1910.

In her export trade, Hungary had no conspicuous trading partner outside the Monarchy. After the 1880s Germany's share of about 10 per cent fell off somewhat, consonant with the decline in the export of wheat and flour to places outside the Monarchy. Until the 1870s and 1880s Hungary's export trade within the Monarchy never exceeded three-quarters of all her exports because of the excellent opportunities to market her grain and flour elsewhere in Europe. By the end of the century, however, the arrival of overseas grain on the European market, and the introduction of protective tariffs, had largely put an end to Hungary's traditional agricultural export trade there, and the Austrian and Czech provinces failed to take up the slack. True, exports of other goods partly made up for the loss of markets for wheat and flour in these years—sugar to England, which took 3 per cent of Hungary's exports outside the Monarchy, and industrial products in sizeable proportions to the Balkans. If the structure of overall exports remained unchanged, the structure of exports to areas outside the Monarchy underwent a fundamental transformation. During the decade of the 1880s grain and flour formed 34 per cent of exports to places outside the Monarchy. Between 1902 and 1911, however, these articles made up only 9 per cent of that trade. By contrast, the share of sugar (in total exports) rose from 1 per cent to 12 per cent, that of timber from 2·5 per cent to 9 per cent.

The Hungarian balance of trade with Austria, except for a few exceptional years, was always passive. Overall, however, Hungarian foreign commerce presents a somewhat different picture. Apart from the five years before the War, trade with areas outside the Monarchy almost invariably closed with an active balance. As a result, the overall balance of trade in the years before 1900 fluctuated. In the first decade of the new century the balance turned active, becoming passive again during the boom of the five years before the War.

# 3 Development of the economy: results, peculiarities, contradictions

The capitalist transformation and modernisation of the economy reached into every area of economic life, from credit and the building of an infrastructure to agriculture, industry, and trade (though not always in equal measure or at the same tempo); in the decades leading up to World War I it brought about a radical transformation of the Hungarian economy.

### THE ROLE OF THE STATE AND OF FOREIGN CAPITAL

In summarising the results of the economy's development, it is absolutely essential to emphasise the role of some special factors.

The Hungarian example makes it plain that, by comparison with Western Europe modernisation and the Western industrial revolution of the eighteenth and nineteenth centuries, the state played an unusual and special role. In this connection it is enough to recall the powerful stimulus and support given by the state to railway construction, at first by a system of guaranteed interest, later by the creation of the state railways; this influence was felt throughout the whole period. Similarly, we might cite state support for industrialisation, which—partly owing to the impossibility of pursuing an independent tariff policy—took more direct forms of aid, including the extension of preferential freight rates and toll charges, tax exemptions, and even direct state subsidy.

The function of the Eastern European state, then, was different from that of its Western counterpart. But even so, it cannot be judged the most notable factor in the modern capitalist transformation. For state intervention, no matter how great an impetus it gave to railway building or the establishment of industry, still could not compensate for the weaknesses springing from low levels of development and capital accumulation. It was able to mobilise no more than the modest resources which stood at the disposal of the country. Direct subsidies for industry made up, as we have seen, only an insignificant fraction of total industrial investment, and the state funds spent on railway construction came overwhelmingly from government loans which drew on foreign capital.

And here, in considering the peculiarities in the process of modernisation in Hungary and Eastern Europe, we arrive at the heart of the matter. By and large, state activity was effective only to the degree that it created attractive conditions for foreign capital, in particular by making investments secure and profitable. Thus the unique factor in the capitalist transformation was not so much direct state intervention as the influx and collaboration of foreign capital.

During the period of modernisation, especially during the first decades, the gap between the soaring demand for capital and the low (or relatively low) level of accumulation was a problem for the capitalist development of every European country, England alone excepted.

In the countries of Western Europe, however, the activity of foreign capital was a purely temporary phenomenon, and generally receded in importance after one or two decades. Thereafter the Western European countries financed their investments from their own sources and indeed, following their own industrial revolutions, became in the last decades of the nineteenth century ever more important exporters of capital themselves (France chiefly from the 1880s, Germany a decade later). Austria herself made use of a significant amount of foreign capital; at the end of the century 35 per cent of the shares and bonds in Austrian industry were in foreign hands. If in the mature Austrian economy capital exports did not *replace* import of capital, as in the typical Western European model, still Austria's capital exports *grew side by side with falling* capital imports. By the end of the century exports of capital had reached 80 per cent of capital imports.

Austrian capital exports were intimately bound up with the development of the Hungarian economy: of the 5,500 million crowns exported from Austria at the beginning of the twentieth century, 4,700 million went to Hungary. As a part of the Habsburg Empire, Hungary from the middle of the nineteenth century became, as we saw before, an important field for the activities of Austrian and Czech capital.

After the Compromise the role of foreign capital in Hungary rather expanded than diminished. Here an important factor was the general rise in capital exports. It was essentially in these decades that the capital-exporting countries of Europe (England excepted) first directed their investments toward Eastern and South-eastern Europe.

Among the main forms of capital import into Hungary in the period extending up to World War I we may single out, above all, state loans. By 1912 the amount of state loans outstanding approached 6,000 million crowns. Only 45·5 per cent of this substantial state debt was domestically owned; well over half (54·5 per cent) was held abroad, 23·2 per cent of it in Austria.

Hungarian government loans were handled principally by the Rothschild consortium, within which key roles were played by the Austrian House of Rothschild and the Creditanstalt (with their Hungarian associates), the French and English Rothschilds, and, increasingly, the great German banks (Darmstädter Bank, Deutsche Bank, Berliner Discontogesellschaft). Little by little the Viennese Creditanstalt and the Berlin Discontogesellschaft gained ascendancy at the expense of the Rothschild interests.

The second form of foreign capital influx was the purchase of municipal bonds and debentures issued in Hungary. The greater part of these (54·7 per cent) was held abroad, 26·6 per cent of them in Austria.

Mortgage loans extended by Austrian banks on Hungarian real property formed the third type of capital inflow. The three largest mortgage-writing institutions alone (Österreichische Centralbodencreditbank, Austro-Hungarian Bank, Österreichische Bodencreditanstalt) held about 500 million crowns' worth of mortgages on Hungarian real estate in 1912.

As a fourth variety of capital inflow we may mention the participation of foreign capital in the building of the Hungarian railway system. Only 30 per cent of all the railway bonds issued were placed at home; the remaining 70 per cent were sold abroad. After Austrian capital, German financial groups played a large part here: they took over 37 per cent of the financial paper of the local railways built at the end of the century.

The fifth and sixth types of capital inflow—and perhaps the most significant, if not quantitatively the biggest—took the form of foreign investment in Hungarian banks and industrial concerns. A significant portion indeed of the shares of Hungarian credit institutions—55–56 per cent—was held abroad; 45–46 per cent of these foreign holdings were in Austria.

The five large banks founded after the Compromise were a creation of Austrian finance, and the leading Hungarian banks at the end of the century also maintained close connections with foreign capital. The Commercial Bank at this time was associated with the Austrian Wiener Bankverein. Nothing demonstrates this Austrian hegemony better than an internal agreement of September 1906, by which the Commercial Bank assured its Viennese partner a 40 per cent share in all its Hungarian banking business. Behind the Credit Bank stood the Austrian Rothschilds; one-third of the shares of the Discount Bank were directly held, early in the twentieth century, by the Austrian Union Bank and Länderbank, and through the latter by the French banks' Austro-French consortium (especially the Crédit Lyonnais).

It was principally from the 1880s that interest quickened in the founding of industrial establishments. For the most part Austrian entrepreneurs or banks were behind the enterprises created during these years. At the peak of this process, at the end of the century, 42 per cent of Hungarian factory industry was directly under foreign control, while another 18 per cent was owned by foreigners in association with Hungarian entrepreneurs. Thus the accelerated pace of industrialisation at the end of the century was essentially a consequence of foreign investments. Though industrial investment continued to rise in the early twentieth century, the growing internal strength and increased capital accumulation of the Hungarian economy considerably reduced the sphere of foreign interests in industry, until just before the war their share stood at only 36 per cent.

This relative reduction in the role of foreign capital in the early twentieth century characterised not only industry but the financing of the economy as a whole. The large-scale influx of capital in the last third of the nineteenth century greatly reinforced the process of domestic capital formation, leading to the general advance of the whole economy. The decline of investments designed to develop the infrastructure also goes to explain the relative contraction of foreign investment in this period. The comparatively modest capital demands of the investments in industry which were now the order of the day, and their quicker return on capital, led to a marked growth of investment from domestic accumulation.

If, then, foreign capital played a decisive part in financing the Hungarian economy in the years up to the World War, one can still recognise in the constantly growing role of domestic accumulation a definite trend towards financial independence and economic development. Between 1867 and 1873 60 per cent of the capital invested in the Hungarian economy was of foreign origin. Between 1873 and 1900 55 per cent of the capital invested in the economy came from domestic accumulation, and the share of foreign capital fell to 45 per cent. Between 1900 and 1913, again, 75 per cent of the financing of the economy was from domestic sources, only 25 per cent from abroad.

RATE OF GROWTH OF THE ECONOMY: RESULTS AND LEVEL
OF DEVELOPMENT ATTAINED ON THE EVE OF THE WAR

The rapid pace of industrial growth in dualist Hungary—6 per cent a year for factory industry, 5 per cent taking into account small-scale manufacture as well—markedly exceeded the rate of increase of agricultural production, which averaged 2 per cent a year. This difference in the rhythm of the two main sectors of the economy allows us to regard industry as the more influential factor in the rise of the national income. Thus it was due primarily to the rapid development of industry that the

Hungarian economy entered a period of really dynamic advance, attaining the rates of growth of Western Europe in the period of industrial revolution.

TABLE 13
*Growth of national income*

| Year | Crowns, millions (at 1900 prices) | Index |
|------|-----------------------------------|-------|
| 1867 | 1·180 | 100 |
| 1900 | 3·497 | 296 |
| 1913 | 5·064 | 453 |

Hungarian national income rose more than four times in the period 1867–1914, at an average annual rate of growth of 3·2 per cent. (According to other calculations, based on gross domestic production, the rate of growth was 2·4 per cent.)

By the eve of the war the dynamic changes characteristic of the industrial revolution had significantly transformed the structure of economy and society. Among the most eloquent indicators of the processes at work, we may point to the changes in the occupational distribution of the population, and in the structure of the production of national income. According to the data of the first census, in 1869, more than 75 per cent of the population of Hungary worked in agriculture. By the time of the census of 1910 the proportion of the agrarian population had fallen to 64 per cent. The preponderance of agriculture was thus diminishing, while, correspondingly, the once insignificant industrial population was growing: it rose from 7 per cent to over 16 per cent.

TABLE 14
*Distribution of gainfully occupied population (%)*

| | 1870 | 1910 |
|---|------|------|
| Agriculture | 80·0 | 64·5 |
| Industry | 8·6 | 17·1 |
| Transport and trade | 2·9 | 6·5 |
| Others | 8·5 | 11·9 |

Sectoral analysis of the national income completes the picture of economic and social transformation already conveyed. At the time of the Compromise agriculture provided 80 per cent of national income, but by the pre-war years the proportion had fallen to 62 per cent. At the same time the share of industry had risen from 15 per cent to 28 per cent.

All in all, Hungary partially reduced her backwardness vis-à-vis several Western countries, kept pace with the developing countries, and to some extent approached or attained the level of development of the countries of Southern Europe. Gross per capita output in Hungary was 40–50 per cent that of the western and northern countries, 70–80 per cent of that of Italy and Austria; per capita output exceeded that of Russia and the Balkan countries by approximately 25–30 per cent. In economic structure Hungary lagged significantly behind Western and Northern Europe, whether from the standpoint of division of national income or from that of the distribution of the population by occupation; it stood close to the level of the Southern European countries, and clearly surpassed that of Eastern Europe.

Relatively rapid advance, combined with a level of development which still remained basically low, turned Hungarian economic life into a peculiar conglomerate, in which sectors reflecting the most disparate economic forms and levels could be found alongside one another. Between the two extremes of the modern estate run on a decidedly capitalist basis, and the small peasant holding scarcely producing for the market, lay a whole range of transitional forms. Naturally the contrast is even sharper if we compare city and village. The cities, especially Budapest, already bore most of the marks of modern Western European development; the villages had scarcely emerged from their medieval backwardness. Another contradiction appeared in the fact that while the greater part of industry still remained at handicraft level, large-scale industry at the same time displayed an extraordinarily high degree of concentration. It was a peculiarity of Hungarian economic development that, despite its marked lag behind Western Europe, there appeared relatively early those phenomena which at the end of the nineteenth century became widespread in the most advanced countries, affecting first the forms of economic organisation but soon coming to permeate the whole economic structure. With the advance of industrial concentration large monopolistic organisations came into existence (in Hungary, mainly cartels); their growing interdependence, and the growing interconnectedness of industrial and bank capital, gave rise to the phenomenon of finance capital. The outgrowth, in the West, of long organic development, finance capital began to gain ground in the Hungarian economy almost at the beginning of industrialisation. All these developments, again, were inseparably bound up with the unique circumstance that Hungary's economic development took place within the broader framework of the Monarchy.

The concentration of banking activity, and the growing monopoly position of the large banks, created (simultaneously with the formation of industrial monopolies) a favourable soil for the emergence of finance capital. In the 1890s, and especially in the first years of the twentieth century, monopolistic financial groups greatly expanded their activities by setting up new industrial enterprises and by extending their network of existing interests based on their monopoly of credit, drawing more enterprises into their spheres of influence. As a result of their gains in the early years of the twentieth century, the leading Hungarian banks multiplied their industrial interests. In 1913 the five largest banking groups already controlled 47 per cent of all Hungarian manufacturing corporations.

## 4 The prime social consequence of economic transformation: emergence of the proletariat and its organisation as a class

The peculiarities of the modernisation process in Hungary strongly influenced the evolution of the working class too, giving rise to many features which diverged from the Western European experience. The special characteristics of Hungarian industrialisation and of the industrial revolution there powerfully affected the course of the development of the working class, and its eventual structure and composition.

The most noticeable effect of the development sketched earlier lay not in the rapid emergence of an industrial working class, but rather in the appearance of a massive agrarian proletariat. In the second half of the nineteenth century the great majority of the population still earned its living from agriculture. In the 1840s there were only about 250,000 outworkers and independent or guild artisans in the country out of a population of 12 million, and even at the end of the century we can scarcely speak of a radical change. The census of 1900 showed that despite the rapid industrialisation of the last years of the century only about 10 per cent of the working population of Hungary made their living in industry. Within the rural majority of the population, however, momentous changes had taken place. In the first half of the nineteenth century most were serfs. The laws of 1848 gave scarcely one-fifth of these the land which they have previously cultivated, and left the vast majority entirely landless (60 per cent), or with only small parcels (20 per cent). In the second half of the century these vast numbers of people became a rural proletariat. Two-thirds of the working population of the country was in agriculture in 1900; and 39 per cent of those who worked in agriculture were farm labourers. As a result of the backwardness of the great estates, only about one-quarter of them lived on the landowners' property as permanent farm servants (*cselédek*); three-quarters were day labourers, moving about the country seeking work at harvest time or in railway and road building. Their ranks were supplemented moreover, by those holders of plots too small to provide a living, who were obliged to sell their labour in order to assure their families' existence. These made up another 15 per cent of agricultural wage-earners. Together the agrarian proletariat and the semi-proletarian rural masses formed roughly one-third of the entire employed population of the country.

Thus even at the end of the nineteenth century this enormous rural proletariat several times outnumbered the industrial working class. Within the industrial sector the number of wage-workers in large and small industry scarcely exceeded 700,000 in 1900, or one-tenth of the country's working population.

The prominence of the agrarian proletariat and the unusually small size of the industrial working class were not the only peculiar features compared with the Western European countries. The development of the industrial proletariat itself differed in many ways. In England and Western Europe at the time of the industrial revolution, factory operatives were recruited predominantly from the ranks of domestic hand workers, journeyman, and former proprietors ruined by modern capitalist competition. At the time of their own industrial revolutions in the later nineteenth century, the Central and Eastern European countries were not able to exploit these kinds of sources so thoroughly because of the relatively heavy demand for labour. Factory industry could satisfy only a fraction of its manpower demands from such sources, because the peculiar course of earlier development had restricted the scope and level of industry. A detailed analysis of the relevant Hungarian figures shows that in the 1840s there were 117,000 independent artisans in the country, about the same number of journeymen, and only about 23,000 factory and domestic workers. The industrial revolution of the second half of the century did not destroy artisan industry; on the contrary, the number of independent masters and their journeymen had risen by 1900 by 400,000 and 300,000 respectively. The tiny number of domestic workers scarcely mattered in the evolution of the factories. Thus the prime source of labour to meet the mounting demand was not small-scale industry, but agriculture: the impoverished village. The increase in the number of factory workers—from 110,000 in 1880 to 320,000 in 1900—came about largely through the conversion of part of the agrarian proletariat into industrial workers.

This difference itself gave rise to other differences. Fresh from the village, the rural masses were unfamiliar with industrial work and for the most part could be used only for unskilled labour. Because of the peculiarities of earlier development, it was impossible to meet the industrial revolution's demand for skilled manpower by turning to domestic workers, easily trained to handle machinery—for these were scarcely to be found in the country. A considerable portion of Hungarian industry's skilled manpower migrated to the country in the last third of the nineteenth century from the Austrian and Czech lands of the Monarchy. In 1875 25 per cent of the workers in Budapest were foreigners; in the production of iron and machinery, dependent on skilled labour, the figure was 35 per cent.

This peculiar genesis of the Hungarian working class had another consequence which made itself powerfully felt in the nineteenth century. The rural origins of most workers, and their use primarily as unskilled factory operatives, contributed to preserving for a long time a transitional type of labourer not yet completely divorced from the village and from agriculture. The whole question is inseparable, however, from another peculiarity of the industrial revolution in Hungary: the revolution in transport preceded the technical transformation of industry, and so railway building and other public works absorbed enormous numbers of the agricultural population, leading to the creation of a special transitional type of worker. Many of these took jobs temporarily in industry, as, for example, seasonally in the food industry, but for a relatively long time they did not permanently become wage-workers.

The belated start of the industrial revolution, and the low level of industrialisation, showed not only in the relatively small numbers of the actual industrial proletariat and in the long-surviving link with the land, but in the unique composition of the industrial working class itself. The peculiarities of industrialisation in Hungary created a demand for a worker of a different type from that in the West. Because of the transport revolution the iron and engineering industries acquired a disproportionate weight, with their demands for the most highly skilled workers and, at the same time, for large numbers of unskilled labourers.

The importance of the iron and engineering industries, in terms of number of workers, appears from the fact that in 1900 nearly one-third of all industrial workers (exclusive of miners) were employed in these branches. It is true that this figure includes the unskilled too, but even without them skilled ironworkers and engineers can still be estimated at one-fifth of the industrial working class. This stratum, which was to form the basis of the emerging Hungarian labour movement, also greatly influenced the physiognomy of the working class as a whole.

Leaving aside these ironworkers and engineers, and the much thinner stratum of skilled workers in other industries (processing) which played such a key role in Hungary's industrial development, employed very few skilled workmen, the great majority of Hungarian workers were unskilled, and among them were many who were employed only seasonally or casually. The preponderant role of this type of labour sprang from the peculiarities of Hungarian economic development. Many branches of the food industry—milling and sugar refining in particular—used seasonal help to a great extent. But a large-scale demand for this sort of transient, completely unskilled worker appeared in the construction industry too. Together, moreover, these two lines employed more than one-third of all Hungarian workers. Their labour needs could be fully met from among the agricultural proletariat, reluctant to break completely with the village and ready to accept any work which permitted a return to the country at the peak working seasons of spring and summer.

The skilled worker—so characteristic a figure of the industrial revolution in England, where he found frequent employment, especially in textiles—was in a small minority in the ranks of the Hungarian working class. Only 6 per cent of the labour force worked in the textile industry in Hungary. Even taking into account other light-industrial employment demanding large amounts of skilled labour (eg, the manufacture of leather goods and other articles of clothing), the number of workers in these light industries did not comprise even a tenth of the industrial working class.

Another characteristic facet of the composition of the Hungarian working class was the relative scarcity (by Western standards) of female and child labour—for it was precisely the largely missing textile industry, requiring skilled machine operators, which might have employed large numbers of women and children. Neither highly skilled work demanding long training nor unskilled work demanding great physical strength offered employment to women and children in large numbers. While the food industry (sugar, tobacco) did employ women in larger numbers, it did not create so great a demand for labour as textiles did elsewhere. In 1900, consequently, women made up less than 15 per cent of the Hungarian working class. The number of working children was even smaller: according to the industrial statistics for 1885 only 12,000 of 354,000 workers were under 16. The census of 1901, relating exclusively to factory industry, still showed only 5·2 per cent of the work force as under the age of 16.

We may assume that the relatively infrequent use of child labour in Eastern Europe was one of the peculiarities of the industrial revolution there, as well as being influenced by the relatively advanced social legislation which had been accumulating in the West for decades.

The special characteristics of the industrial revolution in Hungary created a working class different from its Western counterpart in many ways, in its numerical growth as well as its occupational social structure. The material circumstances of the emerging proletariat, too, were strongly influenced by the peculiar factors discussed earlier—factors to be found, of course, in any of the peasant societies of East-Central Europe. Among these one may single out above all the fact that there, becoming an industrial worker meant social and material decline only for a part of the working class—decayed artisans, guild apprentices, and the like; for farm workers and the village poor, it generally meant an improvement, since industrial wages were higher and even the primitive conditions in the factories were better than those in agriculture. This, again, followed logically from the fact that because of the enormous number of agricultural labourers the gap between the supply of labour and the demand for it on the rural labour market was much wider than in the cities.

In general, agricultural wages lagged far behind industrial wages, much more than was justified merely by the lower cost of living in the villages. Again, unemployment was extremely high among farm workers, as well as partial unemployment (seasonal work), factors which further contributed to the discomfort of their position. Nor can we forget that the plight of the agricultural workers was aggravated, socially and economically, by the survival of substantial remnants of feudal practice.

The Farm Servants' Acts of 1898 and 1907 forbade farm servants to leave their estates or to receive strangers in their homes, and prescribed a penalty of sixty days' imprisonment for inciting to strike. There were no restrictions on working hours; in the summer a sixteen-to-eighteen-hour working day was customary. Farm servants' wages, extremely low to begin with, were paid for the most part in kind. The hired agricultural labourers received most of their wages in money, but their pay was only about 50–60 per cent of that of the average industrial worker. Yet even these low wages were counted to some extent as a stroke of fortune, for according to contemporary calculations only one-quarter of the rural labourers were able to find work for more than 250 days a year.

The living conditions of farm servants are perhaps best illustrated by the fact that 96 per cent of their dwellings were in buildings shared with stables. Disease was rampant in these conditions: tuberculosis ravaged the country people, and infant mortality was very high. The majority of the farm servants and agricultural labourers could neither read nor write.

Compared with these conditions, becoming an industrial worker generally brought with it an improvement in one's circumstances—even if rural tradition, attachment to the land, and a repugnance toward industrial discipline generally made the farm labourer aspire to obtain a piece of land rather than become an industrial worker. In the cities, for one thing, however far down the social scale the workers lived and however wretched their living conditions (as we shall presently see), they were still free of feudal restrictions, arbitrary landlords, and laws restricting the free sale of their labour.

Those who managed to break away from the village, move to the city, and become industrial workers permanently, also very largely freed themselves from unemployment. The late nineteenth century was the dynamic age of capitalism in Hungary; by and large the number of factory workers was constantly growing, and the extension of the cities and other types of construction created a demand for much more labour than the urban work force could supply.

Even if rural unemployment still affected the industrial worker's situation, the favourable relationship between the supply of labour and the demand for it in the cities nevertheless gave rise there to a wage level higher than that of the village. Moreover, the working class could take a direct hand itself, to some degree, in the evolution of industrial wages, via the infant labour movement, through organisation and strikes. All these circumstances contributed to making the industrial worker's wage higher than that of the farm labourer, and his social position and circumstances of life better than those of the rural poor.

Thus, although in Hungary and East-Central Europe generally the advent of capitalism brought lower wages and worse living conditions for the masses than in Western Europe, because of the social and economic backwardness of those countries, the industrial revolution did not bring about a decline in the living standards of broad social strata, specifically in those of the working class. This state of affairs was characteristic of all those countries where industrialisation took place in an environment dominated by a backward system of great estates of feudal origin, where the industrial revolution had to draw almost exclusively upon the agrarian proletariat for new sources of labour.

If, however, we can speak of a certain rise in living standards instead of a decline, that does not contradict the fact which we noted earlier, that compared with the conditions of the workers in the more developed capitalist countries the Hungarian working class lived in a state of dire poverty. The vast mass of agrarian labourers continually influenced the industrial wage level, especially in the case of unskilled workers, but even above and beyond them the reservoir of rural poor acted to depress industrial wages. The average wage of the Hungarian worker was 40–50 per cent lower than that of his counterpart in Western Europe.

Differences in nominal wages do not, of course, express real differences satisfactorily because of variations in the cost of living. In Hungary food was always cheaper because of the agrarian character of the country, and partly for that reason living costs were generally lower. But another factor in the lower cost of living was the general economic and cultural backwardness of the country, the persistence of primitive habits of consumption and the low level of social and cultural demands.

According to one set of calculations, if we take average real hourly wages in England between 1905 and 1909 as 100, then wages in Germany were as 68, in France as 51, but in Hungary —only 30. Even per capita consumption of foodstuffs was lower in Hungary than in the Western countries.

Even while affording a substantially lower living standard than the Western European, these average real wages still concealed within themselves large inequalities. The wages of various strata of the working class, of course, always show great differences within any country. In countries that are behind-hand in their industrialisation, however, these differences appear in a more pronounced form. The reason lies in the fact that to satisfy the demand for skilled workers it was necessary to pay particularly high wages, by local standards, in order to attract skilled craftsmen from more developed countries and to assure them a wage comparable with those found abroad. With the development of capitalism this peculiarity of the wage structure was perpetuated, appearing in later decades in the form of relatively high wages for skilled workers. By comparison the wage level of other categories of workers, determined as it was by the virtually limitless supply of labour, was disproportionately low. While the differential between the pay of skilled and unskilled workers did not reach the same proportions as in the colonial countries, it still led to very marked inequalities. At the beginning of the twentieth century 5–6 per cent of the factory work force was earning three times as much as the average industrial wage, and four or five times as much as the lowest-paid fifth of the working class. While the incomes of the upper categories approached those of the lower strata of employees and petty-bourgeois, the wages of the worst-paid unskilled workers were scarcely enough to keep body and soul together.

The situation of the Hungarian working class, however, with all its special features, was marked not only by a wage level lower than the Western European and by much sharper inequalities within the wage structure, but by a generally more adverse evolution of working and living conditions. In the more developed capitalist countries the superior numbers and organisation of the working class and their decades of struggle, together with the development of productive technology and organisation, brought about a gradual improvement in the inhuman conditions characteristic of the early decades of capitalism. For these reasons substantial changes took place in England and the countries of the western part of the continent between the beginning and the end of the nineteenth century. The most striking progress was made in shortening the working day. In England most trades were working a 53- or 54-hour week by the 1880s. In Germany the average working day at the beginning of the twentieth century was nine and a half hours.

In Hungary, on the other hand, no legislation existed at that time limiting working hours, nor had any meaningful limitations been worked out in practice. In 1901, for example, 10 per cent of all plants worked 12 hours a day or more, and over 60 per cent had a working day of 10–12 hours. Thus fewer than a third of all factories worked less than 10 hours a day. By and large the same proportions held true for numbers of workers too: about three-quarters of all workers put in more than a 10-hour day. A decade later the situation was essentially unchanged. In the 1880s the average working day in Budapest was 12 hours, in the years before World War I 10½ hours.

The long working day was made even more intolerable by the primitiveness of conditions in the factories. By the end of the century the great modern factories of the developed capitalist countries already offered healthier working conditions and some amenities. The reports of the Hungarian industrial inspectors, on the other hand, paint a dramatic picture of Hungarian factory conditions in the early twentieth century, reminiscent of conditions in the early English factories. 'The shops are dirty, smelly holes, with no trace of ventilation or a washroom,' reads one report on a screw factory. 'Tuberculosis was observed to spread to such an extent among the women workers of one textile mill,' the report for 1910 asserts, 'that within a year one-quarter of them fell ill.' Out of 5,000 factories 109 in all had washrooms, 75 had canteens, and 7 had nurseries, with space for but 500 children altogether.

Despite their primitiveness it is clear that industrial working conditions in Hungary, while reminiscent of the overall situation in Europe several decades earlier, were still not identical with the wretched, inhuman conditions of the English industrial revolution of which descriptions from the late eighteenth and early nineteenth centuries speak. The chief credit for this belongs to the European workers' movement of the second half of the nineteenth century, whose international achievements made their effects felt in Hungary.

In Hungary the organisation of the workers began almost simultaneously with the appearance of a working class. Skilled craftsmen coming to Hungary with new industries, from Vienna, Bohemia-Moravia, or even Germany, and Hungarian journeymen travelling abroad in compliance with long-standing custom, introduced the experiences, practices, and ideas of the European labour movement, especially of the German movement. Self-help ideas of the Schulze-Delitzsch type soon lost their base of support in the early organisation of the Hungarian labour movement. The ideas of Lassalle, and especially of Marx and the First International, began to spread widely; the first Hungarian labour organisation, the General Workers' Union of 1868 (Általános Munkásegylet), was inspired chiefly by these ideas, and derived its political and economic goals principally from them. The General Workers' Union created the labour press in Hungary with its newspaper, first published in German; it unequivocally reflected the political objectives of the workers and the beginnings of their organised political struggles. Inseparable from the latter was the beginning of the organised economic struggle: strikes for higher wages and for a shorter working day, leading subsequently to the creation of the first social-welfare institution, the General Workers' Sick and Disabled Relief Chest (Általános Munkás Betegsegélyező és Rokkantpénztár).

During the 1880s the Chest became the organisational and material basis of the labour movement, all the more so as the creation of a party to direct organisation and unite economic and political objectives did not come about until 1890, with the formation of the Social-Democratic Party. In the 1880s the results of the organisation of the working class appeared primarily in the creation of a number of smaller trade unions. Their growth and organisation into a united trade union movement could take place, however, only in the 1890s. In 1899 the first national trade union congress met, setting as its goals the broadening of the mass movement and its more vigorous central direction. In the following years the local unions were gradually organised into national federations. Their membership was between 10,000 and 20,000 at the turn of the century, not more than 2–3 per cent of the industrial working class. By the end of 1904 it had risen to 50,000, almost 10 per cent of the labour force. The best-organised trades were construction, iron and steel, printing, wood-working, and textiles. Organisation was strong in small-scale industry; on the other hand the organisation of factory machine operators and day labourers lagged seriously behind that of skilled craftsmen.

During the great upsurge of the Hungarian labour movement

in the years 1905–7 economic and political objectives appeared side by side, complementing one another. The six-week strike of the ironworkers in the spring of 1905 was followed by strikes of miners and farmworkers. Work stoppages became increasingly frequent: in 1905 40,000 workers struck, in 1906 80,000, and in 1907 75,000, winning wage increases of around 10 per cent. Trade union membership reached a new high in 1906, when 53,000 workers belonged to the various federations. From 1907, however, the movement began to recede. On 10 October 1907, a great demonstration for universal suffrage mobilised 200,000 marchers in Budapest; but thereafter the number of strikes and demonstrations fell off rapidly. In 1908 only 7,000 workers were able to secure wage increases, in 1909 only 10,000, in 1911 25,000. Trade union membership fell by half, recovering after 1910 until it exceeded 110,000 just before the war, some 12–15 per cent of the industrial labour force. The growing influence of the Social-Democratic Party in the political life of the country also enhanced the importance of the unions; thus the government had already taken under consideration the introduction of an anti-strike act.

After three decades of rapid development in the late nineteenth century, the Hungarian labour movement, with its wide-ranging organisation, had become by the early years of the twentieth a political factor of national importance. It was able to mobilise mass support, especially in the capital, but in many provincial districts as well; opposition parties of the left sought its alliance from time to time in order to broaden their own base.

Nevertheless, the labour movement still bore the marks of a narrowness springing from its social and economic circumstances. A minority among the country's predominantly agrarian population, deprived of parliamentary representation by the political system, the Hungarian workers' movement could not directly mould the course of political events.

In Hungary, then, between 1850 and 1914, the process of social and economic modernisation was begun and, in part, completed. It consisted, in essence, of the abolition of traditional feudal relationships and the emergence of capitalist relationships through the economic, technical, and social processes of industrial revolution. This development took place significantly later than in Western Europe. In the tendencies and dynamics of its growth, this process, lagging by half a century, undoubtedly bore many resemblances to the industrial revolution in Western Europe. In Hungary, too, modernisation extended to every sphere of economic life, from agriculture to banking, transport and industry, and set far-reaching social changes in motion.

Despite all this, however, the industrial revolution in Hungary (and in Eastern Europe generally) was far from a simple, belated copy of the industrial revolution in Western Europe. Special conditions of development produced a model of industrial revolution different from that of the western part of the continent. In Western Europe economy and society were radically transformed as a result of modernisation. Within a relatively short period of time, traditional economy and society were made over into modern economy and society. Within a few decades industry became the decisive branch of the economy not merely in its dynamism and effect on other sectors, but in its absolute weight and immediate role in the economy. The Western European countries which had passed through the industrial revolution were turned into industrial countries.

None of this can be said of pre-World War I Hungary. There, the internal and external factors affecting economic growth did not evoke a set of tensions, a 'challenge', to which rapid industrial revolution might have given the response through the industrialisation of the country.

The type of challenge facing Hungary (and Eastern Europe) is to be sought much more in the general European circumstances than in any inevitable tensions of internal development. A post-industrial-revolution but still rapidly industrialising Western Europe offered expanding markets for foodstuffs, which lent a great impetus to the modernisation of Hungary's backward agriculture and hence to the creation of a modern infrastructure and banking system. Industrial development began with the decisive aid of loans and investments from the industrialised West, primarily from the developed western lands of the Austro-Hungarian Monarchy, and always remained oriented toward its creditors' demands for raw materials, their transport and communications interests, and the country's abiding agrarian character. Thus Hungary's social and economic structure underwent substantial change, but it was not fundamentally transformed; moreover its international economic position went essentially unchanged, for Hungary remained a supplier of foodstuffs to the more industrialised areas of the Monarchy.

As a result of this train of causes and effects, not only industry but every branch of the economy, agriculture included, retained many elements of its earlier backwardness. Society showed the effects of peasant predominance, of a stratum of well-to-do peasants aping the gentry, and of a ruling class thoroughly interwoven with the landed aristocracy.

These considerations complete the picture of a belated industrial revolution, inconsistently carried through—indeed never really completed, but rather halted before it was finished. If it attained a higher level than in most of the Eastern European countries, nevertheless at bottom it affected Hungary in much the same way as them.

# 2
# A Stagnant Economy in a New Polity, 1914–44

# 1 Wartime destruction and new economic circumstances

With the outbreak of World War I, that half-century-old process by which Hungary gradually moved from traditional economy on to the road of modernisation came to an end. War not only interrupted the process of development; it also caused serious difficulties for an economy unprepared for the demands of modern warfare. Wartime boom conditions developed only in certain industries as a result of conversion to military production; elsewhere shortages of materials and labour soon appeared, along with a general decline in production. A particularly serious situation came about in agriculture: 50 per cent of the male work force was away at the front and military mobilisation had taken away a substantial part of the stock of draught animals, so that an increasingly large proportion of the soil was left uncultivated and yields fell rapidly. In the last two years of the war agricultural production dropped to 50–60 per cent of the prewar level, and a catastrophic shortage of foodstuffs appeared in the country.

Coal and iron production declined too, even though both were intimately bound up with the wartime economy. As for consumer goods, here the decline in production led, in the last years of the war, to complete economic collapse. By the end of the war it had become impossible to feed and clothe either the civilian population or the troops at the front. Since it proved impossible to cover rapidly mounting military expenditure through domestic loans and other financial devices, the government sought to meet its growing budgetary need through the increased issue of currency. Thus more and more money came into circulation, while at the same time the supply of goods was shrinking. Prices rapidly rose, so that within four years the value of the currency had fallen to 43 per cent of the prewar level.

Thus the collapse of Hungary's wartime economy culminated in a rapidly mounting inflation. By the autumn of 1918 the economic experts were generally aware that the country, and indeed the whole Monarchy, was on the brink of economic disaster and could hardly get through another winter of war. Military collapse and revolution found a country economically ruined. Economic collapse exacerbated existing social problems, making political and economic measures to solve them particularly timely. The movements of autumn 1918 and spring 1919 in Hungary sought to remedy the ills of the Hungarian economy in two distinct phases, and in two different directions. The bourgeois-democratic revolution of October 1918, led by Michael Károlyi, sought primarily to democratise political and social life, by abolishing the vestiges of feudalism; beyond short-run emergency measures demanded by the serious economic situation, its programme affected economic life primarily through its plans for land reform.

The bourgeois-democratic revolution was incapable, however, of solving the economic difficulties. Partly as a consequence, the revolution moved to the left. The masses increasingly went over to the communists, from whom they expected a solution to their grievous social and economic problems, through the creation of a socialist society. The Soviet Republic which came into existence in March 1919 under the leadership of Béla Kun sought to reorganise Hungary's economic life, nationalising the country's industry, mines, and commerce and expropriating the great landed estates. While its actions temporarily improved the situation of the workers, the Soviet Republic could not cope in three months with the economic disorder brought about by declining production, shortages of materials caused by the blockade maintained against Hungary, and the secession of part of the country. Its fall in August 1919, and the succession to power of the counter-revolution, put an end to its longer-range plans.

The postwar revolutions—a historic effort to turn Hungarian society and economy into new paths—ended in defeat. The counter-revolution restored the system of private property in the means of production within a matter of days. In spite of this, however, the Hungarian economy's development after 1919 could not be simply a continuation of what had gone before. The old property relations remained, but the other conditions of economic life had radically changed. Above all, defeat in war led to the triumph of the centrifugal forces which even before had been gaining strength in the Austro-Hungarian Monarchy. The revolutions of autumn 1918 completed the dissolution of the Monarchy, to which the peace treaties of 1919 gave final legal sanction. The old Monarchy—within which the first phase of the Hungarian economy's modernisation had taken place—gave way to three independent states, while in addition other substantial territories were detached to become integral parts of neighbouring countries.

Hungary, within the new boundaries confirmed by the Treaty of Trianon, was completely transformed: its 92,600 square kilometres amounted to only 32·7 per cent of the country's prewar area, and the 7,600,000 inhabitants living within the new frontiers were only 41·6 per cent of the old population. Croatia, formerly affiliated with Hungary, became part of Yugoslavia, along with several southern regions of the Hungarian kingdom, notably the Vojvodina. Transylvania and the border area, the so-called Partium, with its Magyar population, were joined to an expanded Rumania, while the predominantly Slovak uplands became part of the new Czechoslovakia. The western border region, the Burgenland, went to Austria.

In Hungary's case these changes not only led to the creation of an entirely new economic unit; they fundamentally transformed the conditions of economic life. The relative importance of the various industries remaining within the country's new boundaries changed the economic structure, making Hungary a more industrialised country and transforming the inner balance of industry as well. The principal effect of these changes may be designated as the separation of the country from the

TABLE 15

*Structure of gainfully occupied population in 1910 (%)*

|  | Prewar territory | Postwar territory |
|---|---|---|
| Agriculture | 64·5 | 55·8 |
| Mining and industry | 17·1 | 21·4 |
| Trade and communication | 6·5 | 8·7 |
| Other | 11·9 | 14·1 |

nearly self-sufficient economic unity of the former Monarchy: without any period of transition Hungary was forced to become dependent on foreign trade, seeking a place on the world market to replace its secure internal trade connections, now lost.

TABLE 16

*Production of principal industries in postwar territory (% of 1913 output)*

| Iron and metals | 50·7 |
|---|---|
| Engineering | 82·2 |
| Building materials | 59·7 |
| Wood | 22·3 |
| Leather | 57·8 |
| Textiles | 41·8 |
| Clothing | 74·7 |
| Paper | 23·4 |
| Food | 56·2 |
| Chemicals | 54·9 |
| Printing | 89·2 |
| All industries | 55·1 |

But the economy could not function without large-scale foreign trade, conducted at world prices on the world market and burdened with tariff barriers and the need to pay in foreign exchange. Imports in large quantities were indispensable, especially of raw materials. Within its new frontiers Hungary was poor in metal ore and other minerals, and in timber, the country was forced to import raw materials for nearly every industry, textiles included. As a result of the territorial changes a large part of Hungary's industry was separated from its sources of raw materials. To keep the food, textile and iron and steel industries working the import of parts and machinery was of course as essential as the import of materials. And for a time the import of most of the finished goods previously acquired from abroad remained a necessity, even when the economy was developing rapidly.

A large import trade naturally required a correspondingly large quantity of exports to balance it. At the same time many basic sectors of the Hungarian economy now possessed a productive capacity exceeding the ability of the domestic market to absorb their output; this relationship had developed in the setting of the Monarchy and became unbalanced only in the new situation. Thus of their own accord these branches, too, were obliged to seek export outlets. This was true above all of the biggest sector of the whole economy, agriculture. A significant proportion of the output of Hungarian agriculture had always been sold in foreign markets. In 1913 27 per cent (by value) of the agricultural produce of Hungary's post-1920 territory was exported. Although the country had become more industrial as a result of the territorial changes, the domestic market could have absorbed its entire agricultural output only in the event of a very marked rise in the standard of living. For this reason securing export markets for agricultural products was a matter of critical importance. Thus the Hungarian economy became closely linked to the world market.

In these new circumstances, the need to raise the level of accumulation and investment acquired special significance for the Hungarian economy. As it was, the need for capital increased markedly in the new situation. On the one hand, large investments were necessary to create industries capable of producing for export, either by raising the productivity of old lines to make them competitive, or by developing competitive new industries; on the other hand, investment was essential to develop import substitutes.

At the same time, increased demands for capital to reconstruct the economy appeared at a time when the financial mechanisms of the Hungarian economy had also been severely shaken. Not only did the new circumstances put an end to the former unity of the money and credit market, but the Viennese financial groups themselves lost their former influence, Austria herself having become a debtor country. Thus the traditional foreign sources of funds dried up (the temporary eclipse of Germany, Hungary's principal creditor outside the Monarchy, likewise contributed to this result).

All these changes created a complex situation and inevitably brought about grave disturbances. These disturbances, difficult enough to cope with in themselves, were all the more serious in that they occurred at the time of an already critical economic situation, stemming from wartime exhaustion and defeat, the disorganisation of production, accelerating depreciation of the currency, shortages and hunger. Postwar events, including the occupation of a large part of the country, did nothing to relieve the economic exhaustion which had appeared at the end of the war, despite the efforts of the two revolutions of 1918–19. Production continued to stagnate at a very low level.

It followed from the structure of the Hungarian economy that its recovery would largely be determined by conditions in agriculture. We should not forget that prewar Hungary was an agrarian country, where 58 per cent of the national income (within the frontiers of 1920) came from agriculture, while industry contributed only 28 per cent, and trade and transport 14 per cent. For a long time agriculture was unable to recover from the disorganisation into which it had fallen by the end of the war; even in the early 1920s the situation was still catastrophic. In 1920 wheat production hardly exceeded half the average figure for the years 1911–15; in 1921 it reached only 70 per cent of the prewar level. The situation was the same for other crops and for livestock. Agricultural production in 1919 was about one-third of the prewar figure; in 1920 it reached 50–60 per cent of the prewar level.

The low level of agricultural production had a decisive effect on the other sectors of the economy. Given the economic structure of the country, the disorganisation of its agriculture crippled its foreign trade as well. In these years Hungary lost her export outlets almost completely: her agricultural exports in 1920 were 21 per cent of the prewar amount (calculated on the basis of her postwar territory), and in 1921 had reached only 41 per cent of the earlier level. Industrial exports declined too: they stood at

40 per cent of the prewar level in 1920, at 57 per cent in 1921. At the same time, the country was able to obtain only one-fourth to one-sixth of the industrial raw materials it had imported before the war.

All these factors made it virtually impossible to get industry on its feet again. The gravest situation existed in the former war industries, which now were almost completely closed down. Contrary to the Peace Conference's decision of 19 August 1919, the Rumanian government dismantled and shipped home as reparations for war damages machinery and equipment to a value of 1½ million gold crowns (according to contemporary estimates, which are probably exaggerated). Heavy industry generally was in a critical condition. In 1920 industrial production as a whole was 30–35 per cent of the prewar level; by 1921 it had reached only 51 per cent.

Beside the paralysis of production and economic life generally the depreciation of the currency, which had set in toward the end of the war, continued unchecked. In the summer of 1919 the crown stood at 15 per cent of its prewar value; by February 1920 it had fallen to one-eighth of its value of the previous summer.

## 2 Markets and financing: the role of the state and of foreign capital

Hungary came to be reliant on foreign trade, and hence on the world market, at a time when international economic conditions were particularly unfavourable. The postwar world economy was already in the grip of a serious market crisis. In part this stemmed from the virtual loss to European exporters of the Russian market, as a result of the triumph of the October Revolution. Since the war, moreover, Europe's overseas markets had also contracted. The advance of the United States, and the rapid industrialisation of other overseas countries, increasingly threatened the exports of the European countries and in some respects even their ability to acquire raw materials. All these changes sapped the very foundations of Europe's traditional productive activities, making far-reaching adjustments necessary. Industrial production grew much more slowly: even at the peak of production for the postwar decade, in 1929, it surpassed the prewar level by only 28 per cent. The characteristic feature of the postwar European economy, however, was the continued deterioration of foreign trade. In only one of the interwar years (1929) did European foreign trade reach or exceed the prewar level (by 3 per cent); during the other years—including the decade of the 1930s but adjusting for price changes—it remained (20–30 per cent) below the pre-1914 figure.

Europe's possibilities for sales outlets were serious affected by the narrowing of the market for agricultural products. Sharpened competition for world markets, combined with the nationalist passions stirred by the war, led to protectionist tariff policies designed to defend national markets and conquer new ones. France put into effect a series of customs increases; in May 1921, the United States introduced a higher tariff schedule, and England, Switzerland, and Spain followed suit in the summer and autumn of the same year. The new Italian duties of July 1921 were ten to fifteen times higher than before the war.

In Hungary all these tendencies appeared in exacerbated form. Her inability to compete on the world market owing to backward technique and low productivity was only aggravated by the new tariff barriers. At the same time the latter reinforced the existing tendencies toward economic isolation. The situation was no better with respect to the internal market. In Hungary—as in markedly agrarian countries generally—the internal market had never been particularly well developed. After the World War, however, it shrank even more. Because of the contraction of the frontiers the internal market for the most advanced industries narrowed drastically. Economic disorganisation and the privations of war markedly reduced per capita consumption of foodstuffs and manufactures. Breaking up the great landed estates—a demand made largely on social grounds, to be sure—might have served also to extend the domestic market. No such thing happened, however; the land reform of 1921 affected only 5 per cent of the soil, leaving the system of latifundia virtually intact.

The obvious answer to narrow markets and a low, scarcely rising level of consumption was the conquest of Hungarian markets traditionally dominated by foreign goods; this would have widened the market for consumer goods primarily. The worldwide tendency to defend the home market appeared all the more forcefully in Eastern Europe, where it was hoped that economic independence would provide a firm basis for independent national statehood.

Objective conditions favoured such aspirations too. The areas of friction in Europe had multiplied: customs frontiers had increased in length by 6,000–7,000 kilometres, and the former 13 currencies had given way to a total of 27 new ones. Seven independent customs areas now existed on the territory of the one-time Austro-Hungarian Monarchy alone.

In Hungary the implementation of an independent tariff

policy came as the realisation of a demand first formulated in the 1840s, and heatedly reiterated early in the twentieth century. An autonomous customs system was greeted as a decisive, long-sought-after weapon in the struggle for economic development.

No immediate way existed, however, of introducing tariff measures designed to solve the problem of markets by creating an autarchic economy. For the time being international arrangements obliged the newly independent countries to abide by the old customs systems; thus Hungary 'inherited' the old Austro-Hungarian tariff schedule of 1906. These duties, however, had been based on other needs and other circumstances, and were incapable of serving new purposes. Moreover, under the impact of postwar inflation they virtually melted away, for the Monarchy's old tariffs were assessed at a fixed sum in crowns by weight, so that as the currency depreciated these duties fell from 10–20 per cent (sometimes even 30–40 per cent) of the value of the goods assessed, to 1–4 per cent of that value.

Thus the effects of inflation led to modifications of the tariff system. In addition, the Hungarian government soon 'supplemented' the existing duties with strong measures of the kind generally being employed at the time in the Eastern European countries. The government accepted a demand urged in industrial quarters for years past when it revived the wartime system of import prohibitions.

The system of prohibitions served primarily to see the country through the critical years of transition, by encouraging its economic autonomy, cutting traditional ties, keeping out unwanted articles, and by making possible the preparation, behind the screen of protection, of the ultimate weapon for achieving autarchy: a new, independent system of duties. With the political and economic consolidation of the mid-1920s and the expiration of the various temporary restrictions imposed by the peace treaty, the way was opened for a new set of customs regulations.

Preparations began in 1922 and led, amidst heated and sometimes public disputes among the various interest groups, to the acceptance of a vigorous industrial protectionism. The views of the government and of industrial interests triumphed over those of the great landowners, who in order to guarantee export opportunities for their agricultural products first demanded free-trading principles, and later a modified system of protection. In the light of contemporary European realities the landowners were forced to accept the possibility that a high industrial tariff might be the most effective weapon for assuring agricultural exports. They hoped it would lead to mutual tariff concessions which would open the markets of the neighbouring countries to Hungarian agricultural products. The new duties covered more than two thousand items, in contrast with the hundred or so which had been included before.

Another characteristic of the new duties was that they were much higher than the prewar ones. The tariff accepted in 1924 and introduced mostly in January 1925 extended the highest protection, up to 50 per cent *ad valorem*, to the products of light industry (the Monarchy's 1906 tariff, by comparison, varied from 10 per cent to 20 per cent). Duties on heavy-industrial products were generally lower, around 20 per cent, to satisfy certain interests that required their import, while many raw materials and some kinds of agricultural equipment were exempt from duty. The average level of tariffs, around 30 per cent, assured domestic industry of vigorous and effective protection.

The process of growing isolation behind new customs barriers did not, of course, come to an end with the publication of the new duties. The tariff schedules went on being revised right to the end of the decade, generally in the direction of stricter protection.

Between 1913 and 1924 the value of goods shipped to Hungary from the onetime Austrian and Czech provinces—taking into account territorial changes—fell by 60 per cent. By the same token, Czechoslovakia was buying half of its flour requirements and Austria a third of its grain imports from America, while Hungary opened its markets to French and British machinery and equipment, otherwise turning ever more decisively toward the German and Italian markets, so that Austria's and Czechoslovakia's share in her imports fell by two-thirds, and their share of her exports by one-half.

Thus during the postwar decade state intervention by means

of tariff policy created the potential for a broadening of the domestic market and for economic expansion generally. To exploit this potential, however, protectionism had to be capable of encouraging domestic accumulation and the investment of foreign capital in Hungary. In the changed postwar situation, however, domestic accumulation lagged far behind the prewar level. The deterioration of the currency largely swallowed up the deposits and reserves of the banks; yet before the war the greater part of an industrial firm's new investments had been covered not by internal financing, but through bank loans. National income was scarcely 40–50 per cent of the prewar figure, and the share of national income devoted to accumulation fell to an even smaller fraction. Thus during the period of inflation the means of financing the economy were not at hand, even if, as a result of the flight of real values familiar in time of inflation, certain investment opportunities appeared. True, the inflation at one stage passed from a spontaneous phenomenon reflecting the economic collapse to a conscious policy designed to finance the reorganisation of the national economy. This policy took effect in the summer of 1921, after the failure of the first attempt to stem the inflation, and led to an ever faster deterioration of the currency.

In the summer of 1921 17,300 million crowns in banknotes were in circulation. A year later this sum had trebled; by the summer of 1923 it had reached 400,000 million crowns, and by spring 1924, the height of the inflation, 2·5 billion. As a result of the mounting issue of banknotes the value of the currency dropped precipitously. In August 1919 one gold crown was worth 9·9 paper crowns, but in June 1921 it fetched 50·7 paper crowns. By May 1924, finally, one gold crown was equivalent to 18,400 paper crowns. An ever larger fraction of this issue took the form of credits to private business. In 1921 only 10 per cent of the new banknotes came into circulation in the form of state loans to large-scale agriculture and industry, but by the latter part of 1922 this figure had risen to 50 per cent, and in 1923 it was 65 per cent. The value of these enormous loans was not fixed in terms of gold or any other set standard; they were made in rapidly depreciating paper money, so that

TABLE 17

*Depreciation of the gold crown*

| | Value of 100 gold crowns in Swiss francs | Value of one gold crown in inflated crowns (*1 January 1914*) |
|---|---|---|
| 1914, June | 104·28 | 1·01 |
| 1918, October | 44·25 | 2·37 |
| 1919, March | 22·46 | 4·68 |
| 1919, August | 11·62 | 9·87 |
| 1919, December | 3·20 | 34·32 |
| 1920, June | 3·19 | 35·00 |
| 1920, December | 1·24 | 106·38 |
| 1921, June | 2·34 | 50·66 |
| 1921, December | 0·76 | 137·84 |
| 1922, June | 0·56 | 190·33 |
| 1922, December | 0·23 | 466·06 |
| 1923, June | 0·08 | 1,820·00 |
| 1923, December | 0·03 | 6,442·00 |
| 1924, May | 0·0065 | 17,866·00 |

when they fell due they could be repaid at face value in a currency which had meanwhile shrunk to a fraction of its former worth.

Inflation served to cut production costs markedly by reducing the value of wages. Between the middle of 1914 and the beginning of 1924 prices increased 8,000 times, but wages rose only 3,500 times; thus inflation permitted real wages to be reduced to less than half the prewar level. The advantages of inflation benefitted every sector of the property-owning classes; the great landowners in particular took advantage of the inflation to rid themselves of their former debts. During the preceding decades of capitalist development the landlords had accumulated substantial indebtedness. Now they were able to repay, in inflated, nearly worthless paper currency, obligations to the value of 1,300 million gold crowns. (The country's total landed property was valued at about 7,200 million gold crowns.)

Inflation could only bridge the difficulties of financing the economy, of course, for a certain length of time. Its effects were contradictory, and in its later stages they became increasingly negative. The accelerating decline in the value of the currency diverted capital more and more from productive purposes into speculation. Thus the stabilisation of the currency finally became unavoidable.

The demand for stabilisation and for the provision of capital was not an isolated Hungarian affair, but belonged to the most basic political and economic questions in postwar and post-revolutionary Europe: most of the Central and Eastern European countries were in the same position as Hungary and wrestled with similar difficulties. The Western powers, having regained their economic and political stability, sought to prevent a new collapse and new revolutions (and to extend their spheres of influence) by taking a substantial part in the reconstruction of Central and Eastern Europe. In virtually every country financial stabilisation was the initial step in this direction. Austria was the first, in October 1922, with a loan agreement proffered by the great powers in order to stabilise the currency. Between 1922 and 1928 Rumania, Poland, and Bulgaria applied for similar credits, some countries more than once.

In the autumn of 1923 the Hungarian government made known its request for a short-term Western loan of 40–50 million gold crowns, and a long-term loan of 550–650 million gold crowns. At the same time, the government asked that the revenues now under the control of the Reparations Commission be released for its jurisdiction. After a long diplomatic tussle the Hungarians, supported by an English government at pains to counterbalance French influence in Eastern Europe, managed to win the consent of the hesitant French and their allies, Hungary's neighbours of the Little Entente, to the suspension of these pledges and the exemption of the loan from reparations charges. In November 1923 a League of Nations delegation arrived in Hungary, while in London plans for the loan were worked out.

In the upshot the loan did not come up to expectations. Instead of the amount asked for, only 307 million gold crowns were granted. In 1924 the stabilisation plan was passed into law and a Hungarian National Bank was created, as a corporation formally independent of the state, with a monopoly of the issue of currency. The Bank's reserves of gold and foreign exchange were bolstered by a loan of 4 million pounds sterling (82 million gold crowns) from the Bank of England, which also undertook to place sterling at Hungary's disposal in exchange for Hungarian crowns, to any amount presented.

Following these measures, the inflation was finally halted in June 1924. The exchange rate of the crown was stabilised by linking it to the English pound (one pound sterling was equal to 346,000 crowns; one gold crown equalled 17,000 paper crowns). Conversion from the crown to the new currency, the pengő, came only three years later, in 1927, at which time one gold crown was equivalent to 1·16 pengő (£1 = 25 pengő). The month of June was chosen to carry out the stabilisation because the League of Nations loan began to be received at that time. Half this loan was subscribed by England, the rest by six other countries, chiefly the United States, Italy and Switzerland. It was granted on terms which were extremely unfavourable to Hungary.

The uses to which the loan was afterwards put offered some surprises. Although the loan had been sought in order to stabilise finances, only about one-fourth of it (81 million pengő) was actually used to cover the government's budgetary deficit. Since the deficit disappeared in the fall of 1924, much sooner than the two years anticipated, the use of large sums for this purpose became unnecessary. This sum of 81 million pengő could easily have been raised by a once-for-all capital levy, for in after years deficits were successfully overcome using only internal sources of revenue, owing chiefly to a very high rate of taxation, 35 per cent higher than the prewar per capita tax rate. Thus the League of Nations loan merely helped the Hungarian government over its initial budgetary difficulties, sparing the propertied classes the need to make any financial sacrifices, and acted as a reserve or surety for the attainment of a balanced budget. In reality it had no other role than this. The greater part of the borrowed funds went for purposes quite independent of financial reorganisation, half of the amount received to pay off old debts as they fell due, another part of expand the state apparatus.

At the same time the League of Nations loan opened the gates to a veritable flood of Western credits. Among the first to be concluded, in 1925, were a loan for the reconstruction of the Rimamurány Iron Works, and another applied for by 48 provincial cities. Between 1926 and 1929 38 long-term loan agreements were signed. Between 1924 and 1931 long-term credit to a face value of 1,300 million pengő in all flowed into the country. But even this enormous sum was exceeded by the 1,700 million pengő in commercial and other short- and middle-term credit taken out between 1924 and 1931. Of this latter sum, roughly 40 per cent was commercial credit; the rest, because of its early expiration date, could not be used for long-term investment purposes.

Of the loans concluded after 1924 some 60 per cent were in the form of short- and medium-term credits. Prewar debts, postwar loans, and cumulative interest brought Hungary's foreign indebtedness, by the summer of 1931, to 4,300 million pengő. Moreover, a high price had to be paid for these credits. Because the loans were made at a steep discount, Hungary received only 80–90 per cent of their nominal value to begin with. On this reduced sum the high rate of interest, rarely less than 7 per cent, actually worked out to an interest rate of around 20 per cent. All this put a heavy material strain on the Hungarian economy. Because of the large number of old debts, and the high cost and unfavourable terms of the newer loans, more than half of the long-term credits received came to be used to amortise past indebtedness. With the passage of time the ratio between new credits and amortisation steadily worsened, until by 1929 the credits received during the year were less than the sums repaid to foreign creditors on past indebtedness.

The facts cited make it plain that during the 1920s Hungary was the recipient of loans in extraordinarily large amounts. The 400 million pengő received during the average year exceeded even the prewar average of 300 million pengő annually.

The loans of the 1920s, however, were used, for the most part, for investment purposes. Forty per cent of long-term credits went to pay off indebtedness, including prewar debts. The second largest block of these credits, about one-third of the total, went to cities and counties. These sums, split up forty or fifty ways, were spent piecemeal for municipal or communal purposes, in part on socially useful projects (hospitals, roads); but, all in all, they were not investments resulting in increased output. The third largest category, loans of 550 million pengő made on landed property, were likewise not used for investment, for the most part. The large landowners, still not free of the extravagant feudal way of life, spent half of the sums they received on consumption, purchase of land, and articles of luxury; a third was consumed in construction, leaving only about one-tenth for productive investment.

The largest productive investment was the 150 million pengő sunk into industry. But in the end productive investments absorbed only 20 per cent of all long-term credits. Investments in public housing and in the construction of hospitals and schools —not directly related to production—did not exceed 15 per cent of the credits used. Another 25 per cent or so of the long-term loans, moreover, went for expanding the state apparatus, for luxury building, and the like—that is, essentially for consumption purposes.

Put to such uses, these heavy credits created a burden of debt which could not be reduced by any subsequent increase in production. Repaying this constantly growing indebtedness became an ever greater burden, and repayment obligations became more and more difficult to meet. Thus these loans, obtained on unfavourable terms and poorly used, ended by making necessary the floating of new loans, a process leading to financial helplessness and dependency.

Unwise use of the postwar loans was a general European phenomenon, characteristic alike of Austrian, Yugoslav, Bulgarian and Rumanian financial policy during the postwar decade; clearly, then, it was not merely a question of the lack of foresight or financial bungling of the Hungarian government. The postwar loans served primarily political purposes. They contributed to the consolidation of the Central and Eastern European systems and to warding off the danger of revolution.

The immediate economic interests and activities of foreign capital are more easily seen in the investment of working capital than in credit operations. Here, however, the earlier situation was not restored in the postwar years. It is noteworthy that some Czech and Austrian factories or branch factories followed their markets in moving to Hungary, that several leading firms in the electrical industry were acquired by American capital (Ganz, United Incandescent Lamp, Standard Electric), and that German investments were made in the bauxite industry. The Aluminum Ore Corporation (Aluminiumérc Rt), reflected the gains of the leading German aluminum interests (Vereinigte Aluminiumwerke, Ottavi Minen und Eisenbahn Ges). Foreign investors bought about 20 per cent of the industrial stock issued in Hungary in the late 1920s, a decline from the prewar figure. The extent of the decline is shown by the fact that while in 1913 36 per cent of Hungarian industry was under foreign control, by 1929 foreign-owned interests had shrunk to 28 per cent. A similar process took place among the great banks. While early in the century most of the stock of the leading financial institutions (55 per cent) was foreign-owned, by 1929 the Bank of Commerce, the Discount Bank, and the First Domestic Savings Bank of Pest were almost completely in the hands of Hungarian financial interests, and the proportion of Credit Bank stock held abroad (40 per cent) also fell. The share of foreign capital remained substantial only in the newer Italian-Hungarian Bank and Anglo-Hungarian Bank, which were not in the first rank of large institutions.

In the financing of the Hungarian economy, then, direct foreign investment remained relatively unimportant; but when the extension of credit is included, foreign capital still played an important role in supplying the economy with funds. During the postwar decade about as much capital flowed into the country in the form of credits and investments as was accumulated domestically (2·5–3 billion pengő in each case). Because of the differences in the use of the funds, foreign capital played no such role in fixed capital formation. All in all, about one-quarter of all new fixed capital formation stemmed from foreign sources, three-quarters from domestic accumulation.

Thus the amounts invested from foreign and domestic sources were small, even considering the possibilities. The combined sum of capital invested in agriculture, industry, and transport in the postwar decade was about 260 million pengő annually, and the rate of growth of invested capital only around 3 per cent, well below the prewar rate of 5 per cent.

# 3 Effects of the depression: government intervention

The economic crisis which broke out in 1929 interrupted the process of economic recovery in Hungary. This recovery was based upon an expanding internal market protected by high industrial duties, export opportunities for agriculture where prices were favourable, and the role played by imported capital in financing the economy. Falling prices, and a growing inability to sell agricultural produce in foreign markets, led increasingly to the economic isolation of Hungary. This circumstance placed the country in a most unfavourable position not only from a market standpoint but also financially, for it was accompanied by a marked drop in the capital exports of the two largest capital-exporting countries, from £270 million in 1930 to £60 million in 1931, falling in 1932 to almost nothing (£6 million). The impact of all these factors was soon felt in every branch of Hungarian economic life, in the form of declining production, a rapid and uneven fall in prices, loss of foreign markets, and shrinkage of the home market. The first and most serious signs of the depression appeared in agriculture. The price of livestock fell by 50 per cent, the price of vegetable crops more than 50 per cent and that of wheat 65 per cent, destroying the former equilibrium of income and costs in Hungarian agriculture.

As a result the value of Hungarian agricultural exports—reckoned in current prices—fell 60 per cent from 1929 to 1933. The decline is still very great if, excluding the effect of falling prices, we take the stable pre-depression price level as a base. In that case the decline in Hungarian agricultural exports still

TABLE 18*

Agricultural production and prices during the great depression

| Years | Value of output of 1925–7 prices (million pengő) | % | Value of output in current prices (million pengő) | % | Index of agricultural prices |
|---|---|---|---|---|---|
| 1929–30 | 3,971 | 100·0 | 3,270 | 100·0 | 100 |
| 1930–1 | 3,919 | 98·7 | 2,746 | 83·9 | 73 |
| 1931–2 | 3,697 | 93·1 | 2,347 | 71·7 | 74 |
| 1932–3 | 3,897 | 98·1 | 1,987 | 60·7 | 72 |
| 1933–4 | 4,135 | 104·1 | 1,720 | 52·6 | 53 |

* Data from M. Incze (ed), *Az 1929–1933 evi vilaggazdasagi valsag hatasa Magyarorszagon*, Academy Publisher (1955).

amounts to 27 per cent. As a result of the uneven fall of world prices and the emergence of a pronounced agrarian price scissors Hungary received 15–20 per cent less in imports in exchange for the same volume of exports.

If agricultural markets contracted primarily because of the loss of foreign outlets, the market for industrial production was restricted largely by the shrinkage of domestic demand. True, prices of industrial products fell by 25 per cent, but even at lower prices it would not have been possible to sell the same volume of goods. The demand for producers' goods declined to a fraction of the pre-depression level; only one-fifth of the amount of basic industrial materials (iron ore, crude iron, steel) could be sold as before the crisis, and the output of the capital goods industries—iron and steel, machinery, building materials —fell by about one-half. The demand for consumer manufactures fell, as did, indeed, the demand for the products of the food industry. All these factors together reduced industrial production—calculated in constant prices—to a level 24 per cent below that of 1929.

The collapse of the earlier market equilibrium—precarious even before—was aggravated from the summer of 1931 by the financial and credit crisis, which turned it into a depression of the utmost severity. The financing of the economy had relied before on foreign sources to a great extent, and so after June 1931 the drying up of these sources created a radically new situation. It was not only that the credits hitherto available were no longer to be had. That in itself created a gap that was hard to fill, but much more serious were the obligations to repay the principal and interest on the enormous debts accumulated earlier.

The crisis reached its nadir following the summer of 1931, when the effects of the international financial and credit collapse struck Hungary. The debtor countries—among them Hungary—lost their gold and foreign-currency reserves within a few months. The precarious situation of the German and Austrian banks—especially of the Viennese Creditanstalt, which had large interests in Hungary—put the Hungarian banks (above all the Credit Bank) in a desperate position.

This situation was created when foreign creditors, in the wake of one failure after another all over Europe, called in every loan that could be recalled. Between 1 May 1931 and 13 July 1931 the Hungarian National Bank paid out gold and foreign exchange to the amount of 200 million pengő (about £8 million), a sum exceeding its entire reserve of precious metals and foreign currency in April; payment could be maintained only after the National Bank turned for aid to the Bank for International Payments and the leading European credit institutions, at the same time issuing treasury bills to the value of 5 million pounds sterling. At the same time Hungary's foreign indebtedness came to 4·3 billion pengő, whose amortisation cost of 300 million pengő a year would have taken about 10 per cent of the national income, or half the greatly reduced value of exports (almost 100 per cent in 1932).

The immediate danger of an inability to maintain payments and of a bankruptcy of the state threatened. Not only foreign creditors, but long queues of domestic depositors, too, besieged the banks for their money. The sudden demand for payment threatened the Hungarian banking system with possible collapse.

The dissipation of the gold and foreign-currency reserves had to be stopped as well. It was for this reason that, at the same time, controls were instituted over foreign exchange, the most far-reaching of all these various measures. These controls froze the reserves of gold and foreign currency, put an end to the free exchange of the pengő, and made transactions in foreign currency dependent upon the permission of the National Bank.

H

The system of foreign exchange controls later served as the basis for many other measures. Since the government, in applying the controls, had authorised the National Bank to suspend payments in foreign exchange and the conversion of the pengő into foreign currency, it followed that from the time these measures were introduced in the summer of 1931, repayment of debts held abroad ceased as well. Later, in the fall of the year, came the negotiations held between the newly formed National Commission on Foreign Credits (Külföldi Hitelek Országos Bizottsága) and the foreign creditors on a credit freeze, which sanctioned the existing situation. At first the talks turned on the continued payment of interest in foreign exchange, even if repayment of principal in foreign currency was suspended. Soon, however, since the National Bank did not in any case have enough foreign exchange to cover the interest, the government ordered a complete moratorium on transfers, thus officially putting an end to foreign payments. Henceforward Hungarian debtors paid the equivalent of their foreign obligations in pengő to a Foreign Creditors' Fund (Külföldi Hitelezők Alapja) administered by the National Bank. Repayment of short-term debts was organised in the same fashion.

In later years these arrangements were maintained, with minor modifications. In this way the passive balance of payments was reduced and the foreign-exchange earnings of Hungarian foreign trade were released, earnings which otherwise would have been needed to balance the payments account. But it was not only from a balance-of-payments standpoint that Hungary's international economic ties necessitated government intervention. Keeping the balance of trade active required unusual efforts too. Moreover, the way in which exports and imports evolved markedly affected the situation of industry and agriculture. Amid the sharpened competition for markets, Hungarian agricultural exports met serious difficulties; yet, lacking foreign credits and foreign exchange, the import of industrial raw materials, indispensable for the maintenance of economic activity, could have been paid for only out of export earnings. It was thus that measures to increase exports came to form the most important area of government intervention, and foreign trade, thanks to the system of foreign-exchange controls, came under state supervision.

In the bitter struggle for markets many countries turned to the device of devaluing their currency. For the Hungarian government, however, this would have been a two-edged weapon. On the one hand it would indeed have contributed to the winning of new markets and so to achieving an active balance of trade, which would also have helped industry to recover from the crisis. For a debtor country like Hungary, however, a currency devaluation would only have augmented the amount of her foreign obligations, thus wiping out the benefits which the devaluation of various foreign currencies entailed for Hungary's indebtedness.

The government sought to assure the advantages of an appreciation in the value of the currency by introducing into its financial and foreign-trade policy the premium system first worked out in Nazi Germany. The centralisation of foreign-exchange transactions in the hands of the state made it possible to convert foreign currencies into pengő at more than the official rate; ie, a premium was paid for foreign currency. In this way Hungarian products were made cheaper and more competitive in foreign markets, all the more so as the rates were at first set very flexibly, article by article, assuring exporters a premium of 20–50 per cent. In 1935 a new variation of the same system was introduced. The differentials between various articles were abolished, and instead a permanent scale of premiums tied to each currency was established. The highest premium was placed on the currencies of the so-called free-exchange countries, France, Belgium, Switzerland, the nations of the sterling bloc, and other overseas countries. In their case the premium was 50 per cent.

The premium system helped to bridge the difficulties in finding markets and contributed to an improvement of the financial and economic situation and, with import restrictions and protective duties, furthered the monopolisation of the domestic market by Hungarian heavy industry.

The financial and foreign-trade measures described were still not enough, however, to solve the country's market and foreign-exchange problems. Given the special foreign-exchange shortage of the 1930s, placed on a clearing basis, greatly reducing the need for foreign exchange and putting trade on a footing of reciprocal delivery of goods seemed to be able to overcome the problem. Foreign exchange was required only when a reckoning was drawn up at year's end, in order to settle remaining balances. The clearing system spread rapidly in Central and Eastern Europe. Germany concluded trade agreements on that basis with all the countries of the area, and an ever larger share of the trade among them was conducted on a clearing basis. By 1935 63 per cent of Hungary's foreign trade was handled by clearing arrangements.

The clearing regulations were of course closely supervised by the state. They presupposed a trade based on bilateral deliveries. Their use generally went together with regulation of the amount of trade and precise determination of import quotas. This not only helped to solve the financial and foreign-exchange problems of the 1930s but at the same time became a means of winning more of the domestic market for Hungarian production. In this way it became possible to restrict and even virtually exclude foreign goods from the domestic market, much more effectively than with the tariff measures of the 1920s. Restrictions on the import of finished goods opened more of the market to domestic manufactures. Before the depression 30 per cent of domestic textile needs were covered by imports, but by the late 1930s their share had fallen to a mere 1–3 per cent. In 1929 domestic production supplied only 30–40 per cent of paper consumption, but by 1938 it was supplying 70–80 per cent.

With the gradual improvement in business conditions consumption rose until, in the years before World War II, it again reached the pre-depression level.

To exploit the market opportunities for industry, however, some improvement had to be made in financial conditions. Earlier, industry had been financed mainly through stock issues handled by banks and foreign financial groups, and by bank loans. In the 1930s these sources dried up almost completely. After the summer of 1931 foreign investments (with an occasional rare exception) ceased altogether. Following the shock of the banking crisis, the capital position of the financial institutions stagnated throughout the entire subsequent decade. In 1929 the total assets of the Hungarian banks was 4·2 billion pengő; in 1933 it was 4·4 billion, and in 1937, 4·3 billion. Savings deposits, however, were down 11 per cent from the previous peak, and checking account deposits were 13 per cent lower. During the 1930s capital accumulation through the banks came to a complete halt.

Thus industry's financial needs were met exclusively from the internal accumulation of industry itself. In the 1930s the industrial enterprises' self-financing was the only expansive area in the economy and the mainspring of industrial development. The general importance of internal corporate financing is shown by figures indicating that industrial earnings accounted for 60–70 per cent of national capital accumulation during these years. Thus state intervention, and the growth in earnings which it assured, largely solved industry's market and financial problems, making possible a moderate development in this area.

But the general slowness of capital accumulation, the inability of other branches of the economy to accumulate capital, and the absence of foreign funds made any considerable investment activity impossible, especially in agriculture. Restoring the pre-depression level of domestic consumption could not bring any solution to agriculture's market problems. In spite of government intervention, the country's internal economic conditions did not provide a sufficient basis for getting agriculture back on its feet again. That would have become possible only if the crisis in foreign sales had been overcome. Securing foreign markets was inextricably bound up, however, with the political, economic, and power changes going on in Europe in the 1930s, which were dominated by the rapid advance of Nazi Germany.

From the time Hitler came to power Germany exercised a growing influence over the economic situation of the East and South-east European countries. The Neuer Plan in 1937 drastically restricted imports by means of quotas, and completely abolished the old system of foreign trade based on multilateral agreements, replacing it with a system of bilateral agreements. These agreements were made principally with countries which could be paid not in foreign exchange, but with deliveries of German industrial goods, under a system of clearing settlements. With these measures Nazi Germany sought to conserve its supply of foreign exchange for the purchase of strategic raw materials, at the same time directing its buying activity toward countries close to Germany which could be made secure in the event of naval blockade or even war.

These changes made South-eastern Europe especially important for Nazi Germany, which regarded the area as its natural *Lebensraum*. It was from this region that it acquired, besides rich supplies of grain, meat and fats, a significant part of its strategic needs: oil from Rumania, bauxite from Hungary, other metals from Yugoslavia. All these were obtained from close by, and generally without giving up foreign exchange. Since, moreover, the countries of the region were predominantly semi-developed or backward lands producing foodstuffs and raw materials, and likewise had no reserves of foreign currency, stronger ties with Germany and a foreign trade based on a clearing system promised to be beneficial for them too.

As a result of all these factors, the share of the South-eastern European countries in Germany's export trade grew between 1929 and 1937 from 3·8 per cent to 10·5 per cent; their share in German imports rose from 4·3 per cent to 9·4 per cent. The increase was much greater, however, in the case of key German imports. In 1937 37 per cent of Germany's wheat imports came from South-East Europe (against 2·4 per cent in 1929), 35 per cent of her meat imports (7 per cent in 1929), 29 per cent of her metal ores (3 per cent in 1929), and 62 per cent of her bauxite (37 per cent in 1929).

German economic expansion formed an important element in German policy toward this region. It was felt ever more powerfully in Hungary, already inclined toward Nazi Germany by political interest, common revisionist plans, and certain ideological similarities. German-Hungarian trade relations had been virtually paralysed after the onset of the depression, and even after the Nazis took power, by agricultural protectionism; but by 1934 the Nazi economic policy described affected trading relations with Hungary. The most important manifestation of this policy was the signing, in February 1934, of a trade agreement which (though formally only a supplement to the 1931 treaty) actually opened an entirely new chapter in German-Hungarian economic relations. For Hungary, the immediate significance of the agreement lay in the possibilities it offered for substantial exports of foodstuffs. Because of the extremely high agricultural tariffs in force in Germany, Hungarian growers could achieve the agreed export quotas there only because the German government agreed to pay customs rebates to the Hungarian government. In exchange for the export quotas, the Hungarian government guaranteed the import of German industrial articles, through 20–30 per cent tariff reductions and other means. These manufactured goods were in exchange for 90 per cent of Hungarian agricultural exports. The remaining 10 per cent were paid for by the German government in foreign exchange, or in the form of foreign-exchange-earning goods in transit.

At the same time, Hungary acquired opportunities of exporting substantial amounts of foodstuffs through its other ally, Mussolini's Italy. In March 1934 an Italian-Hungarian-Austrian treaty was signed in Rome, supplemented by an economic agreement. One of its main purposes, from the Hungarian standpoint, was to find markets for Hungarian wheat, one of the country's most serious problems during the depression. Under the agreement Italy undertook to take 200,000 tons of wheat. The Austrian government agreed to accept 150,000 tons of wheat and 50,000 tons of flour a year. The quotas for livestock exports were substantial as well.

Not all these agreements turned out well. The value of exports to Italy grew 80 per cent between 1933–4 and 1935, while overall Hungarian exports rose only about 12 per cent in value. By comparison, exports to Austria fell between 1933 and 1935, despite rising prices, by 18 per cent. In 1935 scarcely more than two-thirds of the wheat quota was delivered. In 1935–6 only 38 per cent of the quotas for other commodities was ever used. This was a result in part of Austria's autarchic economic policies, in part of the rise in world market prices for agricultural products, which led to an increase in exports to the free-exchange countries. Not least, it was a consequence of the constant growth of German influence, which brought with it an expansion of agricultural exports to Germany.

During this period Germany rose to be Hungary's most important trading partner. As a result of the trade agreement Germany's share of Hungary's exports jumped from 11 per cent to 22 per cent, and the effective incorporation of Hungary into the German 'living space' began. Between 1933 and 1936 Hungarian exports to Germany trebled, while imports of German goods into Hungary doubled. By 1935–6, for the first time in Hungary's modern economic history, Germany had become its principal trading partner, with 23–24 per cent of Hungarian foreign trade. By this time Germany's share in Hungary's imports was larger than Austria's and Italy's combined.

TABLE 19

*Volume of foreign trade*

| | Imports | | | Exports | | |
|---|---|---|---|---|---|---|
| Year | Value (pengő, 000s) | Index | Germany's share (% of total imports) | Value (pengő, 000s) | Index | Germany's share (% of total exports) |
| 1933 | 61,507 | 100 | 19·7 | 43,701 | 100 | 11·2 |
| 1934 | 63,025 | 103 | 18·3 | 89,866 | 205 | 22·2 |
| 1935 | 91,295 | 148 | 22·7 | 108,098 | 247 | 23·9 |
| 1936 | 113,353 | 184 | 26·0 | 115,198 | 263 | 22·8 |
| 1937 | 125,352 | 204 | 25·9 | 141,334 | 323 | 24·1 |
| 1938 | 123,673 | 201 | 30·1 | 143,350 | 328 | 27·4 |

German expansion, however, was not motivated by normal commercial consideration. Hungarian exports grew much more rapidly than imports from Germany; on the German side it was not the desire to conquer markets which dominated. Hungary's active balance of trade grew steadily during these years: in 1934 it amounted to 15 million pengő, but during the period 1934–6 it was 46 million. Despite official denials, the German government consciously strove to develop as far as possible a passive trade balance with the South-eastern European countries, as is clearly shown by the fact that by the end of 1936 they had accumulated in this manner debts of C.500 million marks ontrary to the usual state of affairs until 1934 the German foreign-trade balance was active—Germany strove for a passive balance, which in the last analysis meant nothing more than obtaining deliveries of goods without paying for them. During the years when Germany could not find credit anywhere but needed large material resources to begin its rearmament, it obtained hidden credits in goods from Hungary and the other South-eastern European countries, by postponing the delivery of its wares in payment for goods already received.

Before 1936 Germany worked partly through covert means to promote its economic expansion, but after that date allowed the process to become ever more open, through increased use of its political position.

This appeared principally in the constantly growing and ever more imperious demands for deliveries of Hungarian goods in this period of intensified German preparations for war, when feverish stockpiling and rapid armament went forward under the four-year plan. In 1936 came the first German demand for deliveries from Hungary; it extended beyond the meat and fats previously shipped, to grain exports as well. The German demands were legally incorporated into the new trade agreement of 1937 (the so-called third supplementary agreement), which brought about a 25 per cent increase in Hungarian exports and a 10 per cent increase in deliveries from Germany.

While the German government was already citing Hungary's obligations to make deliveries—a principle to be emphasised so often later on—the market for agricultural commodities was steadily improving. Between 1933 and 1937 the world price of wheat rose 70 per cent, and the price of meat 100 per cent, and there were more opportunities to sell these commodities for foreign exchange. At the same time the terms of sale on the German market worsened. By now it was not only German indebtedness which had unfavourable effects, but the composition of the German goods shipments sent in exchange as well. Though the system of clearings was still in effect, with settlement for 10 per cent of the value of Hungary's deliveries in foreign exchange or goods in transit, these provisions were increasingly violated by the Germans. The composition of Hungary's imports from Germany became extremely unfavourable. While in 1933 raw materials made up 22 per cent of these imports, by 1936 their share had fallen to 12 per cent, and by 1937 to only 6–7 per cent.

Even in these years Germany was the largest purchaser of Hungarian exports. Of exports in 1937 one-fifth of the beef cattle went to Germany, more than half the bacon and other meats, one-fifth of the milled grain, a third of the legumes, 60 per cent of the seed grain, half the poultry, eggs and feathers, and nearly half the fruit. Only the figure for bulk grain exports was lower: one-tenth of them went to Germany.

After the Anschluss and the dismemberment of Czechoslovakia, German economic influence grew by leaps and bounds. Since Germany had absorbed Austrian and Czechoslovak foreign trade, it now (1938–9) accounted for 52–53 per cent of Hungarian imports and exports. Nazi Germany had acquired a monopoly position in foreign trade, an area of such primary importance for the whole Hungarian economy.

Thus in the later 1930s Hungary pulled out of the grave crisis of agricultural markets, but at the formidable price of being gradually drawn into the Nazi *Grossraumwirtschaft*. In agriculture as in most branches of industry, however, this was no more than enough to permit recovery from the effects of the Great Depression; it did not make possible any substantial advance.

# 4 Development of the economy between the wars

### POPULATION AND SCHOOLING

During the quarter-century after World War I population growth slowed down all over Europe. After the demographic explosion of the nineteenth century Europe's population increased only moderately between 1920 and 1940, by 20 per cent. The population growth of the countries of Eastern and South-eastern Europe during these years considerably exceeded the European average. Hungary's population, however, increased only moderately during this period. Over the entire period the number of births fell faster than the number of deaths, and so the natural rate of increase showed a tendency to decline: in the years before World War I it averaged over 1 per cent, but between 1921 and 1930 it was only 0·9 per cent, and from 1931 to 1941, only 0·7 per cent.

The decline in the natural increase of the population in comparison with the preceding decades was balanced to some extent by the rapid decline in emigration. Emigration almost ceased with the enactment of a new American immigration quota system, while at the same time 350,000 Hungarians moved to Hungary from the successor states between 1918 and 1924. Later the balance of emigration and return migration came to show only a moderate loss: up to 1941 emigration had been responsible for a net loss of 145,000 people, a figure which the larger exodus of 1941–5 raised to only 254,000. As a result of all these factors Hungary's population grew by 17 per cent, from 7,990,000 in 1921 to 8,690,000 in 1930 and 9,320,000 in January 1941.

The growth in population substantially increased the size of the labour force, all the more so as the number of those in the productive ages (between 15 and 60) grew from the prewar figure of 57 per cent to 63 per cent. The number of children under 14 declined from more than one-third of the population to scarcely more than one-quarter, while the proportion of elderly (those over 60) grew from 8 per cent to 11 per cent.

Of the more than nine million inhabitants of the country, nearly 60 per cent lived in the Great Plain (including Budapest); 25 per cent lived in Transdanubia and 15 per cent in the northern regions. In Transdanubia the population grew very little, but in the other regions the increase was above the average. The changes in the territorial distribution of the population were largely a result of urbanisation; still, the process of urbanisation went forward, on the whole, very slowly. Of the more than 3,400 settlements in the country, 227 had a population of 5,000–20,000; Szeged and Debrecen had over 100,000, Budapest over a million. The number of people living on isolated farms, and in other outlying areas, was striking (more than 20 per cent), and indicates the backwardness of urbanisation. The weakness of the process of urbanisation is shown also by the fact that only Budapest and its suburbs displayed any large-scale increase in population.

TABLE 20

*Distribution of Hungary's population according to settlement growth*

| Year | Villages | Towns | Budapest's share of towns' total |
|------|----------|-------|----------------------------------|
| 1920 | 5,353,266 | 2,636,936 | 929,690 |
| 1930 | 5,807,068 | 2,881,251 | 1,006,184 |
| 1941 | 5,995,343 | 3,324,649 | 1,164,963 |

Along with the growth of numbers, improvements in the education of the people took place. Thus economic development was stimulated not only by the existence of a larger and—thanks to the longer average life span—more experienced labour pool, but also by the availability of a better trained and educated work force. Though education still developed only slowly, its importance in the life of Hungarian society grew.

Between the wars elementary education reached 1,300,000

children a year (figures are from the school year 1930–1), or 92 per cent of the school-age population, a modest improvement over the prewar level. More schools were built, which improved teaching conditions considerably. The number of pupils per classroom fell from 60 to 40, and and the pupil-teacher ratio fell from 80 to 47 (and, by World War II, to 42).

For the most part, however, elementary education continued to mean the completion of four to six grades; only a tiny fraction of the children went on to the seventh and eighth grades. During the 1937–8 school year, for instance, the number of first-grade pupils exceeded 200,000; but thereafter the number of elementary schoolchildren fell in a straight line from 185,000 in second grade to 130,000 in sixth grade, while at seventh- and eighth-grade levels together only about 35,000 pupils were to be found.

Secondary education expanded more significantly. In 1930 there were nearly 85,000 high-school students in the country, more than 10 per cent of the population of high-school age (compared with 5 per cent before the war). By the end of the 1930s, however, the number of secondary-school students had fallen to 52,000. The character of secondary education did not change in any way. It remained an extremely narrow, well-supported, high-level élite education.

Illiteracy declined among wage-earners too, most rapidly in agriculture, where before the war more than a third of those employed were still illiterate. By 1930 illiterates numbered only 15 per cent in agriculture. In industry the illiteracy rate was around 5 per cent, in commerce 4 per cent, and in transport 3 per cent, one-half to one-third of the prewar rates.

Between the two wars the number of university students nearly doubled—from 7,000 in 1930 to 12,000 in 1938—and a more modern educational structure contributed to supplying the economy with technical specialists. True, in 1930 nearly 40 per cent of the student body were reading theology or law, but 17 per cent were pursuing technical and commercial subjects, and another 14 per cent were studying medicine or pharmacy. Graduates made up less than 2 per cent of all wage-earners, and most of them found employment in the public service, where they were 8 per cent of all employees. But they were already appearing in larger numbers in trade and transport (2·5–3·5 per cent of all employees), and in mining and industry (0·5–1·5 per cent); in agriculture they were still a rarity (0.2 per cent).

The slow progress achieved in education between the wars did not keep pace with the growing educational requirements of the times.

### STAGNATION IN AGRICULTURAL PRODUCTION

Even before the end of the war Hungarian agriculture entered upon an exceptionally severe decline. By 1918 lack of manpower and losses of livestock had reduced the harvest of grain crops to 60 per cent of the prewar figure. Recovery was extremely slow and long-drawn-out; even in 1921 the yields of the major crops were 30–60 per cent below the prewar levels.

The restoration of agricultural production was closely bound up with the settlement of the land question. The question of land reform, which had come to the forefront during the years of war and revolution, remained Hungary's most burning social problem. The counter-revolutionary regime, which in its struggle against the proletarian revolution appealed not least to the peasantry, could not immediately remove land reform from the agenda. When the time came, however, to fulfil the extravagant promises made while the counter-revolution still desperately needed support it quickly became apparent that there would be no real land reform. Under the Land Reform Act of 1920 130,000 acres were taken, about 10 per cent of the area of the great landed estates; but even of this amount only two-thirds went to peasants owning little or no land. Altogether 400,000 families received unviable parcels averaging 1·5–2 acres. Thus in the end the peasant economy was hardly strengthened, while the great estates remained essentially unharmed. After the political consolidation of the Horthy regime the question of land reform once again vanished into oblivion.

Thus after the war Hungarian agriculture set out on the road to recovery with its old structure virtually unchanged. A further disadvantageous circumstance soon appeared in the shrinking of its external markets. Previously, the boundaries of the

TABLE 21*

Distribution of agricultural holdings, 1895 and 1935
(in comparative territory)

| Size of holdings in hold† | Number of holdings as percentage of total number | | Area of holdings (%) | |
|---|---|---|---|---|
| | 1895 | 1935 | 1895 | 1935 |
| 0 | 53·7 | 72·5 | 6·0 | 10·1 |
| 5 | 35·3 | 21·3 | 24·2 | 21·8 |
| 20 | 10·0 | 5·4 | 23·4 | 20·0 |
| 100 | 0·8 | 0·6 | 13·4 | 18·2 |
| 1,000 | 0·2 | 0·2 | 33·0 | 29·9 |
| Total | 100·0 | 100·0 | 100·0 | 100·0 |

* Data from Szuhay, M., *A parasztság felbomlásának egyes kérdései Magyarországon az első világháboru előtt* (The social structure of the peasantry in prewar Hungary), Studies to the history of capitalism in Hungary, Budapest, 1956.
† 1 hold = 1·4 acres.

Austro-Hungarian Monarchy had determined the structure and potentialities of Hungary's economy and of her agriculture. The appearance of agrarian-protectionist measures in Austria and Czechoslovakia, and the necessity of competing in those markets with Balkan and overseas produce, placed Hungarian agriculture with its rather low productivity and relatively high costs of production in a very serious position.

There was no longer any question of Hungary being able to sell its products on foreign markets in the prewar quantities. In the first years after the war, when there were no surpluses of foodstuffs in Hungary, this caused no problem. But as soon as economic reconstruction was complete, an export surplus reappeared, and agricultural exports became a key issue for the country's foreign trade and balance of payments, and for the whole national economy.

To make Hungarian agriculture competitive on the world market required a substantial modernisation of an extensive and technically backward system of production, still based predominantly on the large estate. For this, large-scale investments would have been necessary. But because of the low level of capital accumulation and the largely unproductive uses (already described) to which the foreign credits of the 1920s were put, such a thing was hardly possible even in the most prosperous years, and became totally out of the question after the depression struck. The critical financial, price, and market conditions of the 1930s made the transformation of agriculture an impossibility.

The structure of cultivation remained virtually unchanged between the two wars. The greatest progress was made in bringing fallow land under cultivation: before the war almost 1,200,000 acres of arable land lay fallow (within the frontiers of Trianon), while at the end of the 1930s less than 300,000 acres remained fallow, only 2 per cent of the country's arable land. Otherwise, however, there was hardly any change: the arable remained, as before, 60 per cent of the cultivated land. The area given to grain, which before the war approximated to 60 per cent of the arable, had in the course of two decades fallen to 54 per cent, but even so it still predominated. Despite the stagnation of sugar-beet production, the area under row crops increased significantly from 25 per cent to over 30 per cent of the whole, thanks to a 20 per cent rise in potato acreage and a growth of one-third in maize acreage. Fodder production rose, largely through an increase in the output of hay. The area devoted to market gardening and vineyards remained the same.

This virtually unchanging structure of cultivation did not, of course, in itself determine the potential for agricultural development. A great deal depended on the technical level of cultivation. In Hungarian agriculture, as previously mentioned, only threshing had been mechanised before the World War I. Between the two wars the mechanisation of tillage and traction brought about a decisive change in world agricultural production. Before 1914 the tractor had scarcely been in use in Hungarian agriculture. During the 1920s the number of tractors rose relatively rapidly: 1,189 were recorded in 1925, 6,800 in 1929. After the depression set in their spread stopped completely and was even temporarily reversed; by 1938 the number of tractors (6,957) only barely surpassed the pre-depression peak. Theoretically, then, there were about 2,100 acres of arable to every tractor, but in practice the acreage per tractor was higher, for during the 1930s only two-thirds of the machines were in actual operation, since it simply did not pay to use the rest in the middle of the agrarian depression.

Progress in agricultural technology was evident not only in the introduction of tractors but also in the modernisation of threshing methods. Horse-driven threshing machines, still fairly numerous before the war (11,000), all but disappeared; on the other hand, the number of internal-combustion-engine threshers rose from 5,700 to 10,800. Apart from the tractor and the thresher, the harvester was the only machine found in agriculture in large numbers. All told, there were 5,000 of these in the country, mainly on the large estates, but even these were not properly utilised.

For the most part, agricultural technique was based on traditional implements and simple machines. Though on an average there was one plough for every holding, most of the small peasant plots lacked even that much equipment. There were very few cultivating machines, and hauling was done by animal-drawn waggons. Hoeing, harvesting, and other operations were performed almost entirely by hand.

Next to mechanisation the use of artificial fertilisers, assuring higher yields and the replenishment of the soil, also acquired special importance in the development of agricultural technique. The use of artificial fertilisers, which spread rapidly in the twentieth century, had only just reached Hungary on the eve of the war. In 1913 an average of almost 19lb of various artificial fertilisers was used per acre. After a severe temporary decline following the war, the use of chemical fertilisers increased again somewhat, approaching an average of 24lb per acre by 1930. Following the onset of the depression, however, the use of artificial manures plummeted to 3lb per acre in 1933, and even by 1938 had not reached 10lb per acre again. On peasant holdings, of course, they were hardly used at all.

The decline in the use of fertilisers, the neglect of soil improvement, and the failure extend to irrigation works prevented any increase in yields. Of about 7 million acres of saline or acid soils requiring improvement, only about 28,000 in all were under treatment, while at the end of the 1930s there were but 33,000 acres of irrigated land. Average yields hardly changed between the wars; in some cases they actually declined. By West European standards yields were low.

TABLE 22

Production of principal crops (quintals, millions)

|  | 1911–15 | 1934–8 |
|---|---|---|
| Wheat | 19·9 | 22·2 |
| Rye | 8·0 | 6·9 |
| Barley | 7·1 | 5·6 |
| Oat | 4·4 | 2·6 |
| Maize | 15·1 | 23·0 |
| Potatoes | 19·4 | 21·3 |

TABLE 23

Value of the principal crops (1925–7 prices)

| Years | |
|---|---|
| 1911–15 | 100 |
| 1925–29 | 103 |
| 1935–38 | 110 |

The production of the main crops still outstripped the capacity of the small domestic market to absorb it. The moderate growth of agricultural production is summarised in Table 23, which gives the value of the output of the chief crops, calculated at 1925–7 prices. Despite a decline in the production of some crops, modest increases in the output of others still generally assured an export surplus from year to year. The very gradual development in production—amounting virtually to stagnation —was compensated to some degree by changes in the composition of the crop, in particular by the development of market gardening.

Some progress was noticeable in the latter field. The area planted to tomatoes, onions, cabbages and peppers increased, and in general their yields also rose. Here average yields were higher than the general level, and the produce soon appeared not only in the big cities but in foreign markets as well. In the 1930s the export of tomatoes, onions, peppers, cucumbers, and other vegetables grew markedly. Progress was even more substantial in fruit growing. The planting of orchards spread considerably during the later 1920s, so that by 1935 there were

50 per cent more fruit trees in the country than at the beginning of the century; in the early 1930s there was an average of almost three fruit trees per acre, and four for every inhabitant.

Greater importance can be ascribed to the role of stock-raising in the modernisation and advancement of agriculture. In European agriculture generally the weaknesses of crop farming were compensated by the considerable results achieved in stockbreeding. In Hungary, however, stock-raising presented an even sorrier picture than crop growing. During the predominantly bad times between the wars Hungarian agriculture never managed to recoup the losses in livestock suffered at the end of World War I, and on the eve of World War II the stock of animals of every important species—calculated on the identical, post-Trianon territory—had not recovered the pre-World War I level.

TABLE 24
Livestock (000s)

| Year | Cattle | Horses | Pigs | Sheep |
|---|---|---|---|---|
| 1911 | 2,149 | 896 | 3,322 | 2,406 |
| 1929 | 1,819 | 892 | 2,582 | 1,573 |
| 1938 | 1,882 | 813 | 3,110 | 1,628 |

This quantitative decline could be only partly compensated for by the improvement of animal breeds. Almost one-third of the pre-World War I decline in the number of cattle was accounted for by the gradual disappearance of the sturdy Hungarian Alföld breed, well suited for drawing the plough but a poor producer of milk and meat; by 1929 only 16 per cent of all cattle were of this variety, by 1938 fewer than 12 per cent. Its place was taken by the Simmental and red spotted varieties. The gradual transition to milk production is indicated by the steady rise in the number of milk cows. As a result, the average yield of milk increased by one-quarter, while the production of cheese doubled and that of butter trebled. Improvements in breeding were observable in pig-rearing too, in a slight increase in the proportion of pigs raised for meat. The most encouraging feature of meat production, however, was probably the upswing in poultry raising, a result partly of changing tastes, partly of export demand for eggs, meat and feathers.

Between the two wars Hungarian agriculture changed little. Its backwardness in comparison with the agriculture of the more developed European countries tended to increase. At the same time, Hungary's lead in development over the other Eastern European countries diminished.

### INDUSTRIAL DEVELOPMENT: STRUCTURAL CHANGES

During the period of moderate growth between the two wars industry became the decisive factor in the economic development of Hungary. Though manufacturing as a whole could progress only modestly, in some sectors there were important achievements. But the innovations had no impact on mining, metallurgy, and power production.

The capacity of Hungary's coal mines was 10–12 million tons a year. Between the two wars a large part of this capacity went unused. The three coal fields of post-Trianon Hungary—the small black-coal basin around Pécs, the extensive better-grade brown-coal deposits around Tatabánya in Transdanubia, and the poorer-quality field near Salgótarján—together produced around 7–9 million tons a year.

Between 1913 and 1938 coal production was raised about 30 per cent from 7,100,000 to 9,400,000 tons, essentially through more thorough exploitation of existing capacity. The mines

TABLE 25
*Output of coal (tons, millions)*

| Year | Lignite | Black coal | Total | index |
|---|---|---|---|---|
| 1913* | 6·2 | 0·8 | 7·0 | 100·0 |
| 1921 | 5·5 | 0·7 | 6·2 | 88·2 |
| 1929 | 7·0 | 0·8 | 7·9 | 111·2 |
| 1933 | 5·9 | 0·8 | 6·7 | 94·8 |
| 1938 | 8·3 | 1·0 | 9·4 | 132·3 |

* Comparative territory.

remained, as before, largely under the ownership of two large concerns, the Hungarian General Coal Mining Corporation (Magyar Általános Kőszénbánya) and the Salgótarján Mining Co (Salgótarjáni Kőszénbánya). Black-coal production was controlled by the Austrian Donaudampfschiffsfahrt-Gesellschaft. The productivity of Hungarian mining, though it rose somewhat in the 1930s, remained low. Output per man-shift ranged from 1,600 to 1,800lb.

The development of the iron and steel industry showed many similarities. With the reduction of iron ore output after the war a good part of the country's capacity stood idle. In 1929 only five of every six furnaces were in operation, during the depression (until 1936) only four in six. Increases in production were

TABLE 26

Output of iron and steel

| Year | Iron ore (tons, 000s) | index | Iron (tons, 000s) | index | Steel (tons, 000s) | index |
|---|---|---|---|---|---|---|
| 1913* | 395·0 | 100·0 | 190·4 | 100·0 | 443·2 | 100·0 |
| 1921 | 36·0 | 9·1 | 71·4 | 37·5 | 166·1 | 37·5 |
| 1929 | 251·7 | 63·7 | 367·9 | 193·2 | 513·5 | 115·9 |
| 1933 | 50·0 | 12·7 | 66·7 | 35·0 | 179·9 | 40·6 |
| 1938 | 297·6 | 75·3 | 334·9 | 175·9 | 647·5 | 146·1 |

* Postwar territory.

achieved by fuller use of existing capacity. Among the few modernising steps taken between the wars were the retirement of the antiquated Bessemer process, which earlier had provided 10 per cent of steel production, and the introduction of the electric-furnace method, which by 1938 was turning out 7 per cent of Hungary's steel. The country's annual crude iron output of 340,000 tons was produced by the state ironworks at Diósgyőr and by the Rimamurány-Salgótarján Iron Works plant at Ózd. These works with the Manfréd Weiss works at Csepel turned out 660,000 tons of steel annually.

An important step in the development of mining and metallurgy was the emergence of an aluminium industry. During the 1920s prospecting in Transdanubia brought to light one of Europe's richest deposits of bauxite, in the western foothills of the Bakony range and in Fejér county. In 1925 the Aluminium Ore Corporation with the co-operation of German capital began to develop the mines at Gánt, which reached an output of ½ million tons by 1929. From then until the outbreak of the war production did not greatly exceed this level. In 1934 the Bauxite Trust built its first plant for alumina (semi-processing of bauxite), with a capacity of 10,000 tons; though it processed only 5–10 per cent of the country's bauxite production, it still laid the basis for an aluminium industry in Hungary. In the same year work began at Csepel on the first aluminium smelting plant, which was put into service in 1935. By 1937 its 48 furnaces were operating with a capacity of 1,400 tons of aluminium a year.

One of the most important steps in the development of the basic industries was the increasing output of electrical energy. In 1921 power production within the new frontiers totalled 276 million kilowatt hours, or 35kwh per person, three times the prewar average. After the war the use of electricity spread widely, thanks to the discovery of cheap new production methods and the introduction of high-tension long-distance transmission lines, which made possible an almost unlimited expansion in the use of electrical power. From 1921 the Electrical Works substantially increased the capacity of its plants. The great coal mining companies began work in 1925 on the construction of new power plants and long-distance transmission lines. One of the most important achievements was the construction, with English co-operation, of the generating plant at Bánhida, connected with Budapest by long-distance lines. By 1929 there were 3,500 kilometres of such power lines in the country, by 1938 almost 12,000. In the decade after 1921 the production of electrical energy nearly trebled, and by 1938 it had more than quadrupled.

The engineering industry took its own special course. The first postwar decade was one of aimless blundering. While throughout the world engineering enjoyed a revival and a strong boom, in Hungary the industry was unable to share in this international progress because of its insufficient capital and narrow markets. In the 1920s about half the engineering output still consisted of agricultural equipment, railway carriages, bridge- and shipbuilding, while electrical equipment made up only 15 per cent and motor vehicles only 5 per cent.

The output of agricultural equipment and rolling-stock stagnated. Many factories were closed down. On the whole engineering marked time; production in 1938 did not exceed the pre-World War I level.

During the interwar period several new, modern branches of manufacture made headway, though slowly. Even in the early 1920s factories unable to sell the traditional kinds of agricultural equipment (Hofherr, MÁVAG) were converting to tractor production. Only a small number of models was produced, however.

Serious efforts were made to introduce automobile manufacturing as well, but in the 1930s, as a consequence of the Great Depression, the manufacture of passenger cars ceased altogether; only MÁVAG and Hungarian Car and Machine continued, as before, to turn out a few trucks.

Motor cycle production, on the other hand, became permanently established in Hungary. In 1925 the Ganz plant initiated the manufacture of diesel trains, and from 1928 was able to enter export markets with its patented 200-horsepower Ganz-Jendrassik diesel train. Unique in its performance and in its place among Hungary's exports, it invaded even the markets of the Western hemisphere. By 1938 some 550 diesel-units of various sizes had been exported. In 1933 the Ganz shipyard began to build river- and ocean-going motor vessels. Four ships had been completed when the war broke out.

Ganz also played an important role in the most rapidly developing branch of industry, the electrical industry. It was only here that modern mass production based on an up-to-date technology permitted Hungary to keep pace with world standards. The Ganz Works, though most of its products had already fallen behind the latest achievements of technology, could still tool up to produce annually 150,000 of the new galvanometers devised by Ottó Bláthy in 1923, and with them penetrate even the American market.

The United Incandescent Lamp Co through its American connections had access to the advances made in the American industry during the war, and strengthened its international position still further by manufacturing the krypton lamp invented by Imre Bródy in 1931. At the same time the company's engineers worked out a new method of producing krypton gas cheaply in large quantities. United Incandescent exported its products to 53 countries.

At the same time, keeping pace with the latest technical demands, it tooled up in 1922 to make wireless valves, and by the end of the 1920s had begun to export them as well. Hungarian production of valves jumped ten-fold in the 1930s, exports twelve-fold. In 1931 United Incandescent bought the Hungarian Wolfram Lamp Co (Magyar Wolframlámpagyár—Orion), in order to concentrate there its radio and wireless valves production. By the end of the 1930s the fast-growing radio industry was turning out 40,000–50,000 receivers a year, three-quarters of them for export. In 1938 electrical equipment was responsible for 30 per cent of the output of the engineering industry, an indication of its rapid expansion.

In Europe chemicals was one of the fastest-growing branches of modern heavy industry. Postwar Hungary, however, failed to reorganise the production structure of this industry, as of so many others. In the 1930s there was more development: this was the Pét Nitrogen Works (Péti Nitrogénművek) set up in 1928 as a state enterprise designed for military purposes, though ostensibly to remedy the virtual absence of nitrogen fertiliser production in the country. From this time on preparations for war, albeit in covert form, began to create a boom in the chemical industry. A characteristic manifestation of this was the remodelling, beginning in 1935, of the Hungária Artificial Fertiliser Works (Hungária Műtrágyagyár). From that date forward the country's largest chemical plant was converted to the production of many industrial chemicals never before made in Hungary.

In the course of similar efforts the pharmaceutical industry, in particular the Chinoin plant, was fitted out for the production of basic pharmaceutical materials. The output of several chemical products doubled or trebled during the 1930s, and the manufacture of many new products was introduced, making the industry one of the fastest-growing between the wars. Its capital doubled, and its production increased almost 50 per cent.

The evolution of the consumer-goods industries during this quarter-century differed in many respects from that of the heavy industries hitherto examined. While the latter mostly stagnated between the wars, attaining a rapid rate of growth only during the years of rearmament, the consumer-goods industries largely followed a contrary pattern. The protected markets of the interwar years brought about a prosperity which even the depression scarcely disturbed, making possible a rapid expansion of output.

The fastest-growing industry between the wars was textiles. The textile factories established in the 1920s absorbed fully one-third of all investment in Hungarian industry. The industry's expansion was greatly aided by the availability of empty factory buildings, old mills, or former war plants; similarly, entrepreneurs were able to buy cheaply from Western European (mainly English) textile manufacturers second-hand equipment no longer needed by industries passing from their great era of expansion into one of technical upgrading. In many cases Czechoslovak textile mills moved to Hungary in order to retain their former markets, or, in the course of converting and developing their operations at home, transferred their old equipment to Hungary and set up subsidiaries there.

The expansion of the textile industry continued even during the depression. The number of cotton spindles grew almost tenfold, from 35,000 in 1921 to 196,000 in 1929 and 324,000 in 1938. The number of cotton looms increased three and a half times, from 4,000 to 12,000 and then 14,000. Spindles for wool doubled in number and looms multiplied six-fold.

Between the wars the textile industry's work force also grew rapidly, to five times its former size (from 13,000 to 64,000). Production in 1925 was twice the prewar level, in 1929 three times as much, and in 1938 four times as much. The textile industry thereby became capable of satisfying the whole of domestic demand, whereas before the war it had supplied only one-third of domestic consumption.

The paper industry enjoyed a prosperity and growth comparable to that of textiles. By 1938 the paper industry had increased its capacity to almost 90,000 tons, and like textile manufacturing it was able to supply most domestic needs. Paper production rose two-and-a-half times between the two wars.

The food industry followed its own special course. With an

output provided 80 per cent by milling, sugar refining, brewing, and distilling, it had been the leading industry of dualist Hungary. In its new postwar situation, however, the food industry's old structure was top-heavy; it had lost its former export position and many of its sources of raw materials, and a large part of its capacity fell idle. In 1912 the leading Budapest export mills ground 940,000 tons of grain, but in the 1920s the amount processed was only 200,000–270,000 tons. One after another the largest mills shut down. But even this constantly shrinking capacity could not be fully utilised: in 1937 the milling industry was still working at only 45 per cent of its productive capacity.

Similar tendencies characterised the other leading branches of the food industry. Little could be done to build up the industry during the postwar decade, but in the 1930s certain new products began to be developed. In the forefront of these was the canning industry, in particular the canning of fruit and tomatoes, which grew into a modern, high-capacity industry even by world-market standards. In 1937 output of canned fruits and vegetables was twice what it had been before the depression. The new industry worked mostly for export, as is clearly shown by the fact that exports of canned fruits and vegetables increased thirteen times over during these years, exports of tomatoes twenty times over.

The technical progress exhibited in a few directions and the advances made through Hungarian inventions in the electrical industry, engineering, and pharmaceuticals, cannot obscure the essential differences between the interwar period and the pre-1914 era of technical development in industry. At the beginning of the century we can speak of the successful adoption of the latest technical achievements by several basic industries covering a broad range of products, and in some important areas of their significant development by Hungarian industry; but after the war the adoption of modern technology was restricted to a few narrow fields and its further development by Hungarian industry became unusual.

Many inventions remained without any economic impact in their own time in Hungary, though they had a place in the general current of technical progress. Among these were György

Jendrassik's gas turbine, Oszkár Asbóth's helicopter, Albert Fonó's ram-jet engine, and János Sklenár's spherical-piston electric motor. Despite successful trial demonstrations, these inventions never went into production in Hungary, and came to be patented only after years of effort, mostly in England or Germany, profiting a more developed Western industry.

Twentieth-century inventions demanded access to large markets. Increasingly it became impossible to apply mass-production techniques in small countries. Thus Hungarian industry, though it was the prime factor of growth in the interwar economy, could not in itself lead to more than modest results.

True, the horsepower available to its factories doubled owing to the progress of electrification, but the record of Hungarian industry is better reflected in the fact that the number of workshops and factories scarcely rose. The growth of industrial production overall was only moderate. Between 1913 and 1938

TABLE 27

*Horsepower and workers in manufacturing industry*

| Year | Total horsepower (000s) | index | Number of workers (000s) | index |
|---|---|---|---|---|
| 1913* | 826 | 100·0 | 246·5 | 100·0 |
| 1929 | 1,330 | 161·0 | 269·9 | 109·5 |
| 1938 | 1,736 | 210·2 | 288·5 | 116·9 |

* In postwar territory.

TABLE 28

*Index of industrial production calculated at constant prices*

| Year | Index |
|---|---|
| 1913* | 100 |
| 1921 | 51 |
| 1929 | 112 |
| 1932 | 84 |
| 1938 | 128 |

* In postwar territory.

industrial output—reckoned on the basis of the post-Trianon territory—increased by only 28 per cent. This was a growth rate of scarcely 1 per cent over the quarter-century period, compared with an average annual increase in production of 5·4 per cent early in the twentieth century. It is striking that the output of the most heavily industrialised countries expanded much faster than Hungary's—44 per cent for England, 49 per cent for Germany, 33 per cent for Belgium. Moreover, some of the smaller European countries were rapidly becoming industrialised: Sweden, Holland and Denmark more than doubled their industrial production during this time, and the situation was similar even in the backward Balkan countries. There was hardly a country in Europe, apart from Spain, Austria, and Poland, whose industrial development did not surpass Hungary's. Hungarian industrial output reached only 43 per cent of the average level of production of the European countries, a slightly poorer showing than the prewar figure of 44 per cent.

At the same time, a relatively moderate tempo of development was accompanied by important changes in the structure of industry. Conspicuous among the structural characteristics of Hungarian industry during the preceding decades of capitalist development was the peculiar relationship of small and large industry.

In the new postwar situation small-scale industry received a new stimulus, and throughout the interwar period continued to employ nearly half (45 per cent) of all industrial workers, while turning out more than a quarter of industrial production. Seventy per cent of this output was accounted for by the clothing, hotel and restaurant, construction, and food industries.

Thus small-scale industry, drawing on cheap labour, held its own. Big industry did not drive out small as in the developed industrial countries, where higher wages and the lower unit-costs of large-scale manufacturing made their effects felt more powerfully, reducing small industry essentially to repair work and to certain necessary functions complementary to big industry. The proportion of workers in factories with over 500 hands fell from 38 per cent to 32 per cent. This decline is to be explained principally by the fact that between the wars it was light industry, and within it chiefly smaller and middling operations, that developed fastest.

The struggle to secure markets amid unfavourable economic conditions led the big firms to measures which were technically and organisationally anachronistic. One of the country's largest heavy-engineering firms, the Manfréd Weiss works at Csepel, manufactured a bewildering array of products. The Hofherr-Schrantz Farm Machinery Co sought by turning out equipment for the paper and textile industries to make up for the loss of business caused by a shrinking market for farm machinery.

These outdated technical and organisational practices, designed to assure markets, ended up by preserving the industrial forms of the nineteenth century. The Hungarian heavy-engineering and iron and steel industries were widely described as a 'general store': their plants simultaneously turned out the most varied products, and in tiny quantities, sometimes even manufacturing a single piece of machinery.

Another unfortunate consequence of the effort to defend markets was the rapid spread of cartel agreements. When the Cartel Act of 1931 came into effect, making it obligatory to report such agreements, there were 256 cartels in Hungary, compared with about 100 early in the century. By the eve of World War II their number had grown to 357. In 1931 cartels governed 32 per cent of the production of large-scale industry, just before the war 42 per cent. To defend their markets a great many firms concluded so-called 'désintéressement' agreements, shutting down several plants in an industry in order to limit production to the industry's few leading enterprises. Early in the century these occurrences were scattered and marginal, in the interwar period with its very modest industrial development they became decisive.

In a few cases Hungarian enterprises which figured prominently on the European market were able, through their foreign financial and market ties, to join international agreements which offered a division of markets and regulation of production, opportunities to develop their technology and specialise their products, and access to patents and capital. The various Ganz plants, for example, belonged to seven different international cartels. United Incandescent Lamp also played an important role in international cartel agreements.

Despite an encouraging start at the beginning of the century

Hungary did not develop modern forms of mass production and the industrial organisation appropriate to them. Only a handful of vertical or horizontal combinations ever came into existence. None the less, important changes took place in the industrial scene. These tended, between the wars, toward abolishing that earlier characteristic of Eastern European industrial structure, the predominance of the food industry. The changes, however, did not take place in accordance with the technical demands of the age, but again bore a peculiarly new Eastern European stamp—the primacy of light industry.

The importance of the food industry decreased considerably in Hungary between the wars: in 1938 it accounted for under 29 per cent of industrial production, against more than 42 per cent in 1913 (reckoned within the frontiers of 1920). But its share of output still ranked it among the strongest industries in the country. Textiles were now the second largest branch of industry with almost 18 per cent of industrial production.

In part these were changes for the better, for besides reducing the unhealthy preponderance of the food industry they point to diversification. None the less in other parts of the world the course of modern industrial development lay in the rapid advance of heavy industry (especially its processing lines), until it accounted for nearly 50 per cent of production. But in Hungary, the share of heavy industry did not increase at all. In 1913 the output of the iron and steel, engineering, electrical and chemical industries (calculated within the frontiers of 1920) was 38 per cent of the total, but in 1938 it was less than 36 per cent. If, then, structural changes acted to reduce the former lopsidedness, Hungarian industry remained backward.

## OTHER SECTORS OF THE ECONOMY

During the preceding period of capitalist development in the second half of the nineteenth century and the early years of the twentieth, in Hungary as generally throughout Central and Eastern Europe, a crucial factor in rapid economic growth was the extension of the infrastructure especially through railway building.

After World War I the dynamism of these sectors was

TABLE 29
*Structure of Hungarian industry,
share of percentages of total output*

|  | 1913* | 1929 | 1938 |
|---|---|---|---|
| Iron and metals | 15·5 | 11·3 | 14·2 |
| Engineering | 13·8 | 10·2 | 9·7 |
| Electrical energy | 1·5 | 4·2 | 4·4 |
| Building materials | 4·3 | 4·8 | 3·7 |
| Chemicals | 7·8 | 7·4 | 9·7 |
| Heavy industry total | 42·9 | 37·9 | 41·7 |
| Textiles | 4·8 | 14·2 | 15·3 |
| Clothing | 1·5 | 2·2 | 2·4 |
| Leather | 2·7 | 3·2 | 3·9 |
| Wood | 2·5 | 3·2 | 2·5 |
| Paper | 0·6 | 1·2 | 2·1 |
| Printing | 2·6 | 2·4 | 1·7 |
| Light industry total | 14·7 | 26·4 | 27·9 |
| Food | 42·4 | 35·7 | 30·4 |
| Total | 100·0 | 100·0 | 100·0 |

* Calculated in current prices of industrial output in postwar territory.

broken. In Hungary the railway system built earlier proved adequate to the transport demands of slow postwar economic growth. Hungary ranked seventh in density of its railway network in Europe (93 kilometres of rail per 1,000 square kilometres) and hardly needed to build new lines. The rolling-stock was adequate too, and its renewal went forward very slowly. The first achievement in the technical advancement of the railways was the introduction of the new 424 locomotive built by MÁVAG in 1923. It was followed by the electrification of the 200-kilometre Budapest-Hegyeshalom line, completed in the early 1930s, and, in connection with the latter, the placing in service of fourteen Kandó electric locomotives. The Ganz Works' advanced diesel trains and motor-trains were produced mainly for export, but several of them were put into service at home, as further contributions to the modernisation of rail transport.

The slowdown in railway development generally observable in the advanced countries was accompanied by the spread of new forms of transport, particularly the motor car. In Hungary, however, the stagnation of the railways was not offset by the development of road transport. Road building made relatively substantial progress, for by World War II the 16,500 kilometres of paved roads existing in 1920 had grown to a network of almost 25,000 kilometres. These roads were more for coach traffic. The number of motor vehicles in use (motor cycles included) leaped from 1,700 in 1920 to 30,300 in 1930, but thereafter the increase stopped, and in 1937 there were still only 30,800, and trucks were relatively few.

Expressing the number of motor vehicles in relation to area and population, one arrives at an average automotive index, so-called, of 5·7 for fourteen European countries in 1930; but the index for Hungary was only 0·5, a fraction of the European average. There were but 2·3 motor vehicles for every 1,000 of population, and even this (by European standards) extremely low figure was made up mostly of passenger cars. Until the war we can speak only of the very beginning of modern truck transport.

Water transport stagnated during these years. The Danube fleet did not expand much, and only the launching of ocean-going river vessels represented any advance. By the late 1930s three regular services marked the beginning of ocean-going navigation. The birth and first achievements of civil aviation deserve mention chiefly from the standpoint of future developments, for in the 1920s only an average 2,000–4,000 people travelled annually by air, rising by the end of the 1930s to 13,000–20,000 per year.

The other important area of infrastructural activity, construction, also dropped off considerably from the level of the pre-World War I decades. The decline in housing construction is indicated by the fact that the 57,700 residential rooms built in Budapest between 1920 and 1929 (an annual average of 5,700) reached only half the prewar building level. Between 1933 and 1938 residential construction in Budapest averaged around 16,000 new rooms a year. The level of construction and road-building activity is illustrated by the fact that in Hungary the average annual consumption of cement was 45–55lb per capita, against an average of 220lb per capita in Western Europe.

Perhaps the most dynamic aspect of infrastructural development was the progress made in the electrification of the country. Before 1913 only about 300 communes in Hungary had electricity, most of them in areas which fell within the new frontiers. In 1920 42 per cent of the population lived in areas provided with electric power, although only 27 per cent actually enjoyed electric light. By 1938 1,100 communes (36 per cent of all cities and communes) had electric power, though 71 per cent of the population lived in localities served by electricity.

Commercial activity also lacked the dynamism of earlier decades. Internal trade suffered a severe blow because of the new postwar situation. Many former commercial centres (Szeged, Miskolc, Esztergom) now found themselves on the periphery of the country, and the commission trade in agricultural produce, organised to serve the entire Monarchy, largely disappeared. The 20–25 per cent increase in domestic trade in the late 1920s, at the height of the boom, did no more than regain the prewar level. Still, some progress can be observed in the development of the network of commercial outlets. The number of stores expanded, partly because of the opportunities created by the wartime boom but, paradoxically, more because of unfavourable postwar economic conditions, which prompted many who were unable to make a secure living in other ways to open little shops. The network of stores which grew up in Budapest between the wars was, as regards density, in no way behind the great European cities: there were 20–25 independent shopkeepers for every 1,000 of population, as in Vienna, Berlin, or Munich. The plethora of tiny shops was, however, not only an indication that the retailing system was well-developed, but also that it was over-extended and old-fashioned. Outside the capital, retail stores remained small, backward, and undifferentiated. As before, there was an average of only one employee for each independent shopkeeper.

The importance of foreign trade increased markedly; opportunities here, however, did not develop favourably because of the effects of a backward, high-cost system of production. In contrast to its 50 per cent growth early in the century, European foreign trade even by 1929 surpassed the 1913 level by only 1 per cent. Hungarian foreign trade rapidly overcame the post-war collapse, exports quadrupling between 1920 and 1925 and imports nearly doubling. But this was merely a return to normal, all the more so as the level of foreign trade did not change appreciably during the second half of the decade. At its peak in 1929, when exports jumped 25 per cent following a record harvest, the value of foreign trade (calculated in constant prices) still remained 15–20 per cent below the prewar level. In the following decade foreign trade dropped off sharply, declining to between one-third and one-half of the pre-depression peak (in current prices).

TABLE 30
Value of foreign trade

| Year | Imports (million pengő) | index | Exports (million pengő) | index | Balance |
|---|---|---|---|---|---|
| 1920 | 484·1 | 100 | 190·6 | 100 | −293·5 |
| 1924 | 815·3 | 168 | 667·0 | 350 | −148·3 |
| 1929 | 1,063·7 | 220 | 1,038·5 | 545 | − 25·2 |
| 1933 | 312·6 | 65 | 391·3 | 205 | + 78·7 |
| 1938 | 410·6 | 85 | 522·4 | 274 | +111·8 |

Despite its reduced volume, however, important changes took place in the structure of this trade. The share of finished industrial goods in imports fell sharply between 1913 and 1937, from 62 per cent to 27 per cent, and the proportion of raw materials and semi-processed goods rose from 38 per cent to 73 per cent. On the other hand, the composition of the export trade hardly altered; indeed, the largest item, the export of foodstuffs and raw materials, even increased its share from 52 per cent to 59 per cent.

TABLE 31
Structure of foreign trade (%)

|  | Imports |  |  |  | Exports |  |  |  |
|---|---|---|---|---|---|---|---|---|
|  | 1913 | 1929 | 1933 | 1937 | 1913 | 1929 | 1933 | 1937 |
| Raw materials | 25·0 | 37·5 | 42·1 | 42·5 | 52·2 | 59·9 | 64·7 | 58·8 |
| Semi-manufactured goods | 13·3 | 22·5 | 28·3 | 30·6 | 10·0 | 6·9 | 7·3 | 10·6 |
| Manufactured goods | 61·7 | 40·0 | 29·6 | 26·9 | 37·8 | 33·2 | 28·0 | 30·6 |

The direction of foreign trade also changed radically. Before World War I 70 per cent of Hungary's external commerce was carried on with the Austrian and Czech lands of the Monarchy. Only in 1929, however, did her interwar trade with the successor states reach more than one-half of her total foreign trade, and by 1937 it had fallen to scarcely more than one-quarter. In the 1930s, as mentioned previously, Germany's (and Italy's) share in Hungary's foreign trade grew rapidly; in 1938 half the trade was conducted with Germany.

Banking in Hungary was affected by development elsewhere in the economy. Before World War I an unusually strong and well-developed banking system grew up in Hungary, as a consequence of the peculiarities of capitalist development there. For that very reason, a further extension of the system was out of the question following the war. At the end of 1924, when the currency was stabilised, there were 2,168 banks in operation. During following years their numbers showed a downward tendency. By 1938 liquidations and mergers had reduced the number of banks in the country to 1,425.

The fall in the number of financial institutions did not spring merely from rationalisation of the financial system, however. Nor does the numerical decrease express adequately the decline in the capital assets and volume of business of the banks.

Before World War I the capital of Hungarian banks exeeded 2,800 million pengő. In 1925, by contrast, it was only 400 million, in 1929 700 million, and in 1938 800 million pengő. Even more striking was the contraction in the supply of funds made available to the banks by their depositors. Before World War I the banks (within the frontiers of 1920) had savings deposits of 4,500 million pengő. In 1925, by contrast, savings deposits were only 300 million pengő, and at their peak in 1930 not quite 1,100 million pengő (a figure not reached again until 1940). Thus even at the interwar peak of prosperity the savings deposited in Hungarian banks did not come to one-quarter of the prewar amount. Current accounts did not display a more favourable trend.

Thus throughout the postwar decades the assets of the banks, and therefore their lending activity, lagged well behind their prewar levels. On this narrowed material base concentration and monopoly increased rapidly. The largest banks extended their influence more and more over previously independent institutions and over the provincial money market.

TABLE 32

Banks and credit institutions

| Year | Number | Capital | Bills of exchange | Mortgages | Deposits | Current accounts |
|------|--------|---------|-------------------|-----------|----------|------------------|
|      |        |         | (million pengő)   |           |          |                  |
| 1925 | 2,533  | 374     | 726               | 8         | 309      | 845              |
| 1929 | 1,941  | 667     | 2,089             | 1,005     | 1,022    | 1,738            |
| 1933 | 1,744  | 806     | 2,387             | 643       | 752      | 1,437            |
| 1938 | 1,628  | 846     | 2,413             | 539       | 866      | 1,711            |

The eight biggest Budapest banks controlled 130 others, either directly or at one or two removes. In this way the group of leading banks commanded 72 per cent of the capital resources of the entire system of joint-stock banks and savings institutions. The Credit Bank and the Bank of Commerce together disposed of over one-third of the capital of the entire credit system.

The ever closer involvement of banks with industrial monopolies was connected with this same phenomenon. The formation of finance capital, first perceptible at the beginning of the century, proceeded with giant steps after World War I. The Bank of Commerce was joined, partly through family ties, in a single interest group with the Rimamurány Iron Works, the Salgótarján Coal Mining Co, and the Manfréd Weiss Works; together they controlled, in 1938, 83 other important industrial enterprises. The Credit Bank and its leading business partner, the Hungarian General Coal Mining Co, included 101 enterprises in their interest group. The two most influential banks, with their interest groups representing nearly two hundred enterprises with assets of 450 million pengő, controlled 50 per cent of Hungarian industry. The other major Budapest banks— except for the Italian-Hungarian Bank, which had virtually no industrial interests—included another 65 important enterprises in their sphere of interest; thus the few great banks controlled not only 72 per cent of all financial institutions but also 60 per cent of Hungarian industry. (In 1913 47 per cent of industry was controlled by the big banks' sphere of interest.)

### GROWTH OF THE ECONOMY: STRUCTURAL CHANGES AND LEVEL OF DEVELOPMENT

The modest performance of the economy, compared with the prewar experience, produced an interwar rate of economic growth which was, all in all, extremely low. The moderate progress of factory industry could not outweigh the poor showing of agriculture, transport and communication, commerce, and small manufacturing. In 1938, national income was only 15–18 per cent above the 1913 level (calculated for the identical post-1920 territory).

Between the two wars, Hungary sank into the ranks of Europe's most slowly developing countries. The average annual rate of growth of national income hovered around 1·5 per cent, but because of the increase in population from 7·9 million to 9·3 million the average yearly rise in national income per capita was a mere 0·8 per cent. The slowdown was conspicuous in contrast with the dynamism of the Hungarian economy in the preceding decades, when it grew at an average rate of about 3 per cent a year.

The change was significant not only by contrast with the previous period of development. The interwar decades brought a halt or slowdown in growth all over the world. But even so, Hungary in this era of general stagnation still belonged, internationally, to that group of countries which showed the feeblest development. Thus while before World War I the growth rate of the Hungarian economy was considered outstanding, after the war its rate of growth lagged behind that of far more highly developed countries. The economic backwardness of the country therefore increased.

Per capita national income, the most comprehensive index of a country's level of economic development, amounted to $120 (£24) in 1937–8 in Hungary (reckoned in 1937 dollars). This was scarcely more than half the $200 (£50) average per capita national income of 24 European countries, and reached only one-quarter to one-third the level of the most advanced countries of Western Europe.

Such changes as there were, were only feebly mirrored in changes in the occupational distribution of the population. While between 1920 and 1940 the non-agricultural population of Europe grew on the average by one-third, in Hungary this increase was more than 50 per cent. In spite of this, the demographic structure of the early twentieth century changed only slightly: according to the 1910 census 57 per cent of the population (within the post-Trianon frontiers) was engaged in agriculture, in 1920 56 per cent, and in 1930, 52 per cent. Even in 1941, during the wartime boom the ratio had fallen to only 49 percent.

Thus the preponderance of the agricultural population remained. Hungary was unable to approach the Western European level of development, where only one-fifth to one-third of all wage-earners still worked in agriculture. Among the European countries only the Balkan states displayed a higher proportion of the population engaged in agriculture (80 per cent) than did Hungary.

The industrial population rose from 21 per cent of wage-earners in 1920 to 23 per cent in 1930, and to more than 25 per cent in 1941; taking into account those employed in transport and distribution, the increase was from 30 to 35 per cent. In the Western European countries the latter figure ranged from 50 to 70 per cent, in the Balkans from 10 to 15 per cent. In the distribution of its working population Hungary reflected the pattern of the other agrarian-industrial countries of Europe—Spain, Portugal and Poland.

The changes in the origin of national income point more clearly to major structural modifications than does the slow transformation in the occupational distribution of the population. During the interwar years the contribution of industry to national income in most European countries exceeded 50 per cent (Austria, Denmark, Norway), or even reached 60–70 per cent (England, Sweden, Germany, Belgium); in the Balkan countries, on the other hand, the share of industry in national income on the eve of World War II reached 20–25 per cent, the level attained in Hungary early in the century.

TABLE 33
*Occupational structure*

|  | 1920 | % | 1930 | % | 1941 | % |
|---|---|---|---|---|---|---|
| Agriculture | 4,449,104 | 55·7 | 4,499,393 | 51·8 | 4,539,000 | 48·7 |
| Industry—Trade | 2,402,799 | 30·1 | 2,806,232 | 32·3 | 3,258,000 | 34·9 |
| Mining and industry | 1,639,653 | 20·6 | 1,998,298 | 23·0 | 2,366,000 | 25·4 |
| Trade, credit | 407,020 | 5·1 | 469,059 | 5·4 | 517,000 | 5·5 |
| Communications | 356,126 | 4·4 | 338,875 | 3·9 | 375,000 | 4·0 |
| Other | 1,128,240 | 14·2 | 1,382,694 | 15·9 | 1,523,000 | 16·4 |
| Total | 7,980,143 | 100·0 | 8,688,319 | 100·0 | 9,320,000 | 100·0 |

In Hungary the most important of the economic changes which took place between the wars was undoubtedly the advance of industrialisation. However slowly and contradictorily, the country was casting off the agrarian character which it still possessed at the turn of the century. Even if agricultural decline played an important part in it, even if a significant lag behind the European standard still persisted, this change was positive: during these two decades the contribution of agriculture to national income fell from 42 to 37 per cent, while the contribution of industry rose from 30 to 36 per cent.

## 5 Changes in the composition and situation of the working class

In contrast with the period before 1914, when economic development was accompanied by broad social changes, the tempo of social change slowed down between the wars; to some degree the social structure rigidified. Those processes which, early in the century, marked the course of social development, persisted into this period, but at a slower pace, and for that reason they did not bring about qualitative changes in the country's social structure. Urbanisation of course continued, but because of the sluggishness of economic development the cities became less and less capable of absorbing the surplus labour of the countryside. In some parts of the country urbanisation completely stopped. The total stagnation of a good many of the provincial cities provides a sharp contrast with the relatively large capacity of Budapest and its environs to absorb newcomers. The flow from the agricultural to the industrial sector did not, of course, stop completely, but since industry's labour needs scarcely grew, its pace was very slow, so that during these two decades the occupational structure of the country changed by only a couple of percentage points. Nearly 50 per cent of the population still worked in agriculture, and the peasantry still formed the most numerous and most important class in the country. The land reform of the early 1920s did lessen somewhat the number of completely landless peasants (the immediate reserve of the industrial proletariat), but in fact these insignificant parcels, mostly of a mere 2 to 3 acres, could not support a family, and so the 300,000 independent agricultural proprietors and especially their dependants were increasingly thrown back on the labour market. Thus the decline in the numbers of the completely landless agrarian proletariat which can be observed between 1920 and 1930 (983,000 wage-earners in 1920; 780,000 in 1930) did not really mean that the oversupply of manpower on the labour market had ceased to exist. On the contrary, because of the decreased demand for labour the oversupply became even more acute.

Of the two strata of the agrarian proletariat, the farm servants of the great estates saw their situation change the least. Though they were often dependent on their lords in almost feudal fashion, they at least had steady work during the years of extreme hardship following the war and could count on regular pay, partly in kind and partly in money. Their number during the whole period varied from 200,000 to 250,000 (taking only wage-earners into account). It was hard for these men to become industrial workers, however, and their mobility was slight. There was a substantial drop, however, in the number of casual farm labourers, from 754,000 in 1920 to 362,000 in 1930. But this decline was not a consequence of the city's power of attraction or the absorptive capacity of industry; it was a result of the land reform, which gave 2- or 3-acre parcels to nearly 200,000 peasants. Though this scarcely provided a good living, it did at least assure a certain subsistence minimum, which in the agricultural labourer's case had largely been lacking before. The demand of the great estates for labour did not increase, for the structure of production remained the same; at most the large estates could go on employing a part of the farm labourers only at seasonal work like harvesting. Their other opportunities for making a living, meanwhile, had almost completely vanished. Railway construction had virtually ceased, and there was little road building either. Thus fewer and fewer of them were able to find work as navvies, and the safety valve of emigration to America had been shut off too. The abundance of manpower made itself felt on the labour market. Agricultural labourers were employed for a maximum of 150–180 days per year; thus at most 50 per cent of their labour was utilised.

The nearly 800,000 landless wage-earners had about the

same number of dependants, and to these we must add those smallholders whose way of life hardly differed, and who numbered 1·5 million (counting owners of 7 acres or less, with dependants). This enormous, pauperised mass—more than 3 million people—determined the social physiognomy of interwar Hungary. Horthy's Hungary was rightly called a country of 3 million beggars.

The other large group of wage-earners consisted of the urban proletariat. Within this category two large strata can be distinguished: the industrial proletariat narrowly defined, employed in workshops, factories and mines, and those in transport and commerce, the great majority of them likewise concentrated in cities. Finally, we may count among the urban proletariat the lower grades of the public services, and that special stratum of the working class, the rather numerous category of domestic servants.

In 1920 the urban proletariat—the designation, if not quite precise, is still useful for the purpose of distinguishing them from the agrarian proletariat—numbered altogether about 900,000, or 23·7 per cent of the entire wage-earning population of Hungary. Within that figure the proportion of the industrial working class narrowly defined was 52·3 per cent (464,445), reflecting the decline of industry at the end of the war. A decade later, in 1930, the numbers of the proletariat had risen to 1,160,000. By reason of the increase of 260,000 the urban working class rose to be 29 per cent of the wage-earning population of the country. Most of this increase was due to a rise in the number of workers employed in industry. As a result of a growth in numbers exceeding the average for the proletariat as a whole, the industrial working class came to form a higher proportion of the total urban proletariat, 56·9 per cent (660,775).

Among the new features determining the development of the industrial working class mention must be made above all of the appearance of mass unemployment. This was almost a natural concomitant of the economic collapse that followed the war, but in fact it persisted as a characteristic feature throughout the interwar period; large-scale unemployment did not cease even

TABLE 34

*Average yearly labour force*

| Year | Industry | Mining | Total | index |
|------|----------|--------|-------|-------|
| 1913 | 213,283 | 33,290 | 246,573 | 100·0 |
| 1921 | 152,591 | 42,126 | 194,717 | 79·0 |
| 1926 | 193,648 | 33,255 | 226,903 | 92·0 |
| 1929 | 235,000 | 34,974 | 269,972 | 109·5 |
| 1933 | 176,237 | 32,110 | 208,347 | 86·0 |
| 1936 | 246,269 | 36,132 | 282,401 | 114·0 |
| 1938 | 288,812 | 41,536 | 330,008 | 134·0 |

during the years of greatest prosperity. During the depression, the 200,000 jobless were one-third of the industrial working class, and their number fell only slowly in the later 1930s, never dropping below the 50,000–70,000 figure of the late 1920s.

The figures for the distribution of the heavy-industrial work force show other important changes as well. Before the war one-third of all industrial workers were employed in the engineering or iron and steel works, but by 1929 they had dwindled to only one-quarter of the industrial work force. At the same time, the number of workers in light industry rose from 16 per cent in 1913 to over 27 per cent at the end of the 1920s. This change throws light on important shifts in the structure of the working class. Whereas the heavy-industrial branches employed skilled male workers for the most part, the rapidly advancing light industries used primarily unskilled or semi-skilled women. Thus during the postwar decade the proportion of female and unskilled labour in the ranks of the Hungarian working class grew significantly.

In 1913 the factories operating within the post-Trianon frontiers employed (according to our estimates) about 50,000 women, or more than 23 per cent of the labour force. Their numbers and their share in the work force were to rise rapidly, from not quite one-quarter to nearly one-third. Though this change was primarily a result of the advance of the textile industry and of light industry generally, it is still worth noting that the proportion of women workers rose in every branch of industry but two.

In prewar Hungary about one-half of all workers were

skilled craftsmen. By and large this remained true of the immediate postwar years as well. In 1921 45·5 per cent of factory workers were skilled, 54·5 per cent unskilled and semi-skilled. Nothing better characterises the great structural changes which took place during the 1920s than the fact that by 1929 the proportion of skilled workmen had fallen to 37·3 per cent, while that of unskilled and semi-skilled climbed to 62·7 per cent.

The rapid and large-scale spread of unskilled and semi-skilled labour at the expense of the skilled craftsman was inseparable from the redistribution of the work force among the various branches of industry, and from the growing role of female labour. The latter is clearly indicated by the fact that while even in 1929 over two-fifths of all male workers still possessed skills, only one-fifth of women workers were skilled. The spreading use of unskilled labour, extending to virtually every industry except clothing and electric power, cannot however be explained solely by the factors previously mentioned. Thus further factors must be sought to explain this development. First among them was the general tendency to replace skilled with semi-skilled labour by employing the latest machinery. Even though the modernisation of industrial technique proceeded very slowly in Hungary during this period, this factor cannot be overlooked.

As a result, the number of skilled workmen in manufacturing had fallen even further by 1938, from 37·3 per cent to 30·3 per cent. Particularly striking was the decline in skilled employment in metallurgy (from 41·8 per cent to 32·8 per cent), in textiles (from 35·2 per cent to 10·6 per cent), and in the lumber and leather industries. There is no doubt, however, that a skilled-unskilled ratio of one to two is misleading—partly because during the 1930s there were among those filling unskilled jobs a great many skilled craftsmen unable to find other work, and partly because the significance of semi-skilled labour in the production process generally grew, until over 50 per cent of those who were not skilled craftsmen were semi-skilled workers.

Finally, we must point to two other important features in the composition of the Hungarian working class. For one thing, because of the general economic backwardness of the country workers in small-scale industry still accounted for about 40 per cent of the entire working class. For another, a disproportionately large part of the working class was concentrated in Budapest and its immediate vicinity. By 1938 61 per cent of factory workers were employed in Greater Budapest, and nearly half of those in small-scale industry worked there as well.

Apart from the areas around Salgótarján and Ózd, whose importance was assured by the mining and smelting activities carried on there, there were only two other large concentrations of workers in the country, at Győr and in the mining region around Pécs. One cannot speak of true industrial areas anywhere else in the country; the 210,000 workers in the provinces were mostly scattered among the $7\frac{1}{2}$ million provincial country- and city-dwellers, and even in the largest of those cities their number scarcely exceeded 10,000 (of whom fewer than 5,000 were industrial workers).

The rigidity of the social structure, the effects of depression, and not least the highly unfavourable political conditions of the day, all put fundamental obstacles in the way of an improvement in living standards. After the defeat of the Hungarian Soviet Republic the social and wage legislation of the two revolutions was immediately abolished, and on top of political persecution a veritable economic war was launched against the masses of workers. The wage level, which had been raised by measures put into effect during the proletarian revolution, was reduced again, on average by 50 per cent. On 13 August 1919, all measures taken by the Soviet Republic in the field of social policy were declared null and void, thus doing away with unemployment insurance, insurance against industrial injuries, and paid holidays. The law introducing the eight-hour day was also repealed.

Thus at the beginning of the 1920s Hungary sank back into the ranks of those few European countries where social legislation scarcely existed, and where even the length of the working day was not regulated by law. These events, followed by the hyper-inflation of the postwar years and later by the long drawn-out effects of the depression, made the material circumstances of the masses exceptionally difficult. Real wages in the interwar period never regained the level of the early years of the century, which was low enough in itself. If we take the prewar level of real wages as 100, then even at the peak of the boom in 1929 the index of real wages stood at only 85–6, and even in the better times of the 1930s, following recovery from the depression, it still lagged 5–10 per cent behind the figure reached at the interwar peak in 1929.

The decline in real wages was all the more serious in that part of the labour force was without steady work. Taking this fact into consideration, the average real wage per worker at the 1927–9 peak was 20 per cent below the prewar level, while between 1934 and 1937 it showed a further drop of 15 per cent.

It was the fall in real income which basically determined the situation of the workers, but the absence of any modern social legislation was also conspicuous. The average working day fell from 9 hours in 1929 to 8·6 hours in 1933, but in 1934 was back to 8·84 hours again. Then in 1935 the 8-hour day was legally introduced (Decree No 6,660, later incorporated in Law XXI of 1937). Its practical application came only gradually, however; in 1938 the average working day was still 8·4 hours. At that time 1·4 per cent of all workers still put in more than 12 hours a day, 10 per cent worked more than 10 hours, and another 10 per cent over 9 hours.

The introduction of the 8-hour day in the mid-1930s does not deserve attention merely for its contribution to limiting working hours, but as a symbol of the regime's new attitude in the field of social policy at this time. The depression of 1929–33, more serious than any before, sharpened class contradictions and made the workers' struggle a serious danger again, by creating severe unemployment and reducing real wages; political factors contributed too, especially the growing threat of war and the mounting fascist onslaught on the working class. The government consciously sought, by making certain concessions, to disarm the workers' movement, passing several more important measures following the introduction of the 8-hour day. Together with legislation on hours of work it introduced minimum wages; this was indeed the second most important facet of social legislation. Such a step had become urgent in the wake of the depression, when high unemployment swelled the supply of labour, offering industrialists a splendid opportunity to drive wages down. In these circumstances the working class demanded a lower limit to wages to stem their uncontrolled fall, and a wage rise for the most poorly paid workers. The government, moved by considerations similar to those which had induced it to regulate hours, set minimum wages for the various trades. This naturally benefited many poorly paid workers and brought with it a certain rise in wages.

Law XXI of 1937, which made the minimum wage and the 8-hour day into law, contained another important social measure: it introduced paid holidays into Hungary. According to its terms any worker who had been employed continuously for one year at the same enterprise could receive six days paid holiday, and in succeeding years the amount of holiday time progressively increased. This provision, though in principle a noteworthy social measure, was meaningless in practice, for as the Trades Union Council's figures for 1935 showed, there were then only 60,000 workers who had worked uninterruptedly in the same plant for a year or more. Thus the number of workers affected by this article of the law was quite small.

The social legislation of the later 1930s was rounded off by Law XXVI of 1938, the so-called family wage law, which prescribed a wage supplement of 5 per cent per month for every child in a worker's family. This measure improved the position of large families. Here we must observe, however, that the average wage level was low, and that the family allowance was the same for each child.

The social legislation of the late 1930s was moderate indeed and often contradictory; but, combined with an upswing in the business cycle and the beginning of rearmament, it undoubtedly brought some improvement in the workers' situation, especially to the most poorly paid strata of the working class. Among the latter we can count the bulk of the textile workers, who as a result of these measures often worked one to two hours less every day and received 10–15 per cent more in wages, while for families with children the improvement was even greater. For workers whose situation was at or above the average, of course, they meant considerably less.

The most important points of this legislation were in operation for only a short time. When war broke out in the autumn of 1939 the government quickly suspended the laws relating to the 8-hour day and paid holidays, even though Hungary remained at peace at that time. The social legislation of the last years of peace did not bring about any basic changes in the living conditions of the working class or of the masses of the population.

Even at the end of the twenties the consumption of most articles in common use remained far below the prewar level. Sugar consumption stood at around ten kilogrammes per capita annually, while in the Western countries it was 25 to 35 kilos. During the 1930s sugar consumption fell again, and even in 1938 it was nearly 10 per cent lower than in 1929. Thus sugar consumption stagnated at the 1914 level, contrary to trends elsewhere.

In the mid-1920s consumption of pork and beef was 50 per cent and 63 per cent, respectively, of the prewar figure, but even at the peak of prosperity it remained 15–20 per cent lower than before World War I. Milk consumption in 1929 was likewise 10 per cent lower than in 1913. Consumption of every one of these articles fell during the 1930s; beer consumption fell by one-half.

The continuing backwardness of housing conditions is indicated by the fact that only about 40 per cent of the workers were tenants in their own right in their dwellings, rather than sub-tenants. Yet 80 per cent of these dwellings were of one room only, with kitchen. Almost three-quarters of these one-room flats were occupied by two to four people, depending on the neighbourhood. Because of the high rents most working-class tenants were obliged to take in lodgers. Nearly 70 per cent of the occupants of one-room flats had lodgers; 17 per cent of them more than two. There is no need to expatiate here on the shanties and cave-dwellings which in Hungary then were far from being merely extreme cases affecting only a few people. A convincing enough picture is given by the data on average housing conditions in working-class Budapest (the best in the country): in 60 per cent of these workers' dwellings there was no plumbing, in 78·5 per cent there was no toilet, and in 50 per cent there was no electricity.

Of twenty-three large European cities, Budapest had the second highest mortality rate and the highest incidence of tuberculosis. In Hungary 179 out of every 1,000 infants died before their first birthday.

The educational level of the workers rose somewhat. By 1929 98 per cent of all Budapest workers could read and write, compared with 92 per cent in 1910. Indeed, by 1929 about 10 per cent of the workers of Budapest had completed four years of middle school. As these data indicate, the problem of providing an adequate elementary schooling had been solved, at least in the capital. They do not demonstrate any more than this, however. Of the pupils in the secondary schools, 1·15 per cent were children of workers or peasants. Of the Budapest workers—and they were the most advanced and politically conscious part of the working class—only one-third read a newspaper regularly, and another 15 per cent frequently. Only one in ten visited a library regularly. A low standard of living, poor nutrition, miserable living conditions, and cultural backwardness characterised the Hungarian working class at a time when, in the developed countries, the progress of technology and the other productive forces was transforming consumption, cultural expectations and living standards in general.

In the West new foods came into common use, while cultural needs grew with the introduction of motion pictures and radio. New forms of recreation—the beach, outings, sports, and the use of new services such as, among women, regular visits to hairdressers—made their appearance as elements of a new way of life. All these changes in styles of living, were scarcely apparent in Hungary. The Hungarian working class ate less and dressed more poorly than before. For the most part they were unable to assure themselves of even the prewar standard of living.

The poor living conditions of the working class between the wars, were connected not only with bad times economically but also with the weakening of the organisation and combativeness of the working class. The defeat of the proletarian revolution in Hungary, and the bloody reprisals and relentless persecution which followed it, set their stamp on organising efforts and on the economic and political struggle during these years. The counter-revolution which came to power in 1919 wished to do more than destroy the political parties of the working class. The Communist Party was decimated and outlawed. The Social-Democratic Party was also exposed to severe persecution; the leaders of its left wing were obliged to go into exile. Severe measures were taken against the trade unions as well. It was made impossible for many unions to function; their premises were closed down and their members put in prison. During the years of White Terror at the beginning of the 1920s a brutal effort was made to do away with the trade union movement once and for all. This effort, however, soon failed. Despite all persecution the working-class base of the trade unions stood by their organisations. Despite the unpunished street murders of trade union members and officials, the membership of the unions in 1920 stood at 152,000; every third worker was a union member, and the percentage of workers who belonged to a trade union significantly exceeded the prewar figure. The largest number of them were concentrated in the metal workers' union, with 50,000 members; also important were the unions of miners, construction workers, printers, and workers in the lumber industry.

The stability in membership and the unbreakable strength of the trade unions lay in the fact that they had retained their prewar character of organisations consisting mainly of skilled workers. It was the factories' best workers, the best educated and most skilful, who preserved the trade unions. The movement drew strength from its links with the Social-Democratic Party, the legal party of the working class at this time, which won 300,000 votes at the 1922 election, and won 24 seats in Parliament. True, the leadership of the Social-Democratic Party was declaredly reformist and ready to seek compromises with the government; none the less, although its actions more than once inhibited the development of the labour movement, it still played a large role in the defence of workers' interests and in the cultivation and spread of democratic and socialist ideas, as the only consistently left-wing democratic party during the Horthy era.

It was thanks to the strength of the trade unions that an unusually stormy wave of strikes swept the country in the course of 1920 and 1921, despite the defeat of the revolution and the reprisals of the White Terror. In 1921 there were strikes for higher wages in 63 factories in Budapest and its vicinity, and similar movements broke out in the coal fields too. In the spring of 1922 12,000 iron and steel workers struck in Budapest, followed in August by a nationwide iron and steel strike. A general strike in the Salgótarján coal basin and the tenacious struggle of the miners of Pécs fed the movement throughout the year. In 1922 352 strikes were recorded, but this figure was far surpassed by the struggles of the following year: in 1923 there were 459 strikes in the iron and steel industry alone. The growing strike movement of the 1920s increased the membership and strength of the trade unions still further: in 1922 there were 200,000 trade union members.

The vigorous workers' struggles and firm trade-union solidarity of the early 1920s were the last ripple of the postwar waves of revolution, a kind of rearguard action following the political and military struggles of the revolution. From the middle of the decade, however, the dynamism of the labour movement slackened. The changes in the structure of industry and the effects of the developing boom of the 1920s weakened the most important strata of the organised workers; the influx of unorganised female and unskilled labour narrowed the objective possibilities of the movement. Strikes fell off; only scattered local struggles were to be found. Nationwide strikes, or strikes embracing all the workers in a craft, no longer occurred. In 1927 only 18,000 workers went on strike, in 1928 28,000. Only an occasional action of the desperate, poverty-stricken miners caused any great stir. In 1926 the miners of Salgótarján with their wives and children set out on a hunger march for Budapest, and two years later the renewal of their bitter struggle once again had nationwide repercussions.

The strikes of the later 1920s were offensive in character,

representing an effort on the part of the workers to win wage increases during those boom years. The onset of the depression, however, created a radically different situation. One-third of the labour force was now out of work, with even higher unemployment in some trades. Thus the possibility of securing wage increases was limited, and the character of the strike movement changed. The depression placed the problem of unemployment squarely in the centre of the working class struggle: at the end of 1932 27·6 per cent of all trade union members were out of work. The high point of these struggles was the great labour demonstration of 1 September 1930. Nearly 50,000 men went out into the streets to demonstrate for unemployment insurance, job opportunities, and decent living conditions; the crowd carried revolutionary political slogans as well. Other movements during the depression were directed against the introduction of methods of rationalising production in the engineering and textile industry, especially the so-called Bedeaux system.

These trade union struggles, however, could at most lessen the misery of the working class, while at the same time severe unemployment completely emptied the trade union treasuries. Income from union dues fell off drastically, and membership gradually declined as well. Organised labour became seriously disorganised. And the hard years of depression had scarcely passed when the government launched a new attack—this time political—against the trade unions, declaring that it intended to nationalise them by introducing a corporative system of interest groups on the model of Italian fascism.

The wage struggles of the working class were now combined with the watchword of defence of the trade unions—as, for example, in the great construction workers' strike of the autumn of 1935. By this time, however, the influence of the trade unions had undoubtedly declined. The number of strikes continued to increase, but at their peak in 1937 they still involved only 25,000 workers. A few outstanding disputes, like the 1934 and 1937 miners' strikes around Pécs and the first significant strikes in the textile industry, proved that a numerically reduced but loyal section of the Hungarian working class, belonging largely to the older generation, still stood by its trade union organisations. But the 80,000–100,000 men who even in this period risked all the political consequences of identification with the trade unions represented only a significant minority of a working class which had grown in numbers.

The new generation, which in the years before World War II found employment mainly in the less-well-organised light industries, rarely joined the trade unions. Mostly of peasant origin and freshly recruited into industry, they had gained from the schools and the press of the interwar period a decidedly nationalistic, religious, anti-labour outlook; among them it was rather nationalistic ideals, fascist demagogy, and the emerging national socialist parties which won increasing loyalty. For these mostly unskilled strata the cautious policy of the trade unions, rejecting all radicalism, and their ageing leadership, did not offer any promise for the future; incapable of weighing the true content and value of political watchwords and objectives, they turned more readily to organisations proclaiming radical and at the same time nationalistic slogans. This turning away from the trade unions was encouraged by the government's social legislation of the late 1930s, already discussed—the introduction of the 8-hour day, family supplements and paid holidays, which were passed explicitly to forestall the 'degeneration of the labour movement'. On the eve of World War II, then, labour had gone on to the defensive; its organisations had grown weaker and its influence was reduced.

## 6 The years of war economy

From 1938 a full-scale war economy emerged in Hungary, following covert preparations since the mid-1930s to put industry on a war footing. Hungarian foreign policy, motivated by the desire to revise the Treaty of Trianon, drew ever closer to Hitler's Germany; at the beginning of 1938 a programme of open rearmament was launched, in case of a joint attack on Czechoslovakia. Throwing off the limitations imposed by the peace treaty, the minister-president declared in a speech of 5 March 1938 that a five-year investment programme involving 1 billion pengő was being started. Sixty per cent of this sum was to go directly for re-equipping the army, the rest for strategic purposes such as improving roads and communications. In order to achieve preparedness sooner the rearmament programme was completed in two years; this intensive investment on the part of the state between summer 1938 and summer 1940 not only improved economic conditions considerably, but also led to the emergence of a full-scale war economy.

It was during these years that a means of financing these governmental investments through hidden inflation was worked out. On paper, the government raised the money for these projects by imposing a special once-for-all levy on property, with a forced loan subscription for larger property-owners. In reality, however, those assessed could turn for loans to the National Bank, which created the necessary sums through the issue of unbacked paper currency. In a single year, from 1938 to 1939, the amount of paper money in circulation doubled. To forestall the undesirable effects of this growing quantity of money, the government in August 1939 introduced state regulation of prices: a price freeze was put into effect, and any increase in prices required the permission of the government. New institutions began to be set up to discharge the state's new economic functions. Among others, a government price commission was brought into being.

These measures created employment in important sectors of industry, so that within a year the 100,000 unemployed were absorbed by the industries thus benefitted. The increased consumption expenditure produced by full employment contributed to an upswing of the consumer-goods industries. From 1938 a broad improvement of the whole economy was discernible.

During these years the prosperity of a wartime economy was as yet unaccompanied by the vicissitudes of war, or by the demands normally made on the population in wartime. After the outbreak of World War II Hungary did not remain neutral, but she did not enter the war either, declaring herself a 'non-belligerent', and up to the time of her co-operation in the German attack on Yugoslavia in the spring of 1941 she took no part in military action. The rebuilt Hungarian army was employed during these years only in colourful parades. To be sure, with German and Italian co-operation the territorial provisions of the treaty system of Versailles were subjected to revision. The so-called First Vienna Award of November 1938 returned to Hungary the southern part of Slovakia, inhabited predominantly by Hungarians. In March 1939, at the time of the German occupation of Czechoslovakia, Hungary recovered the region of Carpatho-Ukraine. These events were followed in August 1940 by the Second Vienna Award, when a German-Italian arbitration board divided Transylvania between Hungary and Rumania. Finally, Hungary's part in military operations against Yugoslavia resulted in her recovering the Bacska region.

These gains nearly doubled Hungary's territory and increased her population by 5,300,000, to more than 14 million. Her war economy was bolstered by a large new supply of labour, important food-growing regions, and fresh reserves of raw materials. The perfecting of the war economy and then, from the time Hungary joined in the German attack on the Soviet Union in the summer of 1941, an economic system functioning under real wartime conditions, determined henceforward the situation of the Hungarian economy.

Hungary's entry into the war opened a new era in the history of her economy. The conduct of modern warfare demands that armies be supplied with vast quantities of weapons and other war material. The state must place enormous orders with industry, especially with heavy industry which plays the most important part in supplying the army, and in particular with the largest enterprises, which from a technical standpoint are best equipped to fill large orders. In Hungary the biggest of these military procurement orders went to the Manfréd Weiss works, the Győr railway wagon factory, the Ganz plants, and the various state engineering works. Orders in the hundreds of millions for various types of tank, for other military vehicles, weapons, ammunition, and anti-aircraft equipment were placed with them. Smaller and middle-sized firms shared in these orders too as sub-contractors.

Military needs made government orders a very important factor in light industry as well. In 1942 nearly two-thirds of the production of the cotton industry went to the army; in 1944 only 10 per cent of cotton-goods production and 20–30 per cent of woollen-goods production was allocated to civilian needs. The situation was much the same in paper, leather, and other industries. Many enterprises stopped producing for civilian consumption.

Apart from government purchasing, state intervention also appeared in the efforts to solve the ever more serious problems of raw materials and energy supply. State direction appeared most unmistakably in the management of raw materials, for here it was easiest to estimate reserves and needs, domestic production and available imports, and to regulate the distribution of stocks on that basis. A system of state allocations replaced the free market sale of essential raw materials.

State intervention had a similar character in agriculture, too. Before World War II the state had been concerned primarily with organising the sale of produce so as to keep prices up.

Early in the war the government was involved mainly with the distribution of existing stocks of food, but it soon came to intervene more and more forcefully in stimulating production to meet wartime needs and in regulating the organisation of production. The system of agricultural deliveries proved incapable of meeting either growing wartime needs or the demands of the Germans. Thus in 1942 a new system of requisitions was put into effect, termed the Jurcsek system after the Minister of Supply; its purpose was to permit the state to secure a fixed amount of agricultural produce. Deliveries therefore were to be calculated against the net income of each acre of arable land.

At the time the Jurcsek system was put into effect a chain of depots was set up to handle the sale of agricultural products. But the government was unable through these measures to overcome its difficulties in supplying the population and satisfying the ever-greater demands of Nazi Germany. It proved impossible to meet the prescribed quotas of some commodities. The quantities of eggs and poultry collected were only 32 per cent and 27 per cent, respectively, of the amount which reached the market before the war.

Other measures of intervention on the part of the state were aimed directly at increasing agricultural production. Such was (among others) the decree compelling farmers to grow industrial crops.

Under war conditions government activity extended beyond direct intervention in production to measures designed to create a balance between supply and demand. Throughout the war supply lagged consistently behind demand; the government sought to right the balance with price controls and restrictions on civilian consumption. At the same time it attempted to hold the rate of inflation within determined limits. The state's regulation of prices did to some extent interfere with profits in the interest of wartime political and economic stability, but at the same time its controls undoubtedly contributed to wages constantly falling farther and farther behind price increases.

By the end of 1943 prices had already reached three times the prewar level. By contrast, repeated official regulation of wages had permitted workers' incomes to rise only 60 per cent. Even though nominal wages actually rose more than this because of the mounting demand for labour, government regulation still succeeded in reducing the purchasing power and the consumption of manufactured articles of those living on wages and salaries.

The government did not succeed in keeping supply and demand in balance, however, even though it made a direct attempt to limit consumption by introducing a system of rationing. Ration cards were issued during the war for every important item of food (bread, flour, fats, milk, butter, potatoes) and for clothing, and with a very low individual ration. Despite an appearance of equality, the rationing system restricted primarily the consumption of the masses of working people, for the ability to buy luxury articles and the emergence of a black market assured the propertied classes of a level of consumption substantially higher than the basic rations.

If military orders and the allocation of raw materials put an end to the free market for the industries turning out producers' goods, price regulation and controls on consumption brought about a decisive change in sectors of the market which had hitherto remained unregulated. Rationing came to take the place of any actual market mechanism. Thus during the war years market freedom ceased to exist for an ever-growing variety of goods, and its place was taken by production and distribution directed by the state.

Similar modifications took place in the money market as well. War production demanded large investments which private capital was unable to assure, even when pressed into service by the state. In many cases private enterprise was not even willing to risk the necessary expenditures. Thus war production came to be financed more and more through state credits and state investments.

To finance the necessary investments the government wished to mobilise capital for purposes of war production. To this end, the government, from the time war broke out against Russia, brought bank credit under its control, putting an end to the freedom of the money market. The banks were obliged to screen requests for loans closely, to determine what purposes borrowers intended to use their loans for; if the requests were not found to be justified, they had to be rejected. Later, these provisions were tightened up on several occasions as, for example, in 1943. If the banks refused to co-operate, the National Bank could refuse to accept their paper. In this manner private bank credit was, for all practical purposes, managed by the state in order to finance war production.

But the government did not stop at regulating the use of available private capital; it also financed the expansion of war production directly by extending large loans to the war industries. New wartime investments, large military orders, and other expenditures connected with the war effort could have been covered only by mobilising the material resources of the state. Government expenditures became so great during these years that they required the mobilisation of an ever greater part of the national income through the state budget. Accordingly the government's budgets rose sharply during the war years.

TABLE 35

*Budgetary expenditure during World War II*

| Years | Budgetary expenditure | National income | Expenditure as % of national income |
|---|---|---|---|
| | (in current prices, million pengő) | | |
| 1938–9 | 1,723 | 5,192 | 33·1 |
| 1939–40* | 4,033 | 9,311 | 43·3 |
| 1941 | 3,807 | 7,526 | 50·5 |
| 1942 | 5,740 | 9,329 | 61·5 |
| 1943 | 8,688 | 12,889 | 67·4 |
| 1944 | 15,993 | 22,298 | 71·7 |

* One and half years.

It was a further characteristic of Hungary's economic life during the war (as we have indicated several times before) that her resources were directly and increasingly pressed into the service of the German war machine. It was not a new ambition of German imperialism to gain control of the economies of South-eastern Europe in order to exploit them more fully. Even in the 1930s the creation of a *Grossraumwirtschaft* had been a leading principle of Nazi economic policy. From 1939, German demands became ever more insistent. Their aims were summarised at the time of the commercial negotiations of 1939: 'The Hungarian economy must become more firmly oriented than before to the needs of the German market.' Accordingly, the Germans demanded that the Hungarian government cease to promote industry and that the free import of German goods into Hungary should be permitted. It was finally decided that Hungarian industry should be reorganised in accordance with the export interests of Germany. The great victories of the first war years and the resulting preponderance of German power in Europe enabled the Germans to make their economic ideas even clearer: 'The countries of south-eastern Europe must accommodate themselves to their natural circumstances. Their industrialisation would be contrary to their agricultural character.' Thus the Nazi government wished to make Hungary a supplier of foodstuffs and raw materials, while allowing its industry to wither or bringing it under direct control.

During the first period of the war, then, German demands focused on increasing Hungary's exports of agricultural products and raw materials essential to the war effort. By 1941 this had reached a point where, in renewing the trade agreement, the Hungarian side promised to ship to Germany half of its wheat and rye surplus, 80 per cent of its maize surplus, and all its oil-seeds. This was supplemented by an undertaking to send the entire foodstuffs surplus of the Bacska region to Germany (with a small portion going to Italy). German economic policymakers for their part interpreted 'surplus' in such a way that the surpluses called for could be achieved only by sharply curtailing domestic supplies.

Apart from the export of grain, meat, fats and other agricultural products, the German government also presented broad and growing demands for deliveries of strategic raw materials, principally oil and bauxite. As early as the July 1941 negotiations the Hungarian delegation undertook to supply large quantities of raw materials. In 1941 and 1942 the Germans demanded nearly a million tons of bauxite, 90 per cent of production; in 1943–4 they demanded a forced increase in production to $1\frac{1}{2}$ million tons, and in 1944–5, 2 million tons. Demands for Hungarian petroleum were constantly raised in the same way.

On the eve of the war 50–60 per cent of oil production was going to Germany, and the quantity increased from year to year.

Hungarian heavy industry soon received orders in hundreds of millions of pengő from Germany. By 1942 a situation had arisen where some branches of war industry were producing more for the German military than for the Hungarian army. Early in 1944 the Germans decided to create a special commission (Deutsche Industrie Commission in Ungarn), ostensibly to supervise German orders, but actually to bring Hungarian industry under German control. A special role in the wartime exploitation of the Hungarian economy was reserved for the joint aircraft programme. Partly because of their own inadequate capacity and partly to escape the bombings, the Germans worked out a programme to build first 1 billion and later 3 billion pengő worth of aircraft, to be carried out by the Manfréd Weiss Works and the Győr railway wagon company. Assembly-line production of Messerschmidts and aircraft engines actually began at these plants and at the newly built Danube Aircraft Factory (Duna Repülőgépgyár) at Szigetszentmiklós, and was brought to an end only by bombing in the summer of 1944. German industrial interests also encouraged Hungarian domestic processing of bauxite. In the 1930s they had blocked this with every means at their disposal, but during the war work was begun on a bauxite-processing and aluminium plant, gigantic by prewar standards.

Incorporation into the German war economy increased the penetration of German capital into Hungarian industry. German capital affected most of all the newly created industries (aircraft, aluminium, and oil). During the war the role of German interests in Hungary's industry and economic life continued to grow.

Large-scale deliveries of agricultural products and industrial raw materials, military orders and contracts, and the growing influence of German capital not only entailed the incorporation of Hungary into the German war economy and the capture of the commanding heights of the Hungarian economy: they also became the means to the direct and open financial exploitation of the country. As time passed the German government did less and less to pay for Hungarian deliveries of goods and for the work contracted out to Hungarian factories. From the summer of 1942 German indebtedness grew so rapidly that international negotiations became necessary to deal with it. At that time the German government declared with its usual cynical frankness that in the future these debts would grow still more; ie, it was not willing to pay for Hungarian deliveries and wished to throw the burden of these on the Hungarian treasury. Litter, a high official of the German Finance Ministry, declared that the bulk of Hungarian deliveries 'actually . . . must be regarded as contributions to the common war effort, whose value will be kept account of. . . . The settlement of the sums recorded in this way is a question which will be raised and decided after the conclusion of the war.'

German debts continued to grow rapidly in 1942 and 1943. At the end of 1941 they amounted to 326 million pengő, but in 1942 they were 558 million, and in 1943, 969 million pengő. During the same period the Hungarian government's war expenditures were 40 per cent less than this. 'Thus we have advanced 60 per cent more in credits to the German treasury than to the Hungarian treasury,' stated the president of the National Bank. 'Here we have a heavy burden indeed!' In 1944 even this enormous sum more than doubled, to 3 billion pengő.

In examining the costs of the war it is not enough, then, merely to take the military expenditures in the government's budget; the enormous sums required to cover these German debts must also be included as one of the most important items of war expenditure in Hungary. Military expenses and German indebtedness together ate up 19·9 per cent of the national income in 1941, 27·9 per cent in 1942, 35·1 per cent in 1943, and 44·1 per cent in 1944.

The state's sources of income could not keep pace with the growth of war expenditure. The deficit rose from 100 million pengő in 1938 to 2 billion pengő in 1943. The government sought to meet the deficit by floating various loans; but it did not back these loans by laying its hands on the capital accumulating in the banks, nor did it limit the profits of those growing wealthy on wartime deliveries; instead it covered the loans by issuing paper money, which only fed inflation. In 1941 the face value of banknotes in circulation was twice that of 1938; in 1943, it was five times the 1938 figure, and in 1944 fourteen times as much.

Inflation and the depreciation of the pengő reduced the purchasing power of wages and salaries, thus contributing to the further impoverishment of the masses of the people who lived by their labour. Hungary followed an inflationary policy not merely to meet its growing expenditures, but to a great extent in order to cover unpaid deliveries to Germany. German debts during the war totalled 4,765 million pengő; at the same time the increase in the amount of currency in circulation between 1938 and 1944 was 11,357 million pengő, so that 42 per cent of the increased issue was traceable to Germany's debts.

Thus the financing of the war economy and war production was relieved through inflation, hidden and gradual at first, but in the last period of the war open and rapid.

Industrial production grew rapidly during the war. Within five years the number of industrial workers increased by about 120,000 (reckoned within the frontiers of 1938 only), more than during the two interwar decades. There was a significant expansion of plant; the horsepower capacity of Hungarian industry grew by about 25 per cent. Production, forced upward by every

TABLE 36

*Value of industrial output in 1938 territory*

| Year | Current prices (thousand pengő) | (1938 = 100) | Unchanged (1938) prices (thousand pengő) | (1938 = 100) |
|------|---------------------------------|--------------|------------------------------------------|--------------|
| 1938 | 3,044,470 | 100·0 | 3,044,470 | 100·0 |
| 1939 | 3,622,275 | 119·0 | 3,677,391 | 120·7 |
| 1940 | 4,316,620 | 141·8 | 4,045,567 | 132·8 |
| 1941 | 4,915,499 | 161·5 | 3,901,190 | 128·1 |
| 1942 | 6,022,848 | 197·8 | 4,119,154 | 135·2 |
| 1943 | 8,642,578 | 283·8 | 4,187,295 | 137·5 |

possible means during the war years, rose substantially. The value of production—disregarding a temporary decline from mid-1940 to summer 1941 which the figures for 1941 reflect—rose steadily, displaying a growth of 37 per cent for the six-year period, which substantially exceeded the pace of develodment during the two prewar decades.

Though the regions annexed to Hungary were relatively underdeveloped industrially, they naturally contributed in some degree, too, to the increased output of Hungarian war industry. Industrial production was 63 per cent higher within the 1943 frontiers of the country than in 1938 (at constant prices). The annexed territories furnished altogether 15 per cent of the country's industrial production. The importance of some regions was much greater, however, particularly from the standpoint of supplying the country with raw materials. Iron ore from the north and key metals from Transylvania, essential to war production, contributed in great measure to the build-up of the Hungarian war economy. Important too were the lumber and foodstuffs of the new territories (46 per cent of the entire country's lumber industry, 23 per cent of its food industry). Their iron and steel industry and other metallurgy, on the other hand, were insignificant (15·64 per cent), and engineering was almost totally absent (1·09 per cent).

The rise in industrial production was only rapid, however, up to 1941—that is, only so long as the wartime boom extended to every branch of industry. From 1941 industrial development acquired a completely one-sided military character. Enterprises producing war material (a large part of heavy industry) continued to increase their output rapidly, but consumer-goods production declined. As a result, total industrial production between 1940 and 1943 (the wartime peak) rose by only a few percentage points.

The disturbing effect of the war on industry appears from the fact that of 120,000 new workers, over 80,000 found employment in iron and steel or in engineering, while at the same time the number of textile and leather workers actually decreased. Coal production rose from 9·3 million tons to 12·7 million tons; pig iron production from 335,000 to 943,000 tons; steel production from 647,000 to 784,000 tons. While engineering, the principal branch of war production, more than doubled its output, the textile mills turned out 25 per cent less and the leather industry 30 per cent less than before the war, and a comparable decline took place in the food industry.

The effects of the war economy were felt, of course, not only in large-scale industry; they brought about changes in the structure of the entire economy, for small producers as well as large.

Nevertheless, the growth of small industry remained slower than that of large. In 1930 small industry's share in the country's total industrial production (mining and metallurgy included) was 28·4 per cent, while in 1940 it was only 25·2 per cent. In agriculture, the changes in the crops grown during the war were most striking. More land was turned over to industrial crops: by 1944 their area had grown to 3·2 times that of the years 1931–8. The area planted to legumes increased nearly as much, trebling by 1943. However, the area under root crops (and until 1942 the area under grain) decreased. As a result of these changes, the structure of cultivation was altered substantially. Industrial crops occupied 1·2 per cent of the arable during the years 1931–8, 3·9 per cent in 1944. The share of legumes rose from 0·76 per cent to 2·3 per cent in 1943. On the other hand, grain acreage fell from 52·6 to 50·3 per cent, that of root crops from nearly 30 per cent to not quite 28 per cent.

A much smaller change was observable in total yields. Measures to increase agricultural production were successful only in the case of legumes and industrial crops. Here, owing to a great expansion of the area sown, the harvest grew by 300–400 per cent; in the case of some crops, like sunflowers, the increase was 900 per cent. On the other hand, output of some crops fell during the war. Shortages of fertiliser, chemicals, machinery, labour, and simple farm tools contributed to this result. Taking the 1929–38 level of production as 100, output of bread grains in 1940 was 83·1, in 1941 84·1, and in 1942 76·2; only the good harvest of 1943 raised it to an index of 101·4. Using the 1935–9 production figures as an index of 100, the output of hay in 1942 was 83·2, and in 1943 78·5. The figures for stockbreeding were no better. Beef cattle herds grew up to 1942, but in 1943 they were 10·6 per cent lower than the previous year, and in 1944 were 11·7 per cent below the 1942 figure. The stock of pigs dropped 32·4 per cent between 1939 and 1943. Thus during the war, as a result of various government measures, agriculture became to some degree more intensive. The structure of production became better balanced. But there was no growth in the output of the most important crops, and thus the overall value of agricultural production did not increase.

As a result of the development of large and small industry and their rapidly growing production, a marked shift took place during the war years in the relationship of the two great branches of the economy, industry and agriculture. In 1929–30 industry's share in national income was 31·1 per cent; by 1938–9 it had gradually risen to 37·5 per cent. After 1938 industry's share rose even faster.

These statistics exaggerate the growth of industry's role, for they do not take into account price changes for agricultural and industrial goods. An undoubted shift in favour of industry is demonstrated, however, by data on the distribution of the population. Here we have only the census figures, which do not allow a year-by-year study of the whole period in question, nor even take in the whole period; but even so they reveal a great deal. In 1930 51·8 per cent of Hungary's population earned their livelihood in primary production, against 23 per cent in mining and industry. In 1941, however—and most of the change took place after 1938—the proportion of primary producers was down to 48·7 per cent, while the mining and industrial population had grown to 25·4 per cent. Taking into account those engaged in trade and transport, the so-called industrial-commercial population rose from 32·3 per cent to 34·9 per cent.

The wartime increase in production lasted only to the end of 1943. In the autumn of that year signs of disorganisation began to appear in industry. Plant and equipment began to wear out for lack of proper maintenance and replacement, while in the mines even the most ruthless exploitation could not expand output.

The occupation of the country by the Germans on 19 March 1944 only increased the pace of economic deterioration. The political and economic effects of the occupation—the transfer to Hungary of the costs of occupation, increased demands for soldiers, the mass deportation of the Jewish population, maximum exploitation of the country's resources and the beginning of resistance and sabotage in production—hastened the disorganisation of the economy. The Anglo-American bombing attacks which followed the German occupation, growing more intensive from the summer of 1944, caused widespread damage. It was the conversion of the country into a theatre of war, however, which brought about the greatest destruction. For six months beginning in October 1944 the front line moved across Hungary, accompanied by heavy fighting. Budapest, the country's industrial centre, was liberated only after a long siege and heavy street fighting. Many cities and districts changed hands several times. The withdrawing German troops, with their Hungarian fascist hangers-on, offered a determined resistance, spreading destruction behind them in an effort to defend in Hungary the frontiers of the Third Reich. In November the Hungarian Arrow-Cross government issued a decree calling for the dismantling or destruction of objects of strategic importance in the event of a withdrawal. Its execution was entrusted to the quartermaster general of the German Army Group South and to individual commanders. Teams of sappers blew up factory power plants, equipment for keeping mines free of water, and a good part of the bridges and railway lines. The most valuable part of Hungary's stock of machinery was loaded on to freight cars and taken to Germany. The same thing happened with the greater part of her vehicles and livestock too. Bitter front-line fighting also caused severe damage.

In the autumn of 1944 only armies moved across wide areas of the country which should normally have been ploughed and sown. In Transdanubia, for example, only one-third of the usual wheat acreage was planted, and the situation was not much better between the Danube and the Tisza. Farm work was neglected, and there was a great loss of livestock and equipment. 1,200,000 cattle—amounting to 44 per cent of Hungary's stock, using the figures of 1938 as a base—were driven off to Austria or Germany or perished, as happened with 56 per cent of her horses (500,000), 79 per cent of her pigs (2,200,000), and 80 per cent of her sheep (1,400,000). The damage caused to agriculture by the war-losses in livestock, the destruction of farm machinery, buildings and equipment reached 3·7 billion pengő. According to calculations of the Hungarian Institute for Economic Research (Magyar Gazdaságkutató Intézet), about one-fifth of the national wealth invested in agriculture was destroyed.

Communications were severely damaged. The withdrawing fascist forces blew up the bridges over the Danube and the Tisza, and many of the smaller ones as well: 36 per cent of the carrying capacity of the country's bridges was destroyed. In many places the roads were impassable. The situation on the railways was catastrophic. Nearly 40 per cent of the roadbed had been destroyed, with over 100 large railway bridges and nearly 900 smaller ones. Of 3,000 locomotives 1,260 were taken away to Germany, and over 60 per cent of those that remained were destroyed or damaged. Of the railways' 70,000 wagons, 47,000 had been taken away, plus nearly 5,000 passenger carriages. Of those that remained about half were destroyed or damaged. Navigation on the Danube and the Tisza was made almost impossible by the sinking of 108 vessels and the removal of the rest of the Danube fleet to the west. War damage to transport came to 3·7 billion pengő at 1938 values, which meant the loss of more than half the country's transport equipment.

This unparalleled destruction to agriculture and transport in itself had a crippling effect on industry. But of course industry was not spared the destructive effects of long, hard fighting and the depredations of the fascist detachments. Factories, amounting to 3,602 (90 per cent of all enterprises), suffered greater or lesser damage; over 2,000 plants, half of the total number, incurred serious damage reducing their capacity by an average of 45·7 per cent. Fifty per cent of plant and machinery, one-third of the generating equipment, and 75 per cent of other machinery was either destroyed or carried away to Germany.

Altogether Hungarian industry suffered 2,042 million pengő of losses from wartime damage: 800 million pengő in stocks of finished goods destroyed or taken away to Germany; 402 million in stores of raw materials lost; 343 million in losses of machinery (exclusive of power equipment); 226 million in damage to buildings; 216 million from destruction of various technical installations; and 55 million from losses in generating equipment. In addition, damage in mining and smelting ran to more than 65 million pengő. The heaviest losses were suffered in engineering, metallurgy, and chemicals. The situation in the textile industry is illustrated by the fact that 49 per cent of all spindles and 37 per cent of all looms went out of production as a consequence of the war. Table 37 summarises wartime destruction and reduction of capacity in several industries.

TABLE 37

*War losses in manufacturing industry*

| Industry | War losses in million pengő (1938 value) | Damaged plant as percentage of total | Loss of capacity (%) |
|---|---|---|---|
| Iron and metals | 236 | 48·1 | 26·3 |
| Engineering | 734 | 44·1 | 36·2 |
| Electric power | 88 | 42·4 | 24·8 |
| Building materials | 43 | 48·1 | 29·4 |
| Wood | 71 | 51·0 | 28·2 |
| Leather | 53 | 46·9 | 16·6 |
| Textiles | 301 | 41·3 | 22·1 |
| Clothing | 49 | 55·7 | 28·6 |
| Paper | 33 | 40·6 | 18·9 |
| Food | 209 | 42·6 | 16·0 |
| Chemicals | 192 | 48·0 | 26·1 |
| Printing | 33 | 35·7 | 17·9 |
| Total | 2,042 | 45·7 | 23·9 |

Damage to housing was also severe. According to a survey conducted in Budapest in March 1945, 3·8 per cent of all dwelling houses had been totally destroyed, and another 23·1 per cent had suffered serious damage. Of the nearly 40,000 residential buildings in Budapest only 26 per cent remained undamaged: 13,588 dwellings had been completely destroyed, 18,775 had been made uninhabitable, and nearly 42,000 had been made partly uninhabitable (through damage to one or more rooms).

World War II destroyed almost 40 per cent of the country's national wealth, making Hungary one of the countries which suffered the heaviest damage from the war.

# 3

# Socialist Transformation and Industrialisation of the Economy Since 1944

## 1 Expropriation and recovery

After half a year of heavy fighting, in April 1945, the advancing Red Army drove the last stubbornly resisting German units from Hungarian soil. With the destruction of the Third Reich the political power of the ruling classes of Hungary also collapsed, and in the changed international situation new social forces and hitherto suppressed political factors came to the fore. The former democratic opposition parties, peasant organisations, and workers' parties became partners in power; above all the Communist Party, forced into illegality before, now emerged with substantial popular influence and with a dynamic programme for the rapid solution of the country's serious economic, social, and political problems. It found mass support in the local organs of popular power through which the initiative of the people emerged with elemental force, but it enjoyed the significant support of the Soviet occupation troops and of an Allied Control Commission under Soviet leadership as well. A radical transformation of the country's social, political, and economic life got under way. Democratic reforms which had waited decades for their realisation were now the order of the day, but almost simultaneously new strivings appeared which aimed at the curtailment of capitalist relationships and the socialist transformation of the country.

The first demand was for the abolition of the system of great landed estates. The implementation of a land reform proved to be decisive for the winning of the peasant majority of the population, the concentration of the forces of the left, and the cooperation of the workers' and peasant parties. For these reasons the programme of the Hungarian Independence Front (Magyar

Függetlenségi Front), drawn up at Szeged in December 1944 on Communist initiative, listed redistribution of the land among its first and most important demands. Even before the complete liberation of the country, on 18 March 1945, the Provisional Government which had been formed at Debrecen issued a decree actually setting in motion the new division of the land. The decree announced the confiscation of former noble estates over 140 acres in size and of peasant properties over 280 acres (with an upper limit of 420 acres for those who had taken part in the resistance against the Germans). The buildings, equipment, and livestock belonging to the land were also expropriated. In principle the former owners had a right to compensation, except for war criminals and members of fascist organisations, whose property was simply confiscated. The execution of the reform was entrusted to local land committees, which in many regions carried it through in a manner even more radical than envisaged in the decree.

The land reform transferred about 35 per cent of the land of Hungary (3·1 million hectares); about 60 per cent of this amount (about 2 million hectares) was distributed to 642,000 peasant families. The rest was turned into state and communal model farms, or used for house-building. Ninety per cent of those who received land were farm servants, agricultural labourers, or those smallholders who held under 3 hectares.

As a result of one of the most radical redistributions of land carried out anywhere after World War II the structure of farm property in Hungary, almost unchanged for a century, was completely transformed.

The agrarian revolution brought about by the redistribution of the land had implications beyond the abolition of feudal vestiges in agriculture, reflecting as it did the anti-capitalist objectives of the workers' parties and other left-wing forces which shared in power. These objectives appeared in the expropriation of land belonging to industrial enterprises, and in the measures taken to restrict the size of the holdings of well-to-do peasants. Anti-capitalist tendencies were evident in the growth of the state's power over economic life, in this case in the development of state farms. These efforts came to fruition much

## TABLE 38*

### Distribution of land in private ownership after land reform in 1945

| Size of holding (in hold†) | Number of holdings | % | Total area (in hold†) | % | Arable land (in hold†) | % | Average size of holding (in hold†) (Total) | (Arable) |
|---|---|---|---|---|---|---|---|---|
| 1·1– 3 | 361,500 | 25·1 | 823,400 | 7·1 | 614,100 | 6·6 | 2·3 | 1·7 |
| 3·1– 5 | 303,200 | 21·0 | 1,323,300 | 11·3 | 1,064,900 | 11·5 | 4·4 | 3·5 |
| 5·1– 8 | 333,400 | 23·1 | 2,319,600 | 19·8 | 1,878,800 | 20·3 | 7·0 | 5·6 |
| 8·1– 10 | 124,600 | 8·7 | 1,169,400 | 10·0 | 958,600 | 10·4 | 9·4 | 7·7 |
| 10·1– 15 | 177,400 | 12·3 | 2,294,300 | 19·6 | 1,860,100 | 21·1 | 12·9 | 10·5 |
| 15·1– 20 | 62,900 | 4·4 | 1,123,200 | 9·6 | 886,200 | 9·6 | 17·9 | 14·1 |
| 20·1– 25 | 30,600 | 2·1 | 716,300 | 6·1 | 561,300 | 6·1 | 23·4 | 18·3 |
| 25·1– 50 | 36,000 | 2·5 | 1,016,600 | 8·7 | 728,100 | 7·9 | 28·2 | 20·2 |
| 50·1–100 | 7,000 | 1·5 | 385,000 | 3·3 | 275,900 | 3·0 | 55·0 | 39·4 |
| Over 100 hold | 4,200 | 0·3 | 521,600 | 4·5 | 418,000 | 4·5 | 124·9 | 99·5 |
| Total | 1,440,800 | 100·0 | 11,695,700 | 100·0 | 9,246,000 | 100·0 | 8·1 | 6·4 |

\* Data from F. Donath. *Democratic land reform in Hungary 1945–47* (Budapest, 1969), 361.
† 1 *hold* = 1·4 acres.

more forcefully, however, in other areas of the economy. Regulation of the biggest monopolies, and nationalisation of several basic industries, figured among the points of the Independence Front's programme. Such measures were taken in many European countries in the years after the war.

The new power structure in Hungary made possible an ever greater degree of state intervention there, too. At the same time postwar economic chaos, severe wartime losses, and general exhaustion demanded that the government intervene vigorously in the economy.

The first forms of state intervention were not merely temporary phenomena of the immediate postwar months. The years of gradual economic recovery did not lead to any slackening off in the government's economic activity; indeed, in many areas the opposite took place. Between 1946 and 1948 stemming inflation and maintaining the value of the currency made an even greater degree of state intervention unavoidable. In Hungary there was no other way to carry through successfully the stabilisation plan introduced in August 1946, relying exclusively on internal resources, with its strict deflationary monetary policy, closely regulated credit policy, firmly centralised wage and price controls, energetic tax policy, and balanced government budgets.

All these measures created a guided economy in which customary market freedom, with market prices determined by the free play of supply and demand, was replaced by strict guidelines and regulation from above. The state acquired a powerful influence over the economy, and the changed social and political character of the government led to firm restrictions on private capital. A special kind of state-capitalist economy emerged.

Caught between a general shortage of funds, limited credit, price controls, and high taxation, most of the industrial enterprises struggled with mounting deficits. The industrial enterprises did in fact incur increasing arrears of taxes and state credits, making them more and more dependent on the state. Government restrictions, and the activities of works committees with wide powers of control over management, prevented any evasion, shutting down of factories, or redeployment of capital. All these measures implied restrictions on capital, foreshadowing its expropriation.

Between 1945 and 1948 these state-capitalist restrictions were characteristically accompanied, in Hungary, by various measures to bring about a partial nationalisation of industry. In December 1945 a law was passed taking the coal mines under government management, as envisaged in the Independence Front's December 1944 programme, and this was followed in the summer of 1946 by the nationalisation of the mines. As a result of this action, and of the fact that several large engineering and iron and steel plants had been in state hands for decades, 22 per cent of all miners and factory workers now came to be employed in state-run enterprises. In November 1946 the four largest firms in heavy industry were taken under state management—formally only until reparations commitments should be met—and the nationalisation of power-generating facilities soon followed. At the end of 1946 more than 46 per cent of all workers were already to be found in the public sector. A further step in this gradual process followed in the summer and autumn of 1947, when the ten largest banks were nationalised. This action not only made the state's monopoly of credit complete, but brought another large group of workers into state employ, raising the total to 58 per cent.

All these measures reached their climax following the political events of the winter of 1947–8, the introduction of the dictatorship of the proletariat, and the dissolution of the coalition government. The policy of a limited state capitalism was abandoned in favour of radical nationalisation of industry. On 25 March 1948 the government declared the nationalisation of all factories employing more than 100 workers, thus raising the state sector's share of industry to 83 per cent (by number of workers).

This turning away from private enterprise affected every area of the economy. It replaced the former government controls and restrictions with complete state direction of foreign trade and wholesale domestic commerce, and initiated the development of a nationalised retail-trade system.

This revolutionary transformation, with very extensive state intervention—though in its radical nationalisation policy only a culmination of trends already at work in the transition period—created exceptionally favourable conditions for postwar recovery. It made possible the mobilisation of all social and economic interests for recovery and economic development, and a maximum concentration of resources and conscious purpose, a matter of special importance in the chaotic conditions of postwar collapse.

TABLE 39

*Public and private sectors in the Hungarian manufacturing industry, at 24 April 1948*

|  | Number of employees | % |
|---|---|---|
| State property or state management | 278,076 | 72·5 |
| Public property | 16,595 | 4·3 |
| Soviet or Soviet-Hungarian mixed property | 13,886 | 3·7 |
| Co-operatives | 4,291 | 1·2 |
| Socialist sector total | 312,848 | 81·7 |
| Foreign property, over 100 workers | 21,023 | 5·6 |
| Private Hungarian property, less than 100 workers | 48,552 | 12·7 |
| Private sector total | 69,575 | 18·3 |
| Total | 382,423 | 100·0 |

The strengthening of the public sector by partial or complete nationalisation of various industries, and by extensive state regulation, led to the development of a mixed economy, creating the conditions for the introduction of central planning. On the initiative of the Communist Party, a three-year plan was worked out early in 1947 and accepted, after a long political battle, several months later. Introduced on 1 August 1947, it became an important determinant of economic progress.

The draft of the plan set recovery as its primary objective. Its goal was to regain the level of 1938 within three years, both in the economy at large and as regards the workers' standard of living. In the light of industry's wartime situation the plan also set certain further objectives: in industry (and especially heavy industry) a level of production was foreseen at the end of three years which would be much higher than the wartime level. Investments were allocated with this goal in mind.

Thus investment policy became a central question of the three-year plan. In 1945–6 the level of investment was extremely low; inflation had rendered worthless large amounts of accumulated capital. Inflation began as soon as Hungary entered the war, and by 1944 it assumed serious proportions. At the end of 1944 there was 24 billion pengő in paper currency in circulation, but by late October 1945 this had risen to 106 billion, and by the end of December, 765 billion pengő. Exhaustion of stocks, low production, the costs of recovery and reparations obligations inevitably produced inflation in the war-ravaged country, and large-scale speculation increased it further. Through the National Bank the government sought to create an investment boom through the use of inflationary credits.

It was a common occurrence for borrowers to use reconstruction credits for speculative purposes: a large part of the state loans, instead of being applied to productive investments, was lent out again at high rates of interest, and advances received on reparations deliveries found their way into the black market. A whole stratum of speculators and black marketeers appeared. Middlemen proliferated in commerce, and the speculative activity of these *nouveaux riches* hastened the dizzy pace of inflation in the first half of 1946. The depreciation of the Hungarian currency in 1946 revealed an inflation greater than the world had ever known. Economic life was carried on in astronomical figures. The 765 billion pengő in circulation at the end of 1945 had risen by the spring of 1946 to 34 trillion, and by the end of June 1946 to 6,277 trillion pengő. On the last day of the inflation the paper currency in circulation reached more than 47 quadrillion pengő.

On 1 August 1946, this unprecedented inflation was brought to an end. New currency was issued, the forint. One forint was equivalent to 400,000 quadrillion 1946 pengő. The gold content of the new forint was lower than that of the prewar pengő: one forint equalled 0·28766 1938 pengő.

The deflationary monetary and credit policy and the shortage of capital which necessarily followed the stabilisation could not, of course, create favourable conditions for large-scale investments. The three-year plan aimed at making available relatively large sums for investment. This was achieved essentially by imposing controls on capital and bringing about a more equitable distribution of national income.

In examining the extent of these investments one must first point out that even in the months of inflation immediately after the war there were large-scale state investments, mainly to assist recovery in transport and (through credits to get the mills working again) in industry. These inflationary investments, however, financed largely by issuing unbacked paper currency, did not approach the scale of the post-stabilisation investments. In 1946–7 net investment amounted to 530 million forints, or 3·7 per cent of net national income; in 1946–7 it was 1,865 million forints, 9·4 per cent of national income. In these years a large fraction of national income was devoted also to meeting international obligations and to rebuilding stocks of goods depleted or destroyed at the end of the war. In 1946–7, for example, 12 per cent of national income went to meet reparations payments and another 5–6 per cent for rebuilding stocks. In 1947–8 the proportions were reversed: 6·5 per cent for international obligations, 12 per cent for building up stocks. Heavy investments assured a rapid rise in national income and a rapid rate of recovery. In 1946–7 the rate of growth of the economy was 76 per cent, in 1947–8 30 per cent.

This unexampled rate of growth, achieved by bringing into play the socio-economic factors already discussed, can be ascribed specifically to two immediate factors. On the one hand, the government assured a high level of investment by mobilising the maximum in material resources, and by directing investment to the areas most essential for recovery; thus smaller investments produced a higher rate of growth. The greater part of investment went toward eliminating the bottlenecks which had appeared in industry as a result of wartime destruction. In textiles, for example, the destruction of 48 per cent of spinning capacity made it impossible to utilise fully the 63 per cent of weaving capacity which had survived undamaged. As a consequence of the effective planned concentration of resources, the returns on the investments made during the period of recovery were very high. These results can be demonstrated quantitatively by examining the amount of investment required to produce a unit of growth in national income (coefficient of capital). In 1946–7 the growth of national income was due not primarily to investment in new plant, but to restoring existing capacity and assuring it of the proper conditions for continued operation. By 1947–8, when reconstruction investments again played a primary role, one unit of investment was generating two-and-a-half units of increase in national income.

The second of the material and technical factors which played an important part in recovery and economic growth was the large surplus of labour available in the economy. In part this stemmed from dislocation of the economy, at the end of the war. After the liberation less than one-third of the old factory labour force resumed work. During the period of inflation the number of workers rose rapidly, reaching 96 per cent of the prewar figure by August 1946. The gradual re-employment of the old labour force was an important source of increased production in 1945, 1946, and to some extent in 1947: these were experienced and, in part, skilled workers, not masses of unskilled labour recently drawn into industry. From 1947, the industrial work force was swollen not only by the return of old workers but by the absorption of new manpower. Other sources of labour were at hand in abundance. Although the land reform enabled most of the village poor, only half-employed before, to gain a bare living, it could not provide employment for the entire rural population. The fact is clearly indicated by the large numbers of unemployed between 1946 and 1948, their ranks constantly fed by the masses of prisoners-of-war returning home.

The census of 1 January 1949 showed 126,000 unemployed, four-fifths of whom may be regarded as industrial unemployed. Thus the large supply of labour opened almost limitless possibilities for drawing new workers into production. Industry seized this opportunity, for given the scarcity of capital the simplest and readiest way to increase production was to employ more workers. Throughout this period a considerable proportion of the workers (and immediately after the war a particularly large number) were engaged not in manufacturing industry but in the work of recovery, clearing ruins, rebuilding, and the like. The lowered productivity of labour and the temporarily worsened physical condition of the workers contributed to the demand for labour as well. As a result, there were 16 per cent more workers employed in industry in 1948—taking the average figure for the year—than during 1938.

All in all, 150,000 new workers were taken into industry (including mining) between 1946 and 1948, an increase of about 80 per cent. Thus the growth of the industrial labour force was a factor of much more than average importance, a special characteristic of the period of reconstruction.

Finally, technical progress and the modernisation of equipment could be an important factor in economic growth, raising the productivity of labour and laying the basis for increased output. Its effects, however, were not felt unequivocally during the postwar period. It is true that the productivity of labour grew rapidly during this time. In the special postwar circumstances, however, this had little or nothing to do with technical progress. At the end of the war labour productivity was so low in industry—43 per cent below the prewar level in 1946—that it could be raised substantially simply by rebuilding the productive apparatus and restoring production to normal. Low productivity was connected with the decline of living standards too, but even more with the fact that industry was short of raw materials, causing stoppages in production, while a significant fraction of the labour force was not engaged in manufacturing production, but was employed in clearing the ruins and in the reconstruction of damaged or destroyed buildings. Thus a mere improvement in this situation was enough to raise productivity markedly in the fiscal year 1947–8, and this was even truer of the year 1948, when the external obstacles to production had largely been overcome. As a result of all these factors combined, the index of net output per worker—taking the 1938 figure as 100—climbed from 43 in 1946 to 73 in 1947, and to 96 in 1948. Thus during the period of reconstruction rising labour productivity played a substantial role in increasing production.

This way of raising productivity was a once-for-all opportunity characteristic of postwar reconstruction. But reconstruction can be accompanied not only by restoration of the old level of productivity, but also by wide-scale improvements in technique. Repairing wartime damage need not mean merely the replacement of old capacity and a return to former modes of production: to some extent it can be combined (though more slowly and gradually, perhaps) with the introduction of new techniques and the replacement of lost capacity with new technology. In our period this would indeed have retarded the growth of output, but at the same time it would have laid the groundwork for further development, compensating, on a longer perspective, for any loss. In the economic circumstances of postwar Hungary, however, there was no chance of any such technical transformation in the course of recovery. On the contrary, ruined equipment was more than once replaced with antiquated machinery bought abroad and put into operation again.

The methods actually followed did, of course, lead in our period to a rapid and large increase in production, and at smaller cost. Industrial production, which in 1945 ran at only 20–25 per cent of the prewar level, and in 1946 scarcely exceeded one-third (36 per cent) of that figure, grew very rapidly thereafter. In 1947 it reached three-quarters of the prewar level, and in 1948 it exceeded by 2 per cent the industrial production of 1938.

At the same time, the reconstruction of industry did not bring a simple restoration of its prewar structure. The attainment of the 1938 level of production was accompanied by a certain restructuring of output, well illustrated in Table 40. In 1948 the food industry and light industry in general still lagged behind the prewar productive level, while output in heavy industry considerably surpassed it. The shift in favour of heavy industry was a necessary consequence of the demands of recon-

TABLE 40

Changes in the industrial structure in the postwar period
(in % by output)

|  | 1938 | 1946 | 1947 | 1948 |
|---|---|---|---|---|
| Heavy industry | 100 | 56·9 | 92·1 | 124·4 |
| Light industry | 100 | 21·7 | 62·2 | 86·4 |
| Food industry | 100 | 29·5 | 65·3 | 93·8 |

struction and reparations deliveries, and also reflected the fact that during the war it was the capacity of heavy industry which expanded most.

Industrial growth in Hungary during the reconstruction period can be regarded as exceptionally rapid, even in comparison with the record of European development generally in the postwar years.

TABLE 41

Industrial production per capita (1935–8 = 100)

| Countries | 1947 | 1948 |
|---|---|---|
| Austria | 47 | 65 |
| Belgium | 81 | 85 |
| Denmark | 90 | 95 |
| Finland | 93 | 102 |
| France | 84 | 95 |
| Italy | 88 | 92 |
| Norway | 88 | 91 |
| Holland | 72 | 77 |
| Sweden | 110 | 116 |
| Great Britain | 106 | 113 |
| Czechoslovakia | 89 | 100 |
| Poland | 87 | 99 |
| Hungary | 87 | 109 |

No such powerful and productive upswing is visible in agriculture. Although agricultural war damage was largely overcome, there were few resources left over, amidst the tasks of reconstruction already described, to further agricultural development. The investment targets for agriculture, as set forth in the three-year plan, were not fulfilled. Instead of the 7,700 new tractors prescribed by the plan, for example, only 4,500 were actually put into use. Restrictions on the development of that portion of the peasantry which raised crops for the market

—particularly the extremely harmful limitations on credit to agriculture—acted as obstacles to growth, as did the appearance, for a time, of an agrarian price scissors. In these circumstances the average yields for 1949 approached but did not reach the prewar levels. For some crops the area under cultivation also lagged behind the prewar figure. Thus it is understandable that agricultural output did not exceed that of the last years of peace. Hungarian agricultural production remained 10–20 per cent below the level of the years 1935–8. But the proportion of agricultural output reaching the market was even smaller, for the poor peasants released from the grip of the latifundia increased their consumption markedly, so that the amount of produce available for market sale was considerably smaller than might be deduced from the crude figures of agricultural production. While the total crop was only a few percentage points smaller than before the war, production for the market in 1949 was only three-quarters of the prewar amount.

With the progress of reconstruction total national income had by 1949 exceeded the prewar level, while at the same time changes had taken place in the structure of the economy, in the form of industrial progress and a reduced role for agriculture.

## 2  Development of a socialist economic strategy

In 1948 and 1949, with the completion of the main tasks of reconstruction, those social and political changes which had begun in 1945 reached their conclusion. Hungary became a member of the socialist camp of nations which had emerged in Europe. With the dissolution of the governing coalition and the unification of the Communist and Social Democratic parties in June 1948, the new Hungarian Workers' Party (Magyar Dolgozók Pártja) came to power. With the proclamation of the dictatorship of the proletariat, the reorganisation of the state as reflected in the new constitution of summer 1949, and the establishment of a Soviet system, new conditions came into being which made possible the immediate realisation of a socialist strategy of economic development.

In taking the socialist path Hungary sought to utilise the only model of socialist economic development then existing in order to make up for many decades of social and economic backwardness. In so doing Hungary was influenced not only by the impressive example of the Soviet Union in overcoming the backwardness of the Tsarist era to develop the economic capacity to resist Nazi aggression, but also by the prevailing war psychosis and the theoretical views on politics then making themselves felt in the world Communist movement. The sharpening of the cold war, the elevation of Soviet Russian practice to the level of universally valid theory, and the labelling of every other course as revisionist, were largely responsible for the fact that in Hungary after 1948 an economic strategy developed two decades earlier, in different historical circumstances, was adopted in almost unchanged form.

In Hungary this strategy began to be carried out essentially from the summer of 1948. At that time appropriate institutions began to be set up for the direction of a new economic system. A new banking system, in which the National Bank, besides acting as a bank of issue, also monopolised the provision of short-term credits, and transfer of money of the various enterprises, was supplemented by a network of banks with special functions. At the same time new ways of guiding industrial activity were created: nationalised companies, formally still independent entities, were brought under the supervision of central industrial authorities and ministries, one for each industry. A central plan adopted by Parliament governed the functioning of the economy. Planning had been introduced in Hungary with the three-year plan of August 1947, which was revised in the second half of 1948. But a fully centralised planning system, with mandatory directives, came into being only in January 1950 with the first five-year plan. This form of planning was based on the classical system of double pricing: a separation of production costs and consumer prices to the complete exclusion of market influences, in which the individual enterprise was a purely fictional book keeping entity and sold at prices independent of real cost and value relationships. In this system the real market operations of buying and selling of course ceased, giving way to a system of distribution directed by the National Planning Office on the basis of the balance sheet of the whole economy.

This system of planning was designed as part of a strategy to realise certain long-term economic goals, and was closely connected with the idea of economic development. Its basic theoretical feature was the belief that under socialist conditions the greatest possible accumulation of capital would automatically lead to the fastest possible economic growth. Starting in 1948, a policy of attaining a maximum rate of accumulation and of maintaining it at a very high level came to prevail. The jump in capital accumulation can be seen with special clarity between 1950 and 1951. During the years 1948–50 national income (calculated at constant prices) grew about 20 per cent, with the share of national income going for consumption rising by only 6 per cent while the share going for investment rose 54 per cent. In 1951, again, the proportion of national income allocated to investment rose by 70 per cent. Between 1949 and 1953 the accumulation of capital proceeded, on average, more than twice as fast as the rise in national income. This process led, during the first half of the five-year plan, to a constant expansion of investments.

On the basis of these prescriptions there began a period of investment activity unparalleled in Hungarian economic history. Of the total national income—allowing for distortions introduced into the data and methods of calculation by the pricing system—nearly 35 per cent was now going for investment. A rate of investment was achieved some six to seven times that of prewar days.

From this maximum level of accumulation and investment the economic authorities expected the automatic attainment of a maximum rate of growth. The February 1951 version of the five-year plan projected an economic growth of 130 per cent during the lifetime of the plan. In industry, a 210 per cent growth was foreseen during these five years. This anticipated (and dictated) high rate of industrialisation was the salient feature of economic policy at this time. The economic authorities wished, through a programme of rapid industrialisation, to achieve within the space of a single five-year plan a fundamental transformation, turning an agrarian-industrial structure into one that would be primarily industrial. For that reason, investments in agriculture were limited to 13 per cent of total investment. At the same time 'non-productive' infrastructural investment—which was running at about 60 per cent of all investment in the developed capitalist countries—was kept to about one-third of total investments. Consequently, during the first half of the 1950s 48 per cent of all investment was devoted to industry. Official policy generally stressed the primacy of heavy industry as a precondition for the growth of the whole economy. Within heavy industry, increased production of basic materials received special emphasis.

Thus the resources allocated to industrial development were concentrated almost entirely on heavy industry, and within it on extractive industries and those engaged in the production of coal, iron and steel. Between 1950 and 1953, when these tendencies appeared in their most characteristic form, nearly 90 per cent of the 26½ billion forints of industrial investment went to heavy industry, with two-thirds of total industrial investment going for the development of mines, foundries, etc.

The maximum possible development of mining and metallurgy was the central theme of this programme for building up heavy industry. At the same time, economic policy did not devote a great deal of attention to the development of the electrical and precision-machinery industries, both of them important from the standpoint of Hungarian industrial tradition, technical progress, and export opportunities.

The objectives of industrialisation, then, displayed two characteristic features: the structural organisation of industry copied Soviet Russian development policies of the preceding decades, and the primacy of heavy industry was equated with the preferential development of mining and metallurgy. Of course, this conception did not prevail simply because it took over Soviet Russian policies born of other, earlier circumstances, but also because it was supported by theories of economic autarchy. In the course of industrialisation the authorities could not count on external co-operation in developing production, for the strain of rapid industrialisation in the other socialist countries everywhere created virtually unrealisable demands for fuel, raw materials, and investment, while the capitalist countries followed a strict embargo policy. The materials needed for development thus had to be raised from the internal resources of the country, to the limits of the possible, and even beyond. Defence considerations reinforced the tendencies of an autarchic economic policy.

Fear of impending war became a decisive factor in economic development; it was one of the principal motives for the successive upward revisions of the plan. Overall the plan allocated half of all expenditures during the entire five-year period to military purposes, and in the first year of the plan outlays for civilian and military purposes were about equal.

Defence considerations affected not only the rate of industrialisation, of course, but also the structure of heavy industry, placing a premium on the production of strategic materials and on efforts to achieve economic self-sufficiency. In these circumstances economic development had to proceed without regard to considerations of profits, cost factors, technical quality, or an up-to-date technological standard. The planners preferred instead to judge on the basis of quantitative growth, without regard to cost factors. In an internal memorandum of 1951 the planning authorities, examining the effectiveness of their investments, openly declared: 'Investment is always determined by political considerations, with economic indicators taking second place.' Similar views were reflected in the proposition that under socialist conditions the depreciation of machinery need not be taken into account. This attitude found expression in serious disproportions between the sums invested in construction and in machinery. During the first half of the 1950s outlays on construction were 5·2 times as great as those on mechanical equipment, and only one-fifth of all investments went toward developing the total stock of machinery. The desire to leap ahead at all costs, and the pursuit of quantitative gains, also led the planning authorities, in the interests of maximising the amount of capital available for development purposes, to withdraw the sums needed for maintenance and replacement, and to cut the amortisation fund by 50 per cent. A 1955 report of the Statistical Office noted, in connection with the fulfilment of the first five-year plan, that, '. . . we have neglected the proper replacement of our mechanical equipment. We deprived our enterprises of a good part of their depreciation funds, which were too small to begin with, largely in order to use them to cover the cost of new investments. . . . This had led to a deterioration in the condition of our existing plant.'

The drastic application of an economic strategy of forced industrialisation in a country like Hungary, poor in capital and natural resources, had led to serious difficulties by the time the first long-term plan was completed. A planned economy did make possible a rapid accumulation of capital, the concentration of material resources, and a rapid rate of development, but in a way that was excessively costly. As a result of this generally wasteful system of management about one-fifth of the increase in national income was lost again through various 'leaks' in the economy. In agriculture, which had furnished most of the capital needed for industrialisation through taxation and a system of forced deliveries at low prices, and where administrative measures to hasten collectivisation had further agitated the peasantry, the situation was extremely grave. Production declined; in the mid-1950s it had not yet recovered the prewar level. Serious supply problems appeared. As a result of these shortages and of the heavy burdens placed on the population by forced industrialisation, in the form of strong inflationary pressures, real wages fell by more than 20 per cent, in place of the 50 per cent rise in living standards called for by the five-year plan. By the middle of the 1950s serious social, economic, and political tensions had arisen, which were to become one of the main sources of the tragic political crisis of 1956.

Mounting economic difficulties, the improvement of the international situation following the close of the Korean War, and developments in the international Communist movement after the death of Stalin led to the recognition among economists and at government level that changes had to be made in the prevailing economic strategy. Certain corrections were made as early as the summer of 1953. In August of that year a new government issued a programme based on a resolution of the Central Committee of the Hungarian Workers' Party in June, announcing and at the same time implementing several basic changes in economic policy. In 1954 and 1955 appeared the first comprehensive critical proposals for overhauling the planning system, although not yet, to be sure, at government level. But the complexity of the new proposals, the strength of retrograde forces, the contradictory character of the measures taken, and another about-turn in economic policy combined to prevent any real progress. In the end the overhaul of economic strategy had to wait for the political changes of late 1956.

The re-evaluation of this strategy started from a critique of the errors and contradictions of the planning and policy of the preceding years. The radically changed leadership which emerged from the political upheavals of 1956, freed from many errors of dogma and practice and free of responsibility for the mistakes committed in the past, was in an incomparably better position to seek new directions for economic policy.

In fact no metamorphosis of the determinants of economic strategy took place. This was primarily so, of course, because rejection of the economic and political policy of the preceding era did not mean complete rejection of all earlier developments. A degree of political and economic continuity was maintained. Among the political and ideological factors working for continuity were the continued low level of international division of labour; despite the declaration of the Berlin session of the Council for Economic Mutual Assistance in May 1956 in favour of greater integration, the progress of real co-operation in production and development remained modest. Even in engineering, where the best results in this respect were obtained, the value of goods produced on a basis of co-operative international specialisation did not exceed 3–4 per cent of production. This circumstance prevented the implementation of a number of important economic lessons. It worked against efforts to overcome autarchy and exercised an unfavourable influence over the distribution of investment.

These retrogressive tendencies continued because many economic insights of the first importance came into conflict with forces that had a stake in the survival of the old planning system, a conflict which in the decade before 1968 became a source of new contradictions. Essentially, efforts to moderate the rate of industrialisation to what was realistically possible had to wait until growth based on the extensive exploitation of resources gave way to growth based on technical modernisation and increased productivity.

The commission of economic experts set up early in 1957 to work out a new economic policy and new planning methods, as called for by the Hungarian Socialist Workers Party's resolution of December 1956, submitted a number of important proposals. The planning system, however, was reformed gradually through piecemeal measures. Thus between 1957 and 1964 a good many alterations were made in the planned economy. Compulsory and low-priced deliveries were also abolished in agriculture. The number of mandatory planning indices was reduced in an effort to overcome the errors of over-centralisation. Profit-sharing was introduced in order to give each enterprise a greater interest in the production and sale of its wares. Funds were allocated for technical development. A 5 per cent tax on capital employed was introduced in order to encourage the most economical and most effective use of investments. All in all, however, these and other measures introduced over an eight-year span did not fundamentally change the system of economic planning and management. Continued disregard for market forces, the retention of obligatory directives, and the survival virtually intact of the system of prices and incentives which went with them vitiated the effect of these individual changes. The system of obligatory directives, which had undergone no basic change, was an organic part of the whole earlier strategy of economic planning, a necessary means of realising a programme of forced industrialisation. Its survival, despite changes in economic thinking, led to a continued stress on attaining quantitative targets, on a model of extensive, forced development, neglect of technical progress, and a lack of interest in the quality and variety of goods to be marketed. Waste remained a prominent feature in investment and production.

Still, important new economic processes were at work from the end of the 1950s. The earlier policy of maximum capital accumulation and investment was rejected. A more realistic estimate of possibilities became the guide in setting economic policy. In the second three-year plan (1958–60) and the second five-year plan (1961–5), for example, an increase of 13 per cent and 36 per cent respectively in national income was projected, while industrial production was planned to grow 22 per cent and 50 per cent respectively. Here the departure from the targets of the first five-year plan was striking. Investments were likewise reduced; from 1954 to 1957 only 10–15 per cent of national income was invested, largely as a short-term tactical measure brought on by political necessities. Between 1958 and 1967 investment generally fluctuated between one-fifth and one-fourth of national income. The tendency to force the pace undoubtedly reappeared during the 1960s; but in any event national income generally grew only 5–6 per cent a year during the decade, a more modest tempo compared with the 12 or 16 per cent record annual increases of earlier days, and growth was smoother, without broad fluctuations or serious failures.

TABLE 42

*Investment in the economy at constant prices*

| Year | Thousand millions Forint | 1950 = 100 | Previous year = 100 |
|---|---|---|---|
| 1950 | 22·3 | 100 | — |
| 1951 | 27·9 | 125 | 125 |
| 1952 | 33·0 | 148 | 118 |
| 1953 | 32·6 | 146 | 99 |
| 1954 | 25·2 | 113 | 77 |
| 1955 | 23·9 | 107 | 95 |
| 1956 | 25·6 | 115 | 107 |
| 1957 | 22·8 | 102 | 89 |
| 1958 | 29·3 | 131 | 128 |
| 1959 | 39·3 | 176 | 134 |
| 1960 | 43·5 | 195 | 111 |
| 1961 | 41·4 | 186 | 95 |
| 1962 | 45·4 | 204 | 110 |
| 1963 | 51·9 | 233 | 114 |
| 1964 | 54·0 | 242 | 104 |
| 1965 | 54·3 | 243 | 101 |
| 1966 | 59·3 | 266 | 109 |

One of the most important adjustments was a more realistic approach to industrialisation, which continued to be a central concern, but was now to be pursued at a slower pace more in keeping with economic conditions, and with a greater sense of proportion. Between 1957 and 1960 industrial output rose 39 per cent, agricultural production 12 per cent, and the index of real wages 12 per cent. Between 1960 and 1965 the figures were 47 per cent for industry, 10 per cent for agriculture, and 9 per cent for real wages.

The more balanced character of this growth is indicated by the fact that while agriculture received only 13 per cent of all investments under the first five-year plan, it was allotted 17 per cent of investment funds from 1954 to 1957 and 18–20 per cent in succeeding years. Infrastructural investment amounted to about one-third of the total during the first half of the 1950s, but between 1956 and 1960 to almost half, and to more than 40 per cent during the 1960s.

This whittling-down of extreme disproportions made itself felt in industry too. On the one hand the share of investment allocated to heavy industry declined from 41 per cent to 34 per cent of all investments, while on the other the internal structure of heavy industry underwent a fundamental change. The primacy of the extractive industries gave way to a greater stress on labour-intensive industries, and on industries of high technology, in particular certain branches of the chemical industry.

Though these changes were far from thorough, their tendency was unmistakably toward meeting the demands of the modern age. The new industrialisation policy not only introduced quantitative modifications in the distribution of investment and the development of production, but also set in motion changes in the basic model of industrialisation. The new development policy which gradually emerged set out from the premise that industrial growth should rest not on a maximum degree of capital accumulation and investment, but on an optimum level of investment. In accordance with this conception, a system of economic management evolved which, while based on mandatory planning directives and centralised direction, also incorporated elements of market incentives and employed indirect means of guiding and influencing the economy.

At the present time this process is still unfinished. Among the important milestones in its development have been the 1965 decision to make a comprehensive reform of the system of economic management, its introduction in January 1968, and the work begun in 1968 and still in progress today to work out a new concept of economic policy within a framework of long-range planning.

Changes in agricultural policy occupy an important place in the revision of economic strategy. Here as in other areas change should be regarded as a process of transition, determined by economic conditions, from the earlier economic policy toward new objectives. New principles of agricultural policy were worked out and published in the summer of 1957. In essence, they called for pursuing collectivisation in conjunction with the development of production and in keeping with actual economic conditions, rather than hastily and as a goal in itself. In the interest of developing production the new policy stressed that 'we must break . . . with the view which has prevailed for years that, despite its large share in national income, agriculture should receive only a small proportion of state investment'. In line with these principles, the share of investment devoted to agriculture did indeed rise. It became a prime goal of agricultural policy to assure an atmosphere of confidence within which productive work could flourish. To achieve this purpose the system of obligatory deliveries was abolished, mandatory planting regulations lifted, restrictions on renting land eased, the purchase and sale of land up to seven acres permitted, and firm measures taken against every kind of illegality.

Emphasising that 'the development of agricultural production and the transition to socialism represent a single, indivisible objective', the planning authorities raised this double goal of collectivisation and increased production to the status of a central principle of agricultural policy. This goal had been stressed in the early 1950s, too, but the new collectivisation programme, like the measures taken to raise production, differed significantly from the earlier one. The new programme firmly declared that the chief means toward collectivisation was the development of the state farms and co-operatives, which in 1957 occupied 22 per cent of the country's arable soil, into 'modern, exemplary, intensively cultivated enterprises'. Great importance was attached to developing more flexible forms of cultivation, wage-payment and distribution, and to the creation of transitional organisational forms such as general co-operatives of cultivators, and special co-operatives for specific technical or productive tasks (ie, collectivising one or a number of branches of agricultural production).

Shortly afterward, however, in December 1958, the economic leadership deemed that political and economic developments in the countryside had 'made it possible for the co-operative movement to proceed faster than before in the coming year of

1959'. It noted that preconditions for collectivisation did not exist uniformly in the various regions of the country. In some places there were opportunities for 'pushing development faster than the overall nationwide tempo'. At the same time it was asserted that 'today the conditions for great and sudden forward advances do not exist. But these conditions can be achieved within a foreseeable time'. At the end of 1958 another resolution took a firm stand in favour of a reorganisation of agriculture by means of producers' co-operatives, while announcing the beginning of a political and educational campaign in the countryside and a shake-up in personnel to facilitate work in the villages. The earliest possible formation of co-operatives was set down as the transitional goal in the reorganisation of agriculture.

Thus in the winter of 1958–9 mass collectivisation began again in Hungary, on the basis of a platform which envisaged socialist reorganisation as a task of the political movement and which regarded conditions as ripe for such a step. Complete collectivisation was achieved in three stages, within a two-year period beginning early in 1959 and interrupted only during the summers, the peak working season in agriculture. By the summer of 1959 over half the country's arable land belonged to the socialist sector, an indication of the rapid success of co-operative organisation.

In the new collectivisation campaign governmental coercion and the impoverishment of the private peasant—practices of the early 1950s—were avoided. New motives were offered for organising co-operatives: obligatory payment of a rental on land, a new solution of the kulak (rich peasants) question allowing co-operatives to decide themselves whether to accept well-to-do peasants (a great bone of contention in earlier years), election of the co-operative's leaders and freedom to decide how it should be cultivated, a more flexible wage system generally more favourable to the peasantry, and freedom to cultivate allotments. Another extremely important factor was the readiness of the state to provide large numbers of agronomists, financial support, and many other kinds of aid far surpassing that available earlier, and well before the main work of reorganisation was begun, in order to assure the stability of the co-operatives. Nor could the historical antecedents of this process be disregarded—the collectivisation of earlier years and the setback suffered a few years before in the attack on the co-operatives—for these were among the factors which made it essential to convince large numbers of peasants of the historical necessity of making changes.

The second stage of collectivisation followed a decision taken by the economic authorities in the early autumn of 1959. Between the autumn of 1959 and the summer of 1960 328,000 families joined co-operatives all over the country; by summer 1960 co-operatives included 72 per cent of the arable land of the country. Finally, in the last period of reorganisation, from the autumn of 1960 to the spring of 1961, another 291,000 families enrolled in co-operatives, bringing with them about 1·85 million acres of land.

As a result of this reorganisation, co-operative enterprises became the key factor in agricultural production. In 1965 the co-operatives, covering more than 77 per cent of all farmland, held 68 per cent of all livestock (state farms, with over 16 per cent of the arable land, had 13 per cent of livestock, private and other enterprises 19 per cent). The co-operatives produced 69 per cent of agricultural output, state farms 15 per cent, individual holdings 16 per cent.

The completion of the collectivisation drive was a historical turning-point in the evolution of the Hungarian economy, a decisive achievement in making socialist relations of production the general rule and creating the socio-economic foundations for socialist transformation.

## 3 Changes in economic structure

SIZE AND LEVEL OF THE LABOUR FORCE: EDUCATIONAL
AND DEMOGRAPHIC ELEMENTS OF GROWTH

During World War II hundreds of thousands of Hungarians died at the front, in the mass extermination of the Jewish population, in the air raids and in the fighting that eventually swirled across the country. In contrast with population increases of 700,000 during the 1920s and 630,000 during the 1930s, Hungary during the decade of the 1940s lost 110,000 people. The census of 1949 found 9·2 million people living in the country. But the postwar years soon saw a renewed rise in population. In 1947 the number of live births again reached the prewar and wartime level of 180,000–190,000 per annum, and between 1953 and 1955 climbed to 200,000–220,000, as a result of strict limitations on abortion. During the 1960s it stood at 130,000–140,000 a year, reaching or surpassing a figure of 150,000 at the end of the decade. The birth rate was about 20 per 1,000 during a ten-year period beginning in the late 1940s; in the following decade it fell to 14–15 per 1,000.

During the same years the mortality rate fell even faster, a consequence of social and economic development, in particular of progress in public hygiene, medical care, and other social measures. From the late 1940s deaths numbered only 100,000–110,000 a year, as against about 170,000 in the 1920s and 130,000 in the 1930s; the mortality rate fell to 10–11 per 1,000.

As a result, the population grew by 1–1·5 per cent annually during the most rapid period of increase, with a yearly rate of increase of 0·2 to 0·5 per cent from the end of the 1950s. In 1960 the population of the country reached 9,960,000, and in the

## TABLE 43

### Size and density of population, distribution of population in different branches of economy

| | 1941 Number (000s) | % | 1949 Number (000s) | % | 1960 Number (000s) | % | 1968 Number (000s) | % |
|---|---|---|---|---|---|---|---|---|
| Population | 9,316 | 100 | 9,205 | 100 | 9,961 | 100 | 10,235 | 100 |
| Density of population per sq km | | | 98·9 | | 107·1 | | 110·9 | — |
| 1 Gainfully occupied people and their dependants | 8,803 | 94·5 | 8,675 | 94·2 | 9,279 | 93·2 | 8,521 | 83·3 |
| (a) Agriculture | 4,573 | 49·1 | 4,524 | 49·1 | 3,540 | 35·6 | 1,499* | 30·7 |
| (b) Industry | 1,888 | 20·3 | 1,889 | 20·5 | 2,602 | 26·1 | 1,639* | 33·6 |
| (c) Building industry | 263 | 2·8 | 234 | 2·6 | 881 | 6·9 | 296* | 6·1 |
| (d) Communications | 373 | 4·0 | 437 | 4·7 | 696 | 7·0 | 323* | 6·6 |
| (e) Trade | 554 | 6·0 | 443 | 4·8 | 531 | 5·3 | 345* | 7·0 |
| (f) Other | 1,152 | 12·3 | 1,148 | 12·5 | 1,230 | 12·3 | 784* | 16·0 |
| 2 Inactive wage earners and their dependants | 513 | 5·5 | 530 | 5·8 | 682 | 6·8 | 1,715 | 16·7 |
| (a) Pensioners | 356 | 3·8 | 435 | 4·7 | 614 | 6·1 | 1,269 | 12·4 |
| (b) Other | 157 | 1·7 | 95 | 1·1 | 68 | 0·7 | 446 | 4·3 |

\* Without dependents

1960s crossed the 10 million mark, reaching 10,240,000 in January 1968.

Even more important for the growth of the labour supply than rising population was the entry into the work force of large numbers who had not worked before or who had been engaged in housework. Although the number of dependents remained about the same (5·3 to 5·4 million), the active wage-earning population grew by almost a million, from 3,910,000 in 1949 to 4,888,000 in 1968. The proportion of women among wage-earners rose during the twenty-year period from 31 to 40 per cent. Thus despite a moderate increase in population the supply of labour grew very rapidly, by almost 25 per cent.

The development of human resources was not, however, limited merely to the numerical growth of the population. Human experience and knowledge, the level of skill of the labour force, was no less important. Certain demographic changes already pointed in that direction, but a large share of the credit must go to the veritable revolution in education which took place in the decades after World War II.

The post-liberation school reform abolished the old elementary schools of four or six grades; in their place, eight-grade general schools offering a uniform elementary education were established. It was only in the decades after the end of the war that the population of school age was able, thanks to the revolutionary social and economic changes which had occurred, to take full advantage of compulsory elementary education. The number of pupils in these schools rose from 1,100,000 in 1938 to 1,500,000 in the early 1960s (falling again to 1,300,000 at the end of the decade as the number of children in this age group declined).

It was only during these years that illiteracy finally disappeared. According to the census of 1960 the rate of illiteracy was a trifle over 2 per cent.

The educational level of the wage-earning population could not, of course, rise in direct proportion to the extension and expansion of schooling. Despite the spread of adult education, important strata of the older generation remained at the old low level of culture. The 1960 census showed that 2·3 per cent of the 5,300,000 wage-earners were illiterate (against 11 per cent in 1930); their numbers, together with those who had completed only one to five years of school, exceeded one-fifth of the wage-earning population. Eighty per cent of wage-earners had had more than five years of schooling. The remaining 13 per cent of wage-earners had had some further education.

Thus the educational level of the labour force had risen rapidly, particularly as regards secondary and higher education. The general broadening of elementary education, mass attendance at primary school, and the improved educational quality of these schools, which first made it possible to realise the prescriptions set down for mass education long before, were the most dynamic aspects of the educational revolution; and they made it possible for mass secondary education to develop.

Before 1945 secondary schooling in Hungary was available to very few children. During the 1930s the number of middle-school students stood at 50,000–60,000, only about 10 per cent of the secondary-school-age population. Here the increase was rapid during the 1950s, and even more so during the 1960s. In 1949 82,000 students were attending middle school, in 1956 120,000, and in 1968, 335,000; by the latter date one-third of the secondary-school-age population was receiving an education.

University education, once extremely limited (17,000 students in 1930, 11,000 in 1938), expanded rapidly from the end of the 1940s. At the same time higher education underwent a structural transformation, bringing it into much closer contact with economic life. During the interwar years about 40 per cent of all university students were in the faculties of law and theology, while another 16 per cent studied medicine and pharmacy, with only 17 per cent altogether enrolled in technical and business schools. In the academic year 1968–9, on the other hand, nearly 39 per cent were pursuing technical studies, with another 10 per cent in economic subjects and 9 per cent in agronomy; the number of law students had fallen to 4 per cent.

Thus the number of people with a secondary-school or university education grew markedly. In 1960 nearly 7 per cent of all wage-earners had completed middle school, and more than 3 per cent were university graduates; over 3 per cent had had some secondary or university education but had left without taking their degrees. These figures, of course, still do not give a complete picture of the qualitative development of the skills of the labour force. We have yet to describe the extent and content of the technical education, on-the-job training of apprentices and others, and the system of extension courses which were so important during this period.

These data clearly show how rapid progress was, especially in industry, where the proportion of those who had received an elementary education rose from one-fifth to one-third, the number of those with a middle-school education trebled, and those with a higher education more than trebled.

The value of this 'human investment' represented a significant portion of the capital invested in developing the forces of production. The amount invested in education was equal to 43 per cent of total investment in the economy. This figure graphically demonstrates the extent of investment in education and suggests its enormous importance for the development of productive forces.

### INDUSTRY

The pace of industrialisation, forced in the early years but rapid even thereafter, led to increases in industrial production unprecedented in Hungarian economic history. The annual rate of growth in the first half of the 1950s was 13·8 per cent, in the second half of the 1950s 7·6 per cent, and in the first half of the 1960s, 7·8 per cent, rising again thereafter; thus on the average the growth rate was approximately 10 per cent.

This historic expansion of Hungarian industry is illustrated by the fact that between 1950 and 1967 the net value of production increased approximately four-fold. As a result, the level of industrialisation of the country, as expressed by the data for per capita industrial production, rose significantly; among the thirty-five leading industrial nations, Hungary by the mid-1960s occupied a place in the middle rank. In the United States, Great Britain, and the German Federal Republic per capita industrial production was 250–370 per cent higher; in Switzerland, Sweden, and Belgium about twice as high, in the

TABLE 44
*Index of industrial output*

| Year | 1950 = 100 | Previous year = 100 |
|---|---|---|
| 1950 | 100 | — |
| 1951 | 124 | 124 |
| 1952 | 150 | 121 |
| 1953 | 167 | 112 |
| 1954 | 170 | 102 |
| 1955 | 186 | 109 |
| 1956 | 170 | 91 |
| 1957 | 196 | 116 |
| 1958 | 217 | 111 |
| 1959 | 238 | 110 |
| 1960 | 267 | 112 |
| 1961 | 294 | 110 |
| 1962 | 317 | 108 |
| 1963 | 339 | 107 |
| 1964 | 369 | 109 |
| 1965 | 386 | 105 |
| 1966 | 412 | 107 |

Netherlands, France, Czechoslovakia, and Austria 50 to 70 per cent higher, and in Italy, Japan, and Finland about the same. In Spain, Bulgaria, and Yugoslavia the level of per capita industrial production was not quite two-thirds that of Hungary's, and in Portugal and Rumania about one-half.

As a result of the progress which it had made, Hungary became industrially self-sufficient. During the second half of the 1960s, only 11 per cent of the industrial goods destined for final use (consumption, investment, building up stocks, or export) were imported articles. The bulk of imports were destined for investment in plant and equipment; between 1964 and 1966 one-half of all newly installed machinery was imported. Of the industrial consumer articles reaching the population, however, only 8–10 per cent were imported, well behind the international average. On the other hand, 85–90 per cent of Hungarian exports were industrial goods.

As industry became the leading productive sector, the proportion of industrial wage-earners in the actively employed population rose. In 1950 the percentage of those employed in industry scarcely exceeded 19 per cent of all wage-earners (while agriculture's share was 52 per cent); but in 1967 industry employed more than 32 per cent, thus surpassing the number engaged in agriculture, which had fallen to 31 per cent of the total work force.

Industry's contribution to the national income rose from 45 per cent in 1950 to 67 per cent in 1965 (in current prices), while by the latter date agriculture was producing only 16 per cent of national income. These proportions, however, are greatly influenced by the pricing system. It is generally known how the price system until the end of the 1960s served the purpose of accumulating capital from agriculture, for investment in industry, by keeping agricultural prices low and industrial prices high (ie, by creating an agrarian price scissors). Thus statistics prepared on the basis of current prices greatly distort the real magnitudes in favour of industry. Somewhat different results emerge from calculations made by the Statistical Office and the Office of National Planning, partly on the basis of so-called cost-proportional prices (distributing accumulation in proportion to fixed capital and wage costs rather than in relation to prices), and partly by adapting world-market prices, instead of current prices in Hungary. These figures show industry responsible for about 40 per cent of national income (at present-day prices, 45 per cent), or that industry's share in generating national income grew by about one-third, while agriculture's share stands at around 30 per cent, having declined one-third, where it remains permanently behind that of industry.

The rapid advance of industry brought about important changes in the structure of industry. Striking among them was the increased concentration of production. The peculiar geographic concentration of production which was a feature of late-nineteenth-century industrial development in Hungary was not substantially modified down to the end of the 1960s: 44 per cent of those employed in industry worked in greater Budapest, and with the extractive industries excluded the proportion reached 50 per cent.

By contrast with the slight changes in regional distribution, comprehensive data point to important modifications in the degree of concentration by enterprise. In 1965 there were 25 per cent more factories than in 1942, and 20 per cent more than in 1955. Among these installations, however, it was the largest which grew faster than the average, indicating a concentration of labour and production. In 1942 47 per cent of all workers were employed in plants with fewer than 500 employees, while nearly 39 per cent were found in plants with more than 1,000 workers. By 1965, however, largely owing to continuing concentration in heavy industry, the number of workers in plants in the under-500 category had fallen to 35 per cent, while more than 45 per cent now worked in factories with over 1,000 hands. In line with the advance of concentration, the largest installations came to dispose of by far the largest share of plant and equipment: between 1942 and 1965 the share of the lowest category of factories in the horsepower capacity of industry fell from 66 to 22 per cent, while that of installations in the highest category rose from 27 to 51 per cent.

Even more important in changing the structure of industry, however, was the transformation in the inter-relationships of the various branches of industry. Industrialisation went forward with an eye to the primacy of heavy-industrial development. From 1950 to 1955 90 per cent of industrial investment went to heavy industry, which between 1961 and 1965 was still receiving 81 per cent of new investment. The extractive industries, particularly coal mining, received a notably large share of this sum. Engineering received 17 per cent of industrial investment, despite large fluctuations and a general tendency for its share to decline. From the late 1950s the chemical industry received larger and larger investments. The traditional leading industries, however—food processing, which had gradually been losing its nineteenth-century predominance but which until the war was still the country's first industry, and textiles, which rose to second place between the wars—lost their earlier primacy. Between 1950 and 1965 the food industry's share in net industrial production fell by an average of nearly 1 per cent a year, and that of textiles by nearly 4 per cent, while the share of engineering rose by an annual 2·5 per cent and that of the chemical industry by 5 per cent.

This process reflected a general world-wide trend and corresponded to changes in consumption habits: the advance of durable consumer goods in the face of a smaller-than-average rise in consumption of food and clothing, a growth in the demand for electricity and mechanical energy as a result of the international upswing in investment activity, and the rapid spread of synthetic materials. The broad character of these tendencies is shown by the fact that during these years the share of the food industry fell by 1–2 per cent per annum in the production of the European countries overall, and that of textiles by nearly 4 per cent, while the share of engineering rose by 1 per cent annually and that of the chemical industry by 3–4 per cent. The same changes broadly characterised the industry of the developing countries. In their case the decline of the food industry (nearly 3 per cent a year) and the growth of engineering (also close to 3 per cent) was greater, although the growth of the chemical industry was much smaller (0·2 per cent altogether).

For the first time in modern economic history, the structural development of Hungarian industry came to parallel the general world pattern. Despite the basically healthy tendencies of this development, however, it was not entirely free of contradictions. For the most part these sprang from its autarchic objectives and the low level of international trade, and partly from outdated methods of development in some industries, pursued without regard for long-term considerations.

Extraordinary efforts were made to develop basic industry and the production of raw materials. Meeting the demand created by forced industrialisation for the largest possible quantities of fuel and raw materials required maximum expenditures on the development of mining and metallurgy. The path of development undertaken in the 1950s determined in part the course of the 1960s too. The forced development of mining, especially coal mining, was one phenomenon that stood in contradiction to the general trend of world economic development. All over the world the number of miners declined, while in Hungary it doubled, an element of backwardness in the occupational structure reflected in the 11 per cent share of mining in overall employment (in contrast with the roughly 5 per cent share of mining in total employment in the developed countries, less in those countries having the most advanced mining industries).

The still highest share of mining in the net value of production (without turnover tax) was also disproportionately high, for in the developed countries it scarcely exceeded 6 per cent (while in the developing countries it was about one-quarter of the value of production). During the period under consideration the output of coal more than doubled, an increase often achieved (until recent years) by very antiquated methods. Hungary's coal output, 9,400,000 tons in 1938 and 13,300,000 tons in 1950, reached 22,300,000 tons in 1955 and a record of 31,500,000 tons in 1964. An excessively large part of the

TABLE 45
Coal output (1950 = 100)

| Year | Tons, millions | |
|---|---|---|
| 1950 | 13·3 | 100 |
| 1951 | 15·3 | 115 |
| 1952 | 18·6 | 140 |
| 1953 | 21·0 | 158 |
| 1954 | 21·5 | 162 |
| 1955 | 22·3 | 168 |
| 1956 | 20·6 | 155 |
| 1957 | 21·2 | 160 |
| 1958 | 24·2 | 183 |
| 1959 | 25·4 | 191 |
| 1960 | 26·5 | 200 |
| 1961 | 28·2 | 212 |
| 1962 | 28·6 | 216 |
| 1963 | 30·5 | 230 |
| 1964 | 31·5 | 238 |
| 1965 | 31·4 | 237 |
| 1966 | 30·3 | 229 |
| 1967 | 27·0 | 204 |

country's energy needs was supplied by coal. The share of coal in world energy production reached a peak of about 80 per cent before World War I, and declined steadily thereafter; during the decade of the 1930s hydrocarbons provided the source of more than 20 per cent of world power production. In

Hungary, a lag of several decades can be seen in the fact that at the end of the 1950s coal still supplied 75 per cent of power needs; the share of hydrocarbons reached 20 per cent only in the early 1960s. In its high degree of reliance on solid fuels and its decision to develop solid-fuel sources Hungary not only lagged behind the rest of the world, but also incurred some of the highest costs of production in the world because of the geology of the coal fields. Hungarian coal costs two-and-a-half times as much as the products of the country's oil refineries, working half with domestic oil and half with the imported article.

It was only in the mid-1960s that new thinking, and new tendencies toward economic co-operation among the socialist countries, brought about a change in the structure of energy production, and hence of coal mining too. By 1967 the use of coal in power generating had fallen to 58 per cent and that of hydrocarbons had risen to more than 36 per cent, a sudden reversal of fortunes. Domestic production of petroleum and natural gas developed, and new fields were discovered near Szeged, raising Hungarian oil production from 1,200,000 tons in 1960 to 1,800,000 tons in 1968; in addition, the import of oil (and gas) played a major part. In 1958 scarcely more than one-fifth of power consumption was supplied by imported fuel, but by 1967 one-third of all power came from imported energy sources. It was only in this manner that coal production could be reduced, beginning in 1965 (though by only 0·4 per cent); but in 1966 a million tons less coal was raised, a reduction of 3·5 per cent. Those mines whose costs of production were the highest were shut down, and the number of miners was reduced, relieving the entire economy of a substantial burden.

The extraction of metal-bearing ores grew much more rapidly than coal mining, yielding a ten-fold increase in output. Most important of these was bauxite mining, whose production rose two-and-a-half times to almost 1·5 million tons. Its growth was connected with one of the prime achievements of Hungarian industrialisation, the solution of the decades-old problem of developing the country's bauxite and aluminium industry. The industry's enormous demands for electrical energy could not be met, given the scarcity of electric power in the country. To be sure, the growth of power production was extremely rapid during the period of industrialisation, rising from 3 million kilowatt-hours in 1950 to 12·5 million in 1967; but this growth barely corresponded to the average increase in industrial production, whereas in most other countries power output rose significantly faster than industrial production (an average of 20 per cent faster in the socialist countries, and nearly 50 per cent faster in the developed capitalist countries). An adequate power supply was indispensable for the proper functioning of the economy. In its absence, restrictions had to be imposed on consumption, and occasionally—as in the mid-1950s, as a result of failures in the generating system—power shortages caused serious disruption of the economy. In the 1950s in particular, frequent shortages of power led to serious economic losses. In the 1960s the chronic shortage of power was overcome, but adequate energy reserves are still not available. Per capita electricity production is still lower in Hungary than in other countries at a comparable level of development. In this respect Hungary only stands ahead of Rumania, Yugoslavia, Greece, Portugal, and Spain among European countries, while many others produce twice as much power per capita or more. In this situation the development of an aluminium industry ran into persistent problems.

The need for international co-operation was obvious. As early as the postwar period of reconstruction, the Hungarian-Yugoslav bauxite and aluminium agreement of 1947 sought to initiate the joint development of the industry in those two countries. But the deterioration of relations with Yugolsavia after 1948 prevented the execution of the plan, and in the 1950s the Hungarian industry began to be developed on an autarchic basis.

The efforts toward economic integration which emerged ever more markedly in the economic policies of the socialist countries from the late 1950s promised a solution to the problems of the Hungarian aluminium industry. The notion of international co-operation repeatedly came under consideration. A Hungarian-Polish bauxite and aluminium agreement was worked out in 1958–9 and signed in 1960. Under the terms of the agreement, Hungary was to supply 80,000 tons of bauxite annually; in return, the Poles would deliver 17,500 tons of raw aluminium to Hungary, while retaining over half the bauxite for their own use. The entire transaction was carried out at world-market prices, deliveries beginning in 1965. Negotiations begun at the same time led to the Hungarian-Soviet bauxite and aluminium agreement of 1962, which called for Hungary to deliver 330,000 tons of bauxite a year when the pact became fully effective, in exchange for 165,000 tons of aluminium from the Soviet Union. These agreements made it possible for Hungary to acquire a quantity of aluminium proportional to its output of bauxite, without the need to develop its own highly costly and hence uneconomic aluminium manufacture; at the same time the country was able to develop bauxite production more rapidly and to lay foundations for the manufacture of aluminium goods. In the years after 1962 the production of semi-finished aluminium goods leapt almost nine-fold, even though really rapid development began only in the late 1960s with the expansion of the stamping and wide-strip rolling mill operations at Székesfehérvár. But even in 1965 Hungary occupied tenth place in the world with a per capita aluminium use of 5·8 kilogrammes.

Although in the case of aluminium a way was finally found to avoid high development costs, the same could not be said for metallurgy as a whole. Metallurgy was one of the most contradiction-laden areas of postwar industrial development. As a result of the industrial policies of the 1950s in particular, the number of workers in the industry rose by more than 70 per cent, and the net value of its output trebled. In iron and steel, the most important branch of the industry, the results were very imposing. Close to 27 billion forints were invested in the industry (at 1967 prices), more than 45 per cent of that sum in the construction of the Danube Iron Works (Dunai Vasmű). Between 1938 and the mid-1960s crude-iron production jumped from 300,000 tons a year to 1·5 million tons, steel production from 700,000 tons to nearly 2,700,000 (steel output increased two-and-a-half times over the 1950 level). The industry was not, however, placed on a really modern technical footing.

## Table 46
*Output of iron and steel (tons, 000s; 1950 = 100)*

| Year | Crude iron |     | Steel   |     |
|------|-----------|-----|---------|-----|
| 1950 | 461·3     | 100 | 1,048·4 | 100 |
| 1951 | 527·3     | 114 | 1,290·0 | 123 |
| 1952 | 619·6     | 134 | 1,459·4 | 139 |
| 1953 | 716·1     | 155 | 1,542·5 | 147 |
| 1954 | 842·9     | 183 | 1,491·3 | 142 |
| 1955 | 867·7     | 188 | 1,629·4 | 155 |
| 1956 | 755·2     | 164 | 1,415·5 | 135 |
| 1957 | 823·2     | 178 | 1,374·8 | 131 |
| 1958 | 1,082·2   | 235 | 1,626·8 | 155 |
| 1959 | 1,104·0   | 239 | 1,759·3 | 168 |
| 1960 | 1,246·3   | 270 | 1,886·9 | 180 |
| 1961 | 1,306·4   | 283 | 2,053·1 | 196 |
| 1962 | 1,381·5   | 299 | 2,332·5 | 222 |
| 1963 | 1,388·1   | 301 | 2,374·0 | 226 |
| 1964 | 1,494·2   | 324 | 2,364·8 | 226 |
| 1965 | 1,577·0   | 342 | 2,520·0 | 240 |
| 1966 | 1,633·0   | 354 | 2,649·0 | 253 |
| 1967 | 1,655·0   | 359 | 2,739·0 | 261 |

As a result of the development of iron and steel making, the industry came to have a larger share in overall industrial production than in the developed countries. In 1965 the metallurgical industry turned out nearly 13 per cent of Hungarian production (value of production before turnover tax), compared with a figure of 7 per cent for the advanced industrial countries. These data, of course, do not at all mean that metallurgy, or within it iron and steel, was in itself an overdeveloped branch of the economy. On the contrary, the progress made during the postwar period achieved a level of production which, in the late 1960s, was essentially in harmony with the demands of the economy; at the most, the overdevelopment of part of its capacity could be contrasted with the inadequacy of other portions. The difficulty sprang rather from the fact that development was undertaken with a reliance on the extremely scanty domestic supply of raw materials and on an insufficiently modernised technology. The decision to develop this industry, with its demands for large amounts of materials and relatively small amounts of labour, did not correspond to the facts of the Hungarian situation; it absorbed too great a proportion of the country's resources. At the same time the industry's large proportional contribution to total production itself tended to perpetuate an obsolete industrial structure, blocking the progress of more modern concepts of development. At the present time the chief element of structural backwardness in Hungarian industry, by international standards, is the extremely large share, almost 25 per cent, that mining and metallurgy has in total production.

The most encouraging feature in the structural transformation of industry was the extremely rapid growth of engineering and chemicals, a trend in keeping with world-wide patterns of industrial development. In engineering the work force more than doubled, and about 17 per cent of total industrial investment went to finance a large-scale expansion of capacity; as a result the output of the industry increased more than six-fold. There were, however, large variations in the rates of development of its various branches. The production of machinery and of articles of mass consumption grew approximately five-and-a-half times, and that of transport equipment a little more than four times; but the output of the telecommunications and vacuum-tube industry grew twelve-fold, and production of machine-tools more than seventeen-fold (figures are for net production in all instances). Thus the rapid expansion of output was accompanied by a marked change in the internal structure of the industry. In 1950 the telecommunications and vacuum-tube industry and the machine-tool industry together turned out less than 10 per cent of the output of the whole industry, but by 1966 their share had grown to 25 per cent. The manufacture of transport equipment fell from 35 to 27 per cent of the total during the same period. In 1950 production of machinery, electrical equipment, and consumer articles together made up about 56 per cent of the whole, while by 1966 their share had fallen to 48 per cent (machinery 22 per cent, electrical equipment 12 per cent, consumer manufactures 14 per cent).

These internal structural changes contributed to a healthy modernisation of the industry, for they pointed toward an industrial structure more appropriate to the natural endowments of the country, in so far as they represented the advance of labour-intensive lines in place of those which demanded large quantities of raw materials.

In many areas engineering production in Hungary is now able to satisfy the domestic demand in its entirety. Among the greatest achievements may be mentioned the development of consumer goods production; the present output of radios, television sets, washing machines, vacuum cleaners, refrigerators and the like essentially covers home requirements. Domestic production supplies more than half the heavy demand for investment equipment, although the interests of technical development require considerable imports of the most modern types of machinery. The greatest stimulus to the expansion of the industry, however, has been its export demand, which has grown nearly six-fold. During the 1960s engineering exports made up nearly half of Hungary's total industrial exports, a very high proportion even by international standards. The extraordinarily brisk export performance of Hungarian engineering, well in excess of the performance of Hungarian manufacturing at large, reflects the successful penetration of the broad markets of the socialist countries, making possible the development of modern assembly-line production and stimulating the growth of several new products. However, this success did not adequately stimulate efforts toward technical modernisation and improvement of product quality, with the result that the products of the Hungarian industry became uncompetitive in the markets of many other countries; thus barely 4–5 per cent of Hungarian exports of machinery go to the developed industrial countries. (There were of course other, primarily structural, reasons for this low figure: the export branches of the industry had been developed with a conscious eye toward meeting the needs of the socialist countries.)

During the 1950s the chemical industry progressed relatively slowly; up to 1957 it had just doubled its output, a record which lagged behind the world performance of the industry. Thereafter, however, growth was more rapid. Chemicals received only one-tenth of all industrial investment between 1950 and

1960, thereafter they received one-sixth of the total; the industry's capital assets sextupled and its labour force nearly trebled. In the 1960s its output was growing at nearly twice the world rate, raising its total production to more than nine times that of pre-1950 days.

Domestic production was able to meet two-thirds of the economy's needs for chemicals. But per capita production of synthetic fibres was only one-quarter to one-half that of the developed European countries, and output of synthetic fibres only one-seventh to one-eighth as great. Only in recent years has the development of synthetic-fibre production and of the petrochemical industry in general achieved high priority. The underdevelopment of the chemical industry by international standards also finds expression in the fact that its share of overall industrial production (before taxes) is still only 8 per cent, far behind the figure of 13–17 per cent for the developed countries.

The food industry and most branches of light industry made not inconsiderable progress, too, during the period of industrialisation, but their share in total production steadily declined. In textiles, the work force rose by 50 per cent but production was only slightly more than doubled. The leather industry trebled its labour force and nearly quadrupled its output; the paper industry trebled its work force, and increased its production three-fold; and the food industry expanded its labour force 70 per cent while raising output more than three-fold. The volume of printing was nearly trebled. But only the wood processing industry (with six-and-a-half times the output and a four-fold increase in employees) and the clothing industry (with a more than six-fold growth in production and three-and-a-half times as many workers) grew faster than the average rate of industrial development.

For many years economic policy devoted very few resources to these industries, causing serious harm not so much in the form of sluggish growth as in their technical backwardness. Most of the progress which they have made dates only from the end of the 1950s.

Apart from the growth of their quantitative output, the

internal structural modernisation of the textile, clothing, and leather industries, which began at the end of the 1950s, also played an important part in their development. In 1955 artificial fibres were still only 12 per cent of all fibres used in the textile industry, but by 1967 they represented 25 per cent, close to the international average.

Despite a rate of growth slower than the average, the food industry was able to process an ever-growing share of the domestic crop, thanks to the even slower increase in agricultural production. In 1938 the food industry was responsible for scarcely more than one-fifth of the value of total food production (ie, agricultural production and food-industry output together). By 1960, however, this figure had risen to 40 per cent, and by 1967 it was close to 50 per cent. In contrast to the slow progress of the traditional leading branches of the food industry (brewing and sugar refining scarcely doubled their output, and milling did not even attain that level), modern processing lines developed rapidly, one of the most important signs of the modernisation of the industry. The food-preserving industry, in which several new lines emerged, had increased its output four-fold even by 1960, and as a result of exceptionally rapid growth in the succeeding years was turning out about nine times its 1950 production by the late 1960s. At the end of the 1950s the food industry, besides supplying the domestic market, was exporting nearly one-fifth of its production; by 1967 this figure had risen to nearly one-fourth. Foodstuffs were a considerable part of total exports.

Thus a substantial transformation took place in the internal structure of Hungarian industry. The share of the food industry in total production had fallen from 29 per cent prewar to 19 per cent by 1965, and that of textiles from over 14 to 7 per cent (for purposes of comparison, gross value of production is used); meanwhile the share of engineering rose from 9 to 25 per cent. Other industries do not display changes of comparable magnitude.

It is a general characteristic of nations whose development has come late, however, that the structure of their industry and economy soon displays features typical of the developed coun-

TABLE 47

*Structure of industry based on total output at 1965 prices* (%)

| | | |
|---|---|---|
| Mining | 6·0 | |
| Electrical energy | 4·3 | |
| Metallurgy | 12·7 | |
| Engineering | 25·3 | |
| Chemicals | 8·9 | |
| Building materials | 3·6 | |
| Heavy industry total | | 60·8 |
| Wood | 3·3 | |
| Paper | 0·9 | |
| Printing | 0·7 | |
| Textiles | 7·1 | |
| Leather | 2·4 | |
| Clothing | 3·0 | |
| Others | 3·0 | |
| Light industry total | | 20·4 |
| Food | | 18·8 |
| Total | | 100·0 |

tries. Level of output per head, techniques, and quality of product catch up more slowly. Distinct contradictions appear between the structural characteristics of their industry and economy on the one hand, and their substantive content on the other. In Hungary the degree of development of the industrial structure of course surpasses the actual state of industrial development. The degree of concentration is much higher than the real level of large-scale industrial production; thus concentration is not accompanied by a correspondingly high level of industrial organisation or the kind of productivity characteristic of large-scale industry. The share of engineering in total production and in exports has attained the level of the advanced industrial countries without the Hungarian industry's being able to compete with them in its products or in its costs of production. A large volume of production often leads to products of inferior quality.

On the basis of this survey of economic strategy it is evident that, in ways not demonstrable through comprehensive indices, technical development during the period of forced industrialisation lagged behind quantitative growth of production and structural reorganisation. The historic change represented by industrialisation was achieved primarily through the use of resources of an extensive character latent in the economy, which could be mobilised to the utmost by the economic strategy employed. The principal source of growth was the infusion into the economy of large amounts of manpower and capital. While employment rose by an average 5·5 per cent a year, the average rate of growth of output per employee was 4 per cent (3·1 per cent in the 1950s, 5·3 per cent in the 1960s). On average, gross industrial production per worker doubled. Thus Hungary was among the countries in which that portion of growth in industrial output attributable to increased productivity was lowest. The extraordinarily low level of productivity is indicated by the fact that in the decade 1958–68 (no reliable figures exist for earlier years) output per unit of productive fixed capital did not rise, but actually declined.

In terms of industrial productivity, then, the relative backwardness of the country grew despite its enormous increase in output. The low level of productivity is shown by the fact that while Hungary was seventh among thirty-five countries in percentage of the population employed in industry, it ranked only twenty-second in net industrial production per capita. In the mid-1960s the productivity level of the Western European countries was generally twice that of Hungary.

The difference was due partly to the generally low efficiency of capital investments, but for the most part to the low, sometimes stagnant or even declining level of technology in industry. The effectiveness of investments was further reduced by the fact that far too long a time often elapsed between investment decision and the actual commissioning of new plant. To begin with, this was because too many investment projects were begun at one time; but the problem persisted throughout the whole period because of inadequate capacity in the construction industry. New plant was often put into service with a delay of from two to four years. It more than once happened that a project considered up-to-date at the time the investment decision was made had become obsolete by the time it went into operation. Much more common and more important, however, was the allocation of too few resources to investments in machinery as a result of the excessive amounts absorbed by the building industry. Often newly installed equipment did not represent the most modern level of technology, and sometimes, as a result of the imperatives of forced industrialisation, necessary replacements of machinery were only partly carried out.

## AGRICULTURE

Amid the historic changes taking place in productive relations in agriculture, and as a result of the strategy which came to prevail in economic development, drawing largely on capital accumulation in agriculture for the resources needed to industrialise, there remained for a long time only few resources left to further agricultural progress. At the same time large numbers were leaving the villages. Thus the growth rate of agriculture could only be very slow and could not possibly keep pace with that of industry.

Even the initial position of agriculture was unfavourable. At the end of the 1940s its productive level, unlike that of industry, had not yet recovered to the prewar level. Stock-raising had almost completely recovered by 1950, but crop production was still down nearly one-fifth, and for that reason gross agricultural output was still 10 per cent lower than before the war. In the first half of the 1950s stockbreeding suffered a serious setback as a result of the economic policies then in force, so that by 1953 the value of its production was 20 per cent lower than in 1950, and even in 1956 output did not much exceed 1950's figure. Crop production was subject to wide fluctuations. Depending on weather conditions, the harvest might exceed the previous year's by one-third (as in 1951) or one-half (as in 1953), or it might be 40 per cent lower (1952) or 20 per cent lower (1956); but overall production stagnated. Thus until 1956 gross agricultural output remained essentially unchanged, exceeding the 1950 level in occasional good years, hovering around or below it in others.

Until the middle 1950s, then, agricultural production did not surpass the level of the last prewar years. Thereafter, thanks to changes in agricultural policy and the stimulating effects of industrialisation, the tempo of agricultural development accelerated markedly. The broad fluctuations were largely ironed out, and after 1961 no serious decline in output took place again. After 1957 the rate of growth was smoother, exceeding 2 per cent per annum, a figure comparable with the average international rate of agricultural development.

Because of the uneven record of the decades following the liberation in 1945, the rate of growth of the period as a whole was only modest: the average annual production of the years 1962–6, compared with the annual average for the years 1934–8, represented a rate of growth of 0·7 per cent. Gross agricultural production in the mid-1960s was 30–40 per cent higher than the 1949–50 level, and roughly one-quarter to one-

TABLE 48

*Gross output of agriculture (excluding forestry and services, at 1959 prices)*

| Year | Million Forint | 1950 = 100 | Previous year = 100 |
|---|---|---|---|
| 1950 | 48,992 | 100·0 | — |
| 1951 | 57,433 | 117·2 | 117·2 |
| 1952 | 42,159 | 86·1 | 73·4 |
| 1953 | 51,534 | 105·2 | 122·2 |
| 1954 | 51,415 | 104·9 | 99·8 |
| 1955 | 57,730 | 117·8 | 112·3 |
| 1956 | 50,030 | 102·1 | 86·7 |
| 1957 | 57,196 | 116·7 | 114·3 |
| 1958 | 60,130 | 122·7 | 105·1 |
| 1959 | 53,062 | 128·7 | 104·9 |
| 1960 | 58,846 | 120·1 | 93·3 |
| 1961 | 59,100 | 120·6 | 100·4 |
| 1962 | 60,255 | 123·0 | 120·3 |
| 1963 | 63,541 | 129·7 | 105·5 |
| 1964 | 67,193 | 137·2 | 105·7 |
| 1965 | 63,557 | 129·7 | 94·6 |
| 1966 | 68,837 | 140·5 | 108·3 |

third more than the volume of prewar agricultural output. Thus the results achieved in Hungarian agricultural development from the end of the 1950s were far from sufficient to compensate for the deterioration of the war years and the stagnation of the 1950s.

Thus the pace of agricultural development in Hungary and the increase in the volume of production attained by the middle of the 1960s—even if somewhat greater than during the prewar quarter-century—were far from sufficient to break out of the agricultural stagnation of the interwar years or to overcome the country's earlier backwardness. On the contrary, the gap between Hungary and the other food-growing and food-exporting countries of Europe and North America widened.

It is not enough, however, in evaluating the achievements of Hungarian agricultural development, to deal with the rate of growth in production and the expanded volume of output alone. Modest results in output went together with a significant transformation of agricultural production and a rising level of cultivation. One of the major factors of change, characteristic of the entire period, was the reduction in the amount of land under cultivation and the mass migration, already described, from country to city. In 1967 there was over 8 per cent less land under cultivation than before the war (17 million acres as against about 18½ million); about 840,000 acres of the difference had been forested, the rest left fallow or used for industrial installations, roads, and the like. At the same time the rural population, virtually stable (as a proportion of the total population) for half a century, began to leave the villages; the active agricultural population dropped by a third, or more than 600,000 people. Thus in agriculture a situation developed which was the exact opposite of that in industry. Production did not grow primarily as a consequence of the application of more manpower; on the contrary, the increase in production—a modest one, to be sure—was achieved in spite of the fact that simultaneously large numbers of the rural population were freed for other tasks. Thus the sole source of growth was rising productivity. Between 1950 and 1965 the gross value of production per worker in agriculture more than doubled, while the gross value of production per acre of farmland increased more than one-and-a-half times.

Among the factors which contributed to a rise in productivity was the fact that disguised unemployment had always been widespread in the Hungarian countryside; the migration of this surplus manpower to the cities in itself helped to raise productivity markedly. Despite the large drop in manpower it is still impossible to employ 15 per cent of the workers in agriculture for more than a few months of the year, at the peak periods in spring and harvest; only 55 per cent of the agricultural work force is employed the whole year round in farming. The chief factors of progress, however, were still the rapid advance of mechanisation, the intensification of production, and a large increase in yields.

The rapid mechanisation of agriculture was indispensable, of course, to replace the manpower which had migrated to the cities, but it was also a natural concomitant of the reorganisation of individual peasant farming into a system of large-scale enterprises. The tempo of mechanisation, with its slow start at the beginning of the 1950s and acceleration from the end of the decade, is suggested by the figures showing the growing number of tractors in use. Between 1949 and 1952 there were on average 13,300 tractors in operation in Hungary, but by 1956 their number had risen to 25,000, and by 1967 to almost 67,000.

During the period of collectivisation the ploughing and cultivation of the soil were mechanised. At the same time another operation demanding heavy physical labour, the grain harvest, also came to be mechanised. Mechanical reapers and threshers made their appearance in Hungary in 1949, and by 1955 numbered more than 2,200; in 1960 there were nearly 4,200 of them, and by 1967 more than 9,800. The use of nearly 5,000 tractor-drawn reapers permitted 92 per cent of the grain crop to be harvested mechanically during the late 1960s, as against 43 per cent in 1960.

In Hungarian agriculture before the war—and indeed from the end of the nineteenth century—only one operation, threshing, had been mechanised. Thus the virtually complete mechanisation of ploughing and grain harvesting was one of the major achievements of postwar development.

The mechanisation of other, more complex operations has not yet been completed, though considerable progress has been made in several areas since collectivisation was begun. The mechanisation of planting is nearly complete: between 1960 and 1968 the percentage of land sown by machine doubled, to over 80 per cent. In 1968 66 per cent of the sugar-beet harvest was harvested mechanically as against 36 per cent in 1960, and the proportion of potatoes picked by machine rose from 12 to 23 per cent between 1960 and 1968. Much hoeing has been mechanised: the amount of land under root crops which is now cultivated by machine has almost doubled. Progress in mechanising other operations, such as corn-cutting and shucking, siloing, milking, and the like, has been considerable, but the level of development attained is still very low.

For raising yields, however, investments designed to intensify production have been much more important. Here the improvement of the soil, primarily through the application of artificial fertilisers, played a special role. Before the war the use of artificial manures was extremely limited in Hungary, and even in 1949 the average was only about 8·5 kilogrammes per acre per annum. Between 1950 and 1954 the average per acre was raised to 18 kilos, to 58 by 1960, and to over 185 in 1966.

The increase in the use of fertilisers, extraordinarily rapid in itself, was still rather slow by international standards, at least until the middle of the 1960s; and the relative gap between Hungary and the developed countries in the use of artificial fertilisers actually grew. The tendency for Hungary to fall ever farther behind the advanced countries in this respect was arrested only in the second half of the 1960s, when an unprecedented increase in the use of fertilisers set in: within two years it rose 60 per cent, to a figure of 250 kilogrammes per acre by 1968 (active ingredients only).

Thanks to these and other factors (irrigation, improvement of plant strains, pest control) average yields of the main crops rose at an unprecedented rate. The average annual yields of wheat, barley, maize and sugar beet between 1963 and 1967 were about 50 per cent higher than the average of the last five prewar years. For other crops the increase was small, and indeed the average yield of some (oats, tobacco, alfalfa) actually declined. Nothing illustrates the growth in yields better than a comparison with the preceding half-century. Between 1891 and 1895 the average yield per acre was only 7·5 quintals of grain; more than a half-century later, between 1946 and 1950, it was still only 7·8. During the next decade and a half, however, it jumped to 13. But even so, the rapid increase in yields was not enough to catch up with international standards; on the contrary, because of the rapidity of world agricultural development Hungary's place in the international rankings did not change even for those products where her progress was greatest.

Another important factor in the modernisation of agriculture was the beginning of efforts to transform the traditional, extensive system of cultivation. One step in this direction was the change in the internal structure of crop production in favour of more labour-intensive, higher-priced crops, suitable for further processing. Before the war, for example, bread grains represented 26 per cent of the value of crop production, but by 1966 only 18 per cent, while the share of maize rose from 17 to 24 per cent. The value of all row crops rose from 27 to 40 per cent.

These changes were accompanied, however, by a gradual decline in the role of field crops as a whole. Their share in the gross value of crop production was only 75 per cent in 1966, as against 83 per cent in 1938. By contrast, the share of market-garden, orchard, and vineyard production rose from 12 to 22 per cent.

The most decisive factor in making agricultural production more intensive, however, has been the growth in the importance of stockbreeding. A characteristic feature of postwar Hungary has been the marked difference between the tempo of growth in stock-raising and in crop production: between 1938 and 1967 the overall rate of growth of crop production was 0·6 per cent a year, while for stock-raising it was 1·8 per cent. Since the late 1950s the value of production from stockbreeding has risen at an annual rate of 3·4 per cent. Thus while crop production represented 63 per cent of the value of Hungarian agricultural output before the war, by the years 1965–7 its preponderance had fallen to a less pronounced 58 per cent.

The number of farm animals rose, largely through increases in the stock of pigs and poultry. In 1968 6·6 million pigs were being raised, against an average of 3·5 million during the years 1934–8, and 28·9 million domestic fowl, against 17·6 million. The stock of sheep also grew with notable rapidity (from 1·4 million to 3·3 million). Cattle herds showed the slowest progress, increasing from 1·8 million head to 2·1 million. The number of milk cows fell, however, from 900,000 to less than 800,000. Agricultural productivity rose somewhat faster than the volume of production (contrary to the case in industry); but even so the average annual increase, from the last prewar years to the end of the 1960s, was only 0·8 per cent (well below the average rate of 1·5–2 per cent per annum for the socialist countries). Internationally such a rate of growth in agricultural productivity counted as very low, for it was during this period that the advanced countries succeeded in 'turning agriculture into an industry': the rise in productivity was conspicuously rapid even in Western Europe, traditionally the home of intensive cultivation, achieving comparison with increases in industrial productivity.

### SERVICES AND THE INFRASTRUCTURE

Investments in infrastructure and services were about one-third of total investment in the first half of the 1950s, rising to about one-half in the second half of the decade; in the first half of the 1960s they were set somewhat lower, at 44 per cent. By and large the Hungarian figures were comparable with those for the other socialist countries or even somewhat better, for in most of those nations investment in infrastructure and services was under 40 per cent in the 1960s, and in some (Bulgaria, Rumania) it was only 25·30 per cent. In the advanced countries, however, it was around two-thirds of total investment.

In Hungary the effectiveness of this already rather low level of investment was further jeopardised by unusually violent swings in the amounts allocated. The fluctuations characteristic of investment activity in general were even more marked in the case of infrastructural investments. Investment in transport varied from 6 to 18 per cent of total investment, for example, investment in residential construction from 11 to 25 per cent. These fluctuations caused frequent and often harmful alternations of expansion and contraction in the industries affected.

As a result, social overhead capital grew much more modestly

(71 per cent) than that of manufacturing and mining (127 per cent). The trend of development over our entire period, moreover, was unfavourable to the former. In 1960 the growth in the capital assets of the infrastructural and service industries since 1953 was over two-thirds of that in the goods-producing industries, but in 1966 the increase over 1960 was only a little more than half the rise in the capital stock of the latter.

The labour force in the infrastructural and service occupations also grew slowly, so that in 1967 as in 1950 the same 16·17 per cent of the total work force was employed in those occupations.

As a result of all these factors, the net value of services grew more slowly than national income, declining slightly from the 10 per cent figure of 1960.

The sluggish development of this sector became particularly evident in transport. In this area no effort to modernise was made for a long while. The rapid development of the economy naturally placed increased demands on the transport system: between 1950 and 1967 the number of passenger-miles logged increased three-fold times, and the number of ton-miles of goods carried nearly quadrupled. To handle this increased demand the carrying capacity of the transport system had, of course, to be expanded. Relatively large investment efforts were made in the 1960s, so that investments in transport were finally doubled. Even this increase, however, is still far less than the 25 per cent of investment in the production industries. For these reasons the structure of transport is antiquated; railways are still the predominant carriers of domestic freight traffic.

The modernisation of the transport system began only in 1963-4. On the railways significant progress was made in overhauling rolling stock and accelerating the introduction of diesels; by the late 1960s diesel or electric locomotives provided over half of rail traction, as against only 10 per cent in 1950. Only a beginning was made, however, in modernising railway roadbeds.

More important changes took place in highway transport. As a result of works undertaken primarily in the 1960s, the proportion of paved roads quadrupled, until half the highway system was paved. The average width of road surface was increased from 3·8 to 4·7 metres. The number of motor vehicles grew rapidly, passenger cars eleven-fold, buses seven-fold, and trucks ten-fold; but one-quarter of all motor vehicles are more than nine years old. As a result, a quickening in the development of the transport structure was evident by 1967: at that date railways were carrying only 72 per cent of domestic freight (in 1950: 92 per cent), while road transport's share had risen to 24 per cent (in passenger transport the proportions were 57 and 42 per cent respectively).

All the various transport indices demonstrate that in its development the transport system lags significantly behind the general economic level of the country. The number of passenger cars, for example, is only half what one would expect on the basis of the international ratio between per capita national income and number of cars. The proportion of national income allocated to road building and maintenance is little more than half the proportion used for those purposes in Europe generally.

#### FOREIGN TRADE

The import needs of the Hungarian economy grew by leaps and bounds during the decades of industrialisation. More and more raw materials and capital goods were needed, and these could be secured only by a corresponding increase in exports. Imports and exports thus became an important factor in economic growth, sometimes lending it new impetus, but at the same time setting limits to its potential.

The demands of industrialisation for increased investments in machinery and equipment could to a large degree be met only through imports. Between 1950 and 1956 imports of these articles jumped six-fold. At the same time, keeping a constantly expanding productive capacity in operation, given the country's shortage of natural resources, required a large-scale increase in imports of raw materials and semi-processed goods. Imports of these commodities rose more than three-fold. The value of all imports multiplied about five-fold.

Only a corresponding quantity of exports could cover the

cost of these enormously increased imports. In earlier decades foodstuffs and other agricultural products had formed the traditional leading category of Hungarian exports. Until the end of the 1950s, however, the slow growth of agricultural production and a simultaneous marked rise in domestic consumption hindered the growth of agricultural exports, preventing them from regaining the prewar level. That level was reached in 1959–60, and its attainment was followed by a pronounced increase. Between 1950 and 1958 agricultural exports had stagnated, but by 1966 they had risen two-and-a-half times and had come to exceed the prewar figure by 75 per cent. This, however, was still far from enough to cover the cost of imports. For that purpose the products of the most dynamically growing industries were needed. During this period the export of consumer articles, semi-processed goods, and raw materials increased five-and-a-half times, and that of machinery and equipment six-and-a-half times. Total exports rose nearly five-fold.

TABLE 49

*Foreign trade*

| Year | Imports | Exports | Total | Imports | Exports | Total |
|------|---------|---------|-------|---------|---------|-------|
|      | *(million Forint)* | | | 1950 = 100 | | |
| 1950 | 3,706·4 | 3,857·0 | 7,563·4 | 100 | 100 | 100 |
| 1955 | 6,506·5 | 7,055·4 | 13,561·9 | 176 | 183 | 179 |
| 1960 | 11,455·4 | 10,259·8 | 21,715·2 | 309 | 266 | 287 |
| 1965 | 17,848·5 | 17,721·3 | 35,569·8 | 482 | 460 | 470 |
| 1966 | 18,378·5 | 18,705·1 | 37,083·6 | 496 | 485 | 490 |

The rate of growth of foreign trade thus significantly exceeded the rate of growth in production and national income. For every 1 per cent rise in national income there was a 1·25 per cent increase in foreign trade in the early 1950s, and a 1·84 per cent increase in the 1960s. These data reflect the differences between the two periods of development, in particular the significant expansion of international economic ties during the 1960s.

The sensitivity of the Hungarian economy to foreign trade, its so-called open character, which had grown up between the wars, was now markedly enhanced. In 1959 imports and exports amounted to about 25 per cent of national income, in 1967 to about 40 per cent. The economic importance of foreign trade grew in keeping with the geographical character of the country, its resources and products, and in its magnitude largely came to resemble the place of foreign trade in the economic structure of the developed European countries having a territory or population comparable with Hungary's.

As an examination of the divergent rates of growth of the main import and export items indicates, this greatly increased foreign commerce went hand in hand with changes in the structure of the trade. In imports, the proportions of the chief categories of goods in total imports do not show radical changes. Before the war about 30 per cent of imports were finished industrial goods (machinery and industrial consumer goods), while 62 per cent were raw materials and semi-finished goods, and 8 per cent foodstuffs and other agricultural products. Up to 1967 the proportion of industrial finished goods in imports rose sharply to 37 per cent, as a result of large imports of machinery (27 per cent) and imports of industrial consumer goods (6 per cent). Since agricultural imports remained about the same, the share of raw materials and semi-finished goods fell to 56 per cent.

These structural changes reflect worldwide trends in foreign trade, in particular the rapidly growing role of industrial finished goods on the world market as a result of the scientific and technical revolution of the 1950s and 1960s. Trade in machinery and equipment rose from one-sixth to one-fourth of the total on the world market, and the share of raw materials and foodstuffs fell as a result of more intensive production and changes in consumption habits (from 55–57 per cent of world trade at the beginning of the 1950s to 45–47 per cent).

Much more radical changes are apparent from the data reflecting the shifting structure of exports. Before the war foodstuffs and other agricultural products made up about 60 per cent of Hungarian exports; finished industrial goods amounted altogether to about 13 per cent. The most important effect on exports of the transformation of the economy was a precipitous decline in the share of foodstuffs and agricultural products, to

20–25 per cent in the late 1960s. Since the share of raw materials and semi-finished goods remained relatively stable, the most important export articles were now machinery (27–33 per cent) and manufactures (22–24 per cent). Thus manufacturing's share of total industrial exports now slightly exceeded 50 per cent. Even the reduced agricultural exports themselves had acquired more of an 'industrial' character, since before the war two-thirds of agricultural exports were raw produce, while by the mid-1960s much more than two-thirds of these exports consisted of processed commodities. The data showing the distribution of exports reveal a genuine turning-point. Hungary's character of a backward country supplying raw materials and foodstuffs completely vanished, and in its place an export structure appeared comparable with that of the advanced industrial countries.

It is true of the structure of exports to a pronounced degree, however, that countries whose development has begun late reach the level of the advanced countries sooner in their structural characteristics than in the substantive content of those structures. Hungary's export structure was of course considerably more advanced than the economy as a whole. Its transformation was due largely to the fact that the trade of the socialist countries, cut off from world markets and thrown back on trading among themselves under a system of mandatory planning targets, bore all the marks of a barter economy: a strict bilateral exchange of goods in quantities determined in advance for each commodity. Under these conditions of direct international exchange of goods the quality and technical characteristics of the product, and its costs of production, played hardly any part; the market could not measure the level of marketability so as to render inferior goods uncompetitive and unsaleable. Under these hothouse conditions an export structure developed which was not at all in line with the qualitative level of production. In those markets where this kind of protection did not exist—the markets of the capitalist world—Hungary's export structure had to adjust itself according to the calibre of products, and here the structure of exports developed in quite a different way.

Agricultural commodities still form over half of Hungarian exports to the West, and a large part of these are still in unprocessed form. In 1967 cattle on the hoof and animal products formed two-thirds of Hungary's exports to the capitalist countries. Half of total beef production was exported, either dressed or on the hoof, and this item alone accounted for one-sixth of all exports to the West. At the same time the export of machinery, which played a dominant role in Hungary's trade otherwise, made up only 10 per cent of exports to the capitalist countries, a percentage that was no greater during the 1960s than at the beginning of the 1950s. Moreover, the bulk of machinery exports are purchased by the developing countries, for machinery and equipment sold to the advanced industrial countries account for only 4 per cent of Hungarian exports bought in the markets of the developed world.

Everything that has been said until now about the development of Hungarian foreign trade clearly indicates how fundamental a change took place in its distribution by region. Between the two world wars the traditional economic links connecting the countries of Central and Eastern Europe were broken, reducing their trade with one another to a mere 10–13 per cent of their total external commerce. After 1945, as a result of the fundamental political and economic changes which took place in the wake of the war, there was a turn for the better; in 1949 trade with the CEMA countries was about one-half of Hungary's foreign commerce. At the beginning of the 1950s, owing to the effects of international political events, the planning system, and other factors, the wheel had come full circle: between 1950 and 1955 two-thirds of Hungary's foreign trade was carried on within the framework of the Council of Economic Mutual Assistance. During our period, then, imports from the socialist countries grew more than five times, imports from the capitalist countries only a little more than three times. Exports to the socialist countries likewise increased nearly fivefold, while exports to the capitalist countries rose not quite four-fold. Thus the proportions which developed in the early 1950s displayed only minor fluctuations in later years, generally in the direction of a slight further decline in trade with capitalist partners. Throughout the 1960s trade with the socialist countries was in the neighbourhood of 67–70 per cent of all Hungarian foreign commerce. Thus trade with the capitalist world sank to around one-third of Hungary's total foreign trade right at the beginning of the era of socialist development and very largely remained at that level throughout.

RATE OF GROWTH: CHANGES IN ECONOMIC STRUCTURE
AND LEVEL OF DEVELOPMENT

During the decades of socialist economic development Hungary underwent exceptionally rapid economic growth. These years brought with them the most dynamic period in the entire modern economic history of the country. The country's economic structure was thoroughly transformed, bringing about a fundamental change in the level of economic development.

TABLE 50

*Annual changes in national income (%)*

| | |
|---|---|
| 1951 | 16 |
| 1952 | − 2 |
| 1953 | 12 |
| 1954 | − 4 |
| 1955 | 8 |
| 1956 | −11 |
| 1957 | 23 |
| 1958 | 6 |
| 1959 | 6 |
| 1960 | 10 |
| 1961 | 6 |
| 1962 | 5 |
| 1963 | 6 |
| 1964 | 5 |
| 1965 | 1 |
| 1966 | 8 |
| 1967 | 9 |

Until the end of the 1950s the rise of national income was marked by rather broad fluctuations. Thereafter its growth became steadier and more balanced.

Alternating stretches of rapid development and relative stability, interspersed with periods of sudden advance, stagnation, or decline, led in the last analysis to a rapid rate of growth of the economy. Between 1950 and 1967 national income rose two-and-a-half times, from 80 to 200 billion forints; in the light of a 10 per cent increase in population, per capita national income rose 2·3 times, at an average annual rate of 5·1 per cent. At world-market prices, the annual rate of growth was about 4 per cent, mainly as a consequence of the large share of agriculture, which developed more slowly, in Hungarian national income.

TABLE 51

*National income (1959 prices)*

| Year | Thousand million Forint | 1950 = 100 | Previous year = 100 |
|---|---|---|---|
| 1950 | 78·8 | 100 | — |
| 1951 | 91·8 | 116 | 116·0 |
| 1952 | 89·6 | 114 | 97·6 |
| 1953 | 100·7 | 128 | 112·4 |
| 1954 | 96·2 | 122 | 95·5 |
| 1955 | 104·2 | 132 | 108·3 |
| 1956 | 92·4 | 117 | 88·7 |
| 1957 | 113·4 | 144 | 122·7 |
| 1958 | 119·6 | 152 | 105·5 |
| 1959 | 127·3 | 162 | 106·4 |
| 1960 | 139·5 | 177 | 109·6 |
| 1961 | 148·1 | 188 | 106·2 |
| 1962 | 155·1 | 197 | 104·7 |
| 1963 | 163·9 | 208 | 105·7 |
| 1964 | 171·7 | 218 | 104·8 |
| 1965 | 173·7 | 220 | 101·2 |
| 1966 | 188·2 | 239 | 108·4 |

Thus Hungary's economic growth speeded up immensely in the era of socialist economic development, becoming incomparably more rapid than in any previous epoch. With respect to rate of growth Hungary was one of the most slowly developing countries in the world between the two world wars, while in the postwar period it stepped into the ranks of the fastest-growing countries. A more rapid tempo of development was attained only in the socialist countries overall (an average of nearly 7 per cent growth per annum in national income), Japan (7·4 per cent), and the German Federal Republic (5·5 per cent), while Italy and the Common Market countries generally achieved comparable rates (4·9 and 4·5, respectively).

A rapid rate of growth, based on the pre-eminence of industrial development, transformed the structure of the economy. The role of industry, as has been seen, expanded significantly. It came to employ nearly one-third of all wage-earners, in place of the earlier one-fifth, while the agricultural population fell from over half the whole to less than one-third. At the same time industry took first place in the generation of national income; its share grew by one-third, so that industry is now responsible for 40–5 per cent of national income. Agriculture's contribution, by comparison, fell by one-quarter to one-third, and now amounts to only about 30 per cent of national income.

Thus Hungary, once underdeveloped and reliant to a great extent on foreign capital, was able to keep pace with an unusually rapid international rate of growth in the postwar decades, essentially through exploitation of its domestic resources alone, and even to surpass the average world rate of development. Through a substantial modernisation of her economic structure, it was able to reduce the degree of underdevelopment which had characterised it earlier.

On the basis of per capita national income, the most comprehensive index for comparing economic development internationally, we can determine Hungary's ranking in terms of development, and the changes that have taken place in the last three decades. For purposes of a better comparison we have taken, instead of official national-income figures, calculations based on 24 natural indicators, which adjust for national differences in price systems and methods of calculation, revising the official figures by an average of 10–12 per cent. In 1937 average per capita national income in Hungary (in 1960 dollars) was $244, in 1965 $500. The earlier figure was equal to 47 per cent of the prewar per capita national income of the Common Market countries before 1973, while the latter was 52 per cent of per capita national income in those countries in 1965. Before the war the Hungarian figure was 95 per cent of that for the more backward European capitalist countries (Greece, Spain, Portugal), but in 1965 it exceeded theirs by nearly 30 per cent. Overall, the Hungarian level of national income rose from 46 to 53 per cent of that of the European capitalist countries. Thus the scissors which opened wide between the two world wars have begun to close, if slowly, and the progress which has been made in comparison with capitalist countries on a comparable level of development is especially noteworthy.

# 4 Social consequences of economic development

The profound political and economic transformation which took place in Hungary in the postwar years was accompanied by radical social changes. The collapse or destruction of the old state apparatus following the liberation, the parcelling of the great estates, the expropriation of capital, the collectivisation of agriculture and the organisation of small urban producers into co-operatives, the restriction of the private sector to a narrow sphere—all these measures, accompanied by the emergence of a new political and economic leadership from the ranks of the working class and peasantry in the quarter-century following the triumph of the dictatorship of the proletariat, completely transformed the structure and character of Hungarian society.

Between 1945 and 1953 the former Hungarian ruling classes, together with various groups of their hangers-on and certain petty-bourgeois strata, lost their earlier position in the social hierarchy. This was a social movement of broad dimensions: approximately 350,000 to 400,000 families lost their former position and were obliged to seek a new place in society.

At the same time, however, an opposite social movement set in. Fresh elements from the working class and peasantry rose in large numbers to fill leadership positions at various levels of government and the economy, and many blue-collar workers moved into white-collar occupations. Taking together the changes of the immediately preceding years, the members of these 'rising' groups must have numbered, with their dependents, almost a million people. By the beginning of the 1960s only 15 per cent of those in professional and managerial posts came from professional or managerial families, while 40 per cent were from workers' families and 26 per cent from peasant families.

The characteristic features of the old proletariat were transformed. The mass influx of workers into positions of leadership in itself indicates the process of change. The picture is more complete if one considers that this process was not restricted merely to a certain number of changes of occupation, but also removed the barriers previously existing to the advancement of workers' children. The extent of the change is shown by the fact that in the early 1960s over 44 per cent of secondary students, and 33 per cent of all university students, were children of industrial workers' families.

Thus the position of the working class in society had undergone a fundamental change. Historic shifts in the internal structure of the proletariat were also discernible. Among the characteristic structural features of the old working class was the fact that even after World War I half its members were farm labourers (the proportion was still more than one-third during the World War II boom years), while about 10 per cent were domestic servants; and of the workers in industry—scarcely more than one-third of the total—close to half worked in small craft workshops.

Among the most decisive aspects of the transformation of the proletariat was the virtually complete disappearance of the farm labourer. At the beginning of the 1950s there were only about 200,000 workers and other employees in agriculture, compared with nearly 800,000 in state-owned industry; thus their number had dropped to only about one-fifth of the total of wage-earners in industry and agriculture. By the mid-1960s their proportion had fallen further, to one-sixth. Domestic servants had virtually disappeared. Within the working class the ranks of industrial workers had swollen; they were now 60 per cent of all workers.

The modernisation of the social structure found expression in a rapid rise in the number of workers, and in changes in their distribution throughout the industrial structure as well. Between 1950 and 1963 the number of workers and other employees in manufacturing and construction nearly doubled, from 1,057,000 to 1,963,000. As a result of the expansion of employment in transport, exchange, and other activities the proportion of the wage-earning population employed in outside agriculture rose from 45 to 70 per cent.

This tremendous increase in the numbers and social weight of the working class was only possible, of course, because of the vast influx of people into the ranks of the working class, perhaps the single most important phenomenon among all the social movements of the era of industrialisation. During this period (and allowing for normal replacement of those leaving the work force) not quite half the new recruits to the industrial labour force came from the working class itself—mostly from the younger generation, but partly from the ranks of women who had not worked before, and about 10–15 per cent from among former small craftsmen—while more than half came from other social strata. The influx from the peasantry was especially large, of course, while former self-employed persons, white-collar workers, and other elements made up the remaining one-fifth. The incorporation of these elements, of course, greatly swelled the ranks of the young Hungarian working class. Half the workers of the 1960s came from peasant families.

This large internal migration in itself suggests the transformation in the position of the peasant in Hungarian society and the far-reaching changes which took place among the peasantry. The two characteristic groupings of the prewar Hungarian village—the well-to-do peasant on one side and the masses of farm labourers on the other (39 per cent of those engaged in agriculture were landless labourers or farm servants)—disappeared during our period. The former were restricted in their scope, the latter received land as a result of the 1945 land reform (at which time only 13 per cent of those engaged in agriculture were left landless); presently nearly all became members of co-operatives or found work in industry, often changing their status several times before eventually finding a new place in society.

The small peasant producer, too, went through enormous changes. First his numbers were greatly increased by the hundreds of thousands of those who had newly received land.

The proportion of individual proprietors shrank from 90 per cent to less than 5 per cent.

Side by side with this historic transformation went a growth in social mobility and the vanishing of the traditional isolation of the peasantry. Many men and women of peasant background made their way into leading positions in state and economy. The rapid increase in opportunities is shown by the fact that while before the war scarcely more than 1 per cent of secondary students, and only 1·5 per cent of university students, were children of poor peasants or farm servants, three decades later 17 per cent of secondary students, and 11 per cent of university students, came from peasant families. The most common form of mobility, of course, was from the peasantry into the working class.

Under the impact of economic growth and social transformation profound changes took place in the circumstances and consumption habits of the population, lending impetus to the modernisation of their way of life. One of the most important changes was the enormous influx into the cities and the urbanisation of various semi-urban settlements. The pace of urbanisation, proceeding side by side with the advance of industrialisation, emerges with striking clarity from the figures showing the rise in urban population: since 1949 the population of the cities has grown by 28 per cent, or about one million people. At the beginning of 1949 only a little over one-third of the population lived in cities or settlements of urban character, while at the end of the 1960s their inhabitants considerably exceeded half the total population.

Urbanisation drastically changed the living conditions of a great part of the population. Many exchanged village homes without comforts or modern conveniences, extremely limited cultural opportunities of the countryside, and a way of life determined by village custom, for city flats with running water and other amenities and the educational and cultural opportunities of the city. Under the influence of this new urban environment, the transformation of the style of life and habits of the new urban population got under way.

Leaving aside the sometimes serious shock of transition and

the contradictory human effects of adjustment to the new environment, urbanisation opened the way to a more modern way of life. Still, the unpleasant effects of the process cannot be ignored, among them persistent and increasing crowding, mass transport difficulties, and growing air pollution. A typical and —for the large numbers of people affected—serious transitional problem is the phenomenon of 'commuting' on a mass scale. Some 350,000 workers travel daily or weekly from their homes in the country to jobs in Budapest and five other large industrial cities. Settlements sprawl out unhealthily in the vicinity of the big cities, particularly Budapest, often accompanied by the spread of temporary buildings unfit for permanent habitation.

Little by little some of the changes characteristic of urbanisation are reaching out to the countryside as well. The electrification of the villages affords the country population some opportunity to take advantage of the latest advances of civilisation (although 700,000–1,000,000 residents living in scattered settlements still do not have electricity). The rapid spread of modern amenities is indicated by the widespread use of gas stoves in the villages: between 1960 and 1969 the number of rural consumers of propane-butane gas jumped from 129,000 to 1,200,000. A regular, frequent inter-urban bus service has completely revolutionised travel between the provincial cities and villages: in 1969 450 million passengers used inter-urban buses, compared with a mere 28 million in 1950.

A trend toward abandonment of the most primitive isolated farmsteads has become evident: in 1949 17 per cent of the population lived on individual farms, but by the end of the 1960s their proportion had fallen to 7 or 8 per cent. Thus a larger portion of the rural population than before now live within the limits of a village commune, which better assures their prosperity. Their circumstances have considerably improved, above all as a result of the brisk home-building activity of the 1960s. Housing conditions have improved markedly by comparison with the preceding decades. All these changes are inseparably bound up, of course, with the general social development of the village, in particular the emergence of the co-operative peasant's new way of life. The spread of large-scale co-operative farming and the mechanisation connected with it have transformed the conditions of life and labour in the countryside. The nature and organisation of the work, the methods of utilising the working day, and the opportunities for enjoying leisure all point to profound changes.

Employment grew very rapidly as a result of the forced pace of industrialisation, soon eliminating the chronic mass unemployment of earlier days. A high and still-rising level of jobs assured the absorption of all the manpower being released from agriculture. Full employment was accompanied, however, by such undesirable side effects as wasteful use of manpower.

Thoroughgoing legal regulation of working hours was not really carried through in Hungary until after World War II. The establishment of a 48-hour week and the regulation of overtime and overtime pay were followed by the first attempts to shorten working hours further. In some occupations hazardous to health a shorter working day has been introduced (in many factories, six hours), and in several industries a beginning has been made toward eliminating Saturday work.

In the wake of legislation on hours great progress was made in extending various kinds of social-welfare measures. The introduction of universal social insurance may be mentioned as one of the most significant achievements. The social legislation of the 1930s extended such protection to only about 31 per cent of the population, but by 1949 41 per cent of all Hungarians enjoyed coverage, by 1960 85 per cent, and by 1967, 97 per cent. In the course of the past quarter-century free medical care, and virtually free medicines, have been made available to practically everyone, which has resulted in a greatly increased demand for these services (consumption of medicines has risen five-fold). The number of holiday resorts has grown markedly. At the beginning of the 1950s 5 per cent of active workers were able to have a holiday at low-cost trade union or co-operative centres; by the end of the 1960s 15 per cent of a greatly increased work force was using such holiday opportunities.

Because of the inadequacy of earlier social legislation—and indeed as a natural reaction against it—social benefits were often extended at a rate that outstripped practical possibilities, creating new difficulties in certain areas. It was for this reason, for example, that the achievement of universal free medical insurance, quite exceeding in its extent all real material possibilities, gave rise to crowded conditions which often affected adversely the quality of treatment, to the search for private treatment, and to the offering of extra fees in the hope of superior treatment. For the same reason, the unusually low age limits set for eligibility for pensions for all (60 for men, 55 for women), in defiance of existing material resources, led to a system of pension payments which were for the most part very low, sometimes affording only a bare minimum.

Like the rapid expansion of once-neglected social-welfare measures, the spread of the technical wonders of the twentieth century was also an important factor in changing the Hungarian way of life. During the postwar period, for example, the number of radios per 1,000 of population nearly quadrupled, until at the end of 1969 there was practically one radio for every four Hungarians; thus on the average every family had a radio. The spread of television, introduced only belatedly in the second half of the 1950s, went on with unparalleled speed. At the present time there is one set for every six or seven people, or one for every second household, at least; more than two-thirds of all workers' and white-collar employees' homes have television. During the last decade television has become perhaps the most powerful factor affecting styles of life, the use of leisure time, and the pursuit of entertainment, information and culture. The effects of television are, of course, extremely uneven and contradictory. It obviously does more than any previous medium to raise the cultural level of the village by bringing drama, films, and educational programmes to a mass audience in the countryside, but at the same time its tendency to affect adversely such valuable leisure activities as reading, discussion and the active pursuit of knowledge is evident, especially among the younger generation.

The spread of technical innovations which greatly affect the circumstances of life was particularly marked in Hungary from the end of the 1950s. Among these was the rapid increase in the use of motor cars and motor cycles. Although their number is still very low by European standards, the trend is clearly indicated by the fact that between 1960 and 1969 the number of families with cars or motor cycles nearly trebled, from 9 to 25 per cent of all households.

Household appliances began to come into more common use. In 1960 only washing machines were at all frequent, but by 1968 more than half of all families owned washing machines, every fourth household had a vacuum cleaner, and every fourth or fifth family had acquired a refrigerator.

Despite these gains, and despite a doubling in the volume of consumption, the structure of consumption still bears the marks of only a middling degree of development. This situation is reflected in the relatively large proportion of income spent on food, relatively low expenditures on clothing (only half the proportion spent on clothing in the advanced industrial countries), and the even lower consumption of consumer durables (only one-third the share of income spent on these items in the advanced countries). The same state of affairs can be seen by examining the make-up of food consumption itself. Of the daily average intake of 3,054 calories, 45 per cent is provided by cereals and 17 per cent by fats. Only 6–8 per cent of food consumption is supplied by processed (canned or frozen) foods. Thus the structure of food consumption changes only slowly, and presents an even less favourable picture in international perspective, by comparison with the general situation elsewhere. Custom and the power of tradition play a large part, of course, in this resistance to change.

Expenditure on clothing has grown only a little during the past two decades. Clothing still tends to be used a long time before it is replaced; many are still obliged to wear articles of clothing which are practically worn out.

The most noteworthy factor in the evolution of consumption has been the rise of so-called consumer investments (ie, acquisition of building materials and consumer durable goods). The value of such purchases rose particularly rapidly in the 1960s, twice as fast as consumer expenditures in general, reaching one-fifth of the total expenditure of the population.

The existence of social benefits and the general rise in the standard of living made possible a significant development of the cultural level and of leisure occupations. One typical index of cultural standing is the extent of newspaper reading. Between 1950 and 1970 the total number of copies of newspapers published more than doubled.

In 1938, 17·3 million copies of books and periodicals were published in Hungary; by 1969 this had risen to 87 million copies, a clear indication that reading had become a regular habit for large numbers of people. In the late 1960s all family members above 8 years of age were regular readers in one-fifth of Hungarian families, and in more than 40 per cent of the remainder at least one family member reads regularly. At the same time the number of families in which no one is a regular reader is still rather high (nearly 40 per cent).

Finally there is the increase in visits to the theatre, cinema, concerts, and museums. Between 1950 and 1969 annual admissions to theatres, cinemas and concerts rose from about 3 million to about 7 million, in a nation of 10 million people; half of these were in Budapest. Attendance at lectures was a steady 4 to 5 million a year throughout the 1960s, while the number of museum-goers rose from the 2-million level of the 1950s to between 5 and 6 million. Thus reading, theatre, cinema, and attendance at other cultural events became a permanent feature in the daily lives of broad masses of the population.

An integral part of this changing way of life was the remarkable increase in travel compared with the interwar period, as a result of group excursions, the organisation of group travel, the spread of cars and motor cycles, and the increase in holidays and other leisure time. In 1969 2½ million people used the country's hotels, tourist homes, and camping grounds on an individual basis, and another 700,000 as members of trade unions or employees of enterprises; together they totalled almost one-third of the population, in comparison with the prewar figure of 200,000 holiday-makers annually. In the late 1950s the possibility of foreign travel opened once again, following its virtual suspension earlier in the decade. Most travellers visited the socialist countries, but after 1961 the beginnings of travel in the West gave a new impetus to tourism. In 1960 nearly 300,000 Hungarians travelled abroad, 92 per cent of them in the socialist countries. By the end of the decade the number of travellers was five times what it had been before the war, reaching 1 million.

Thus by the end of the 1960s the number of Hungarian travellers abroad and holiday-makers at home was about 4 million a year. Of course nothing like this number of Hungarians actually took holidays or travelled at home and abroad: we must take into account the fact that as a result of social and material distinctions a narrower section of the population was able to travel more often, or take frequent weekend trips. Still, tourism touched at least one-third of the population, a dramatic advance over interwar conditions, and one which indicates the effect on Hungarian habits of the new worldwide vogue of travel since World War II.

All these developments, however, not only affect different social strata unequally; they scarcely even affect the least advantaged elements in Hungarian society. For families with many children and for old people living on small pensions, there is little hope of holidays or travel; for them, indeed, the problems of securing a day-to-day livelihood are far from solved. The living conditions, consumption standards, and other habits of one-quarter of the people have scarcely gone beyond the bounds of traditional society. Other obstacles to the spread of culture and material civilisation still exclude large numbers of country-dwellers from the enjoyment of many benefits.

# Bibliography

## I WORKS IN HUNGARIAN

Berend, Iván T. *Ujjaepites es a nagytoke elleni harc Magyarorszagon, 1945–1948* [Reconstruction and the struggle against capitalism, 1945–1948] (Budapest, 1962)

———. *Gazdasagpolitika az elso oteves terv meginditasakor, 1948–1950* [Economic policy during the first years of the five-year plan, 1948–1950] (Budapest, 1964)

Berend, Iván T. and Ránki, Gy. *Magyarorszag gyaripara, 1900–1914* [Hungarian manufacturing industry, 1900–1914] (Budapest, 1955)

———. *Magyarorszag gyaripara a masodik vilaghaboru elott es a haboru idoszakaban, 1933–1944* [Hungarian industry before and during World War II, 1933–1944] (Budapest, 1958)

———. *Magyarorszag gazdasaga az elso vilaghaboru utan, 1919–1929* [Hungarian economy after World War I, 1919–1929] (Budapest, 1966)

———. *Kozepkelet-Europa gazdasagi fejlodese a 19-20 szazadban* [The economic development of East-Central Europe in the nineteenth and twentieth centuries] (Budapest, 1969)

Buzas, Jozsef and Nagy, Andras. *Magyarorszag kulkereskedelme, 1919–1945* [Hungarian foreign trade, 1919–1945] (Budapest, 1961)

Fazekas, Bela. *Mezogazdasagunk a felszabadulas utan* [Hungarian agriculture after 1945] (Budapest, 1967)

Ferge, Zsuzsa. *Tarsadalmunk retegzodese* [The structure of Hungarian society] (Budapest, 1969)

Gunszt, Peter. *A mezogazdasagi termeles tortenete Magyarorszagon, 1920–1938* [The history of agricultural production in Hungary, 1920–1938] (Budapest, 1970)

Incze, Miklos (ed). *Az 1929–1933 evi vilaggazdasagi valsag hatasa Magyarorszagon* [The effect of the great depression in Hungary] (Budapest, 1955)

Kornay, Janos. *A gazdasagi vezetes tulzott osszpontositasa* [The over-centralisation of the economy] (Budapest, 1957)

Kovacsics, Jozsef (ed). *Magyarorszag torteneti demografiaja* [The historical demography of Hungary] (Budapest, 1963)

Lacko, Miklos. *Ipari munkassagunk osszetetelenek alakulasa* [The formation and structure of the working class in Hungary] (Budapest, 1961)

Orban, Sandor. *Agrartarsadalom atalakulasa Magyarorszagon, 1945–1970* [The transformation of Hungarian agriculture and rural society, 1945–1970] (Budapest, 1972)

Ormos, Maria. *Az 1924-evi magyar allamkolcson megszerzese* [The history of the state loan from the League of Nations] (Budapest, 1963)

Ránki, György. *Magyarorszag gazdasaga az elso haromeves terv idoszakaban, 1947–1949* [Hungary's economy during the first three-year plan, 1947–1949] (Budapest, 1963)

Sandor, Vilmos. *Nagyipari fejlodes Magyarorszagon, 1867–1900* [Hungary's industrial development, 1867–1900] (Budapest, 1957)

Szabo, Istvan (ed). *A parasztsag Magyarorszagon a kapitalizmus koraban, 1848–1914* [The peasantry in Hungary during the age of capitalism, 1848–1914] (Budapest, 1965)

Szterenyi, Jozsef and Ladanyi, Jeno. *A magyar ipar a vilaghaboruban* [Hungarian industry during World War I] (Budapest, 1934)

Szuhay, Miklos. *Allami beavatkozas es a magyar mezogazdasag as 1930-s evekben* [State intervention in Hungarian agriculture in the 1930s] (Budapest, 1969)

Timar, Matyas. *Gazdasagi fejlodes es iranyitasi modszerek Magyarorszagon* [Economic development and economic mechanism in Hungary] (Budapest, 1968)

Varga, Jeno. *Magyar kartellek* [Hungarian cartels] (Budapest, 1912)

We have also used various archive sources, including those of the more important banks and businesses, of the various economic ministries, of the Foreign Office, of the Socialist Workers Party of Hungary, and of the German Foreign Ministry.

Statistical material used includes the censuses taken every ten years since 1869, Statistical Year Books since 1890, and industrial, agricultural and trade statistics.

## 2 WORKS IN WESTERN LANGUAGES

Bandera, V. N. *Foreign capital as an instrument of national economic policy* (The Hague, 1954)

Basch, A. *The Danube basin and the German economic sphere* (London, 1944)

Berend, Iván T. and Ránki, Gy. *Die Deutsche Wirtschaftliche Expansion und das Ungarische Wirtschaftleben zur zeit des Zueiten Weltkrieges* (Budapest, 1958)

——. *The development of manufacturing industry in Hungary* (Budapest, 1960)

Eckstein, A. *National income and capital formation in Hungary, 1900–1950.* Income and Wealth series, vol 5 (London, 1956)

Ellis, H. S. *Exchange control in Central Europe* (Cambridge, 1941)

*Die Frage des Finanzkapitals in der Österreichisch Ungarisch Monarchie* (Bucharest, 1965)

Gratz, G. and Schüller, R. *Die Wirtschaftliche zusammenbruch Österreich-Ungarn* (Vienna, 1930)

Hertz, F. O. *The economic problem of Danubian states. A study of nationalism* (London, 1947)

Matolcsy, M. and Varga, I. *The national income of Hungary, 1924/5–1936/7* (London, 1938)

Moore, W. *Economic demography of Eastern and Southern Europe* (Geneva, 1945)

Offergeld, W. *Grundlangen und Uhrsachen der Industriellen Entwicklung Ungarns* (Jena, 1914)

Sandor, V. *Die Grossindustrielle Entwicklung Ungarns* (Budapest, 1958)

Sandor, V. and Hanák, P. (eds). *Studien zur Geschichte der Österreichisch-Ungarischen Monarchie* (Budapest, 1961)

*Socio-Economic Researches on East-Central Europe* (Budapest, Studia Historica, 1971)

Spulher, N. *The economics of Communist Eastern Europe* (London, 1957)

Warriner, D. *Economics of peasant farming* (London, 1939)

Zagorov, S., Végh, J. and Bilimovich, A. *The agricultural economy of the Danubian countries, 1935–1945* (Stanford, 1955)

# Index

accumulation and investment, 30, 33, 34, 51, 73, 103, 104, 109, 110, 117, 137, 167, 171, 191, 192, 198, 199, 200, 201, 203, 204, 205, 206, 207, 214, 224, 229, 236, 237
agrarian proletariat, 77, 78, 79, 80, 82, 84, 154
agriculture, agricultural (production, yields), 41, 42, 43, 44, 45, 46, 47, 96, 97, 111, 112, 128, 129, 130, 131, 150, 151, 152, 178, 179, 180, 181, 195, 196, 205, 207, 208, 209, 230, 231, 232, 233, 234, 235, 236; credit, 32, 41, 42, 43, 71; mechanisation, 41, 44, 128, 129, 195, 233, 234; population, 74, 150, 151, 232; prices, 111, 112, 196
American capital, 106, 109
animal husbandry, 47, 48, 131, 178, 180, 209, 230, 235, 236
Austro-Hungarian Bank, 17, 42, 43, 71
Austro-Hungarian Compromise, 16, 24
Austrian (Austro-Hungarian) State Railway Co, 50, 53, 57
Austrian capital, 36, 42, 51, 52, 53, 70, 71, 72
autarchy, 101, 203, 221

banks, banking system, 28, 29, 30, 31, 32, 33, 34, 42, 71, 72, 76, 103, 113, 117, 147, 148, 149, 172, 188, 198
bauxite and aluminium industry, 109, 133, 134, 173, 174, 220, 221, 222
big estates, *see* land tenure
birth rate, *see* population growth
Budapest, 26, 34, 35, 52, 54, 58, 64, 65, 75, 79, 86, 88, 124, 134, 144, 153, 158, 161, 162, 164, 180, 182, 216, 251, 255

capital accumulation, *see* accumulation
cartels, *see* monopolisation
chemical industry, 63, 136, 182, 217, 218, 224, 225
coal mining, 49, 50, 53, 56, 63, 132, 133, 177, 200, 217, 218, 219
collectivisation, 202, 207, 208, 209
commerce, trade, internal market, 64, 65, 112, 145
Commercial Bank, *see* Hungarian Commercial Bank of Pest
concentration, 75, 76, 148, 217, 228
credit, 32, 33, 41, 42, 43, 103, 171
Creditanstalt, 29, 30, 71, 113
Credit Bank, *see* Hungarian General Credit Bank
crisis, *see* depression
customs (customs union), tariffs, 16, 17, 18, 19, 41, 44, 65, 66, 67, 99, 100, 101, 102, 103, 119, 127

## Index

Danube Steamship Navigation Co, 38, 50, 58, 132
death rate, *see* population growth
Debrecen, 35, 124
depression (crisis): of 1873, 30, 37; of mid 1870s in agriculture, 43, 44; of 1929–33, 111, 112, 113
Diósgyőr, 53, 57

education, 26, 27, 28, 124, 125, 126, 162, 212, 213, 214, 250
electrical industry, electrification, 59, 134, 135, 136, 251
employment and unemployment, 82, 83, 155, 156, 159, 168, 192, 193, 212, 215, 218, 219, 229, 232, 237, 252
emigration, 25, 123
engineering, 51, 54, 58, 63, 134, 135, 174, 177, 182, 217, 224, 225
English capital, 36, 71, 106, 134
export, 43, 44, 65, 66, 67, 96, 97, 102, 111, 114, 115, 118, 119, 120, 121, 146, 173, 225, 227, 239, 240, 241, 242

female labour, 81, 156, 157, 212
finance capital, 76, 149
First Domestic Savings Bank of Pest, 28, 31, 109
food processing, 49, 51, 52, 53, 54, 62, 63, 64, 137, 138, 142, 177, 182, 194, 195, 217, 218, 226, 227
foreign capital (loans, investments), 29, 30, 31, 36, 42, 52, 55, 70, 71, 72, 73, 96, 97, 105, 106, 107, 108, 109, 113, 114, 116, 133, 134, 137, 174
foreign trade, 43, 44, 56, 65, 66, 67, 68, 95, 96, 99, 102, 114, 115, 116, 118, 119, 120, 121, 122, 127, 145, 146, 147, 173, 174, 215, 220, 225, 227, 238, 239, 240, 241, 242, 243
French capital, 36, 70, 71

Ganz Works, 50, 51, 54, 58, 59, 109, 135, 141, 143, 169
German capital, 36, 70, 71, 72, 109, 133, 174

Győr, 158
Győr Waggon Factory, 58, 169, 174

Habsburg empire (dissolution), 14, 15, 17, 94
Hofher, Schrantz, Clayton & Shuttleworth Co, 58, 135, 141
Hungarian Commercial Bank of Pest, 28, 31, 32, 72, 109, 148
Hungarian Discount and Exchange Bank, 31, 109
Hungarian General Coal Mining Co, 56, 132, 148
Hungarian General Credit Bank, 29, 30, 31, 32, 72, 109, 113, 148
Hungarian National Bank, 105, 106, 113, 114, 167, 172, 175, 190, 198
Hungarian State Railway Machine Works, 54, 135, 143

illiteracy, 27, 125, 212
import, 56, 95, 96, 102, 116, 120, 121, 122, 146, 215, 220, 238, 239
industry, industrial (production, structure, growth), 49, 50, 51, 52, 53, 54, 55, 56, 57, 58, 59, 60, 61, 62, 63, 73, 98, 99, 112, 132, 133, 134, 135, 136, 137, 138, 139, 140, 141, 142, 143, 176, 177, 178, 181, 182, 194, 195, 200, 205, 206, 214, 215, 217, 218, 219, 220, 221, 222, 223, 224, 225, 226, 227, 228, 229; population, 49, 74, 150, 151
inflation, 93, 98, 103, 104, 106, 167, 176, 187, 190
investments, *see* accumulation and investments
iron and steel industry, 50, 51, 53, 54, 56, 57, 63, 133, 177, 182, 200, 222, 223

labour movement, trade unions, worker parties, 80, 86, 87, 88, 163, 164, 165, 166, 184, 189, 197, 202, 203
land reform, 93, 100, 126, 153, 154, 184, 185, 249

land tenure (big estates), 41, 42, 100, 126, 127, 186
leather industry, 60, 63, 177, 182, 227
living standard, see wages, living standard

Manfréd Weiss Works (in Csepel), 58, 133, 141, 148, 169, 174
Miskolc, 145
monopolisation (cartels), 32, 76, 141, 148, 187

national income (rate of growth), 74, 97, 149, 150, 151, 175, 179, 191, 192, 196, 198, 199, 204, 205, 216, 237, 239, 243, 245, 246
nationalisation, 93, 187, 188

occupational distribution of population, 49, 74, 95, 150, 151, 179, 211, 245
Ózd, 56, 133, 158

paper industry, 60, 63, 137, 182, 226
peasantry, 77, 90, 153, 154, 155, 185, 208, 209, 247, 248, 249, 250
Pécs, 50, 132, 158, 164, 165
population growth, 24, 25, 26, 123, 124, 210
planning, 189, 190, 191, 198, 201, 202, 203, 204
prices, 111, 112, 168, 170, 216
productivity, see technical progress

railway, 32, 35, 36, 37, 38, 41, 69, 143, 181, 237, 238
reparation, 98, 105, 188, 190, 191
revolution of 1848-9, 15, 16, 24, 40; of 1918 and 1919, 93
Rimamurány Iron Works, 51, 53, 56, 107, 133, 148
road and water transportation, 38, 39, 144, 237, 238
Rothschild, 29, 30, 31, 35, 36, 71, 72

Salgótarján, 57, 158, 164

Salgótarján Coal Mining Co, 56, 132, 148
serfdom (abolition), 14, 15, 16, 40
skilled workers, 79, 80, 81, 84, 85, 157
social legislation, 81, 82, 158, 159, 160, 161, 166, 252, 253
stabilisation (financial), 105, 106, 187, 190, 191
state intervention, 36, 37, 55, 69, 70, 71, 113, 114, 115, 116, 117, 167, 168, 169, 170, 171, 172, 173, 174, 175, 176, 187, 188, 189
State Iron Works, 53, 57, 133
strikes, 88, 164, 165
Szeged, 35, 124, 145, 220
Szolnok, 35

Tatabánya, 132
technical progress, productivity, 44, 45, 52, 53, 54, 55, 58, 59, 60, 139, 143, 193, 194, 203, 226, 228, 229, 232, 236
textile industry, 50, 55, 59, 60, 62, 63, 64, 137, 142, 177, 182, 217, 218, 226, 227
trade unions, see worker movement

unemployment, see employment
United Incandescent Lamp Co, 109, 135, 136, 141
unskilled workers, 80, 84, 156, 157
urbanisation, 26, 124, 153, 250, 251

Vác, 35
Vienna, 29, 35, 96; awards, 168

wages, living standard, 82, 83, 84, 85, 86, 104, 158, 159, 160, 161, 162, 202, 205, 215, 253, 254, 255, 256
war destruction, 92, 180, 181, 182
Wiener Bankverein, 56, 72
working class, industrial proletariat, 49, 77, 78, 79, 80, 81, 82, 83, 84, 85, 153, 155, 156, 158, 161, 162, 163, 247, 248, 249

WITHDRAWN FROM CLARK UNIVERSITY
LIBRARY

CLARK UNIVERSITY
A16400079361